Guide to the National Parks
East & Midwest

American Moose, Isle Royale National Park

NATIONAL GEOGRAPHIC

Guide to the National Parks
East & Midwest

National Geographic
Washington, D.C.

4

Lake of the Woods

Boundary Waters Canoe Area Wilderness

VOYAGEURS N.P.

ISLE ROYALE N.P.

Lake Superior

Apostle Islands Nat. Lakeshore
Keweenaw Peninsula

Huron Mts.

Apostle Islands Country Drive

Sturgeon River Gorge Wilderness Area

MINN.

Black River Waterfalls

Minneapolis St. Paul

Porcupine Mts. Wilderness S.P.

WIS.

Lake Michigan

MICH.

Madison

MILWAUKEE
Lansing

DETR

Madison

IOWA

CHICAGO

ILL.

IND.

O

Springfield

COLUM

INDIANAPOLIS

Jefferson City

Missouri

Big Bone Lick S.P.

Daniel Boone N.F.

ST. LOUIS

Frankfort

MO.

Bernheim Arboretum and Research Forest

KY.

Pine Mt. S.R.P.

Blanchard Springs Caverns

Dale Hollow Lake S.R.

MAMMOTH CAVE N.P.

Buffalo National River

Obed N.W. & S.R.

GR

Hot Springs to Harrison Drive

Ozark N.F.

Nashville

SM
MTS.

Hola Bend N.W.R.
Magazine Mt. S.P.

ARK.

Fall Creek Falls S.R.P.

MEMPHIS

TENN.

Little Rock

Ouachita N.F.

HOT SPRINGS N.P.

Arkansas

Cherokee N.F.

Chattahoochee N.F.

Nantahala N.F.

Beavers Bend State Park

Crater of Diamonds State Park

Mississippi

ATLANTA

MISS.

ALA.

Tall
Gorge

LA.

Jackson

Montgomery

G

Florida N.S.T.

Baton Rouge

Tallahassee

NEW ORLEANS

MAP KEY

☐ National Park

☐ Excursion Site

miles
0 ——— 300

kilometers
0 ——— 400

National Key Deer Refug
Great White Heron N.W.
Florida Keys Driv
DRY TORTUGAS N.

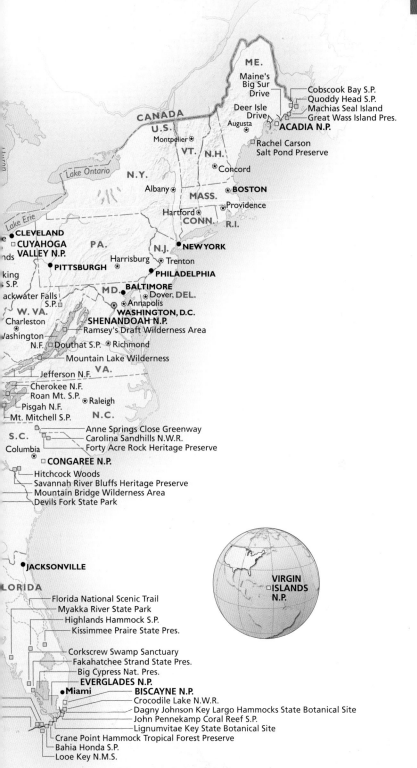

Contents

Photos: Cover, Lighthouse, Acadia National Park; pp. 2–3, Great Smoky Mountains at sunset; opposite, Children on a lakeshore, Voyageurs National Park

Treasures of the East and Midwest

IF THE DIVERSE NATIONAL PARKS of the East and Midwest have one thing in common, it's water. From the turquoise coves of the Virgin Islands to the ice-cold lakes of Voyageurs, the 13 eastern and midwestern national parks are awash in water.

Six of the parks, in fact, are primarily islands and their surrounding waters. Two parks—Congaree and Cuyahoga—center on rivers. Two others—Mammoth Cave and Hot Springs—owe their existence to underground water. If not for a steady bath of slow-moving water, the Everglades would be no more. And even those titans of eastern national parks, Great Smoky Mountains and Shenandoah, count on copious rain-fall to water their dense forests and replenish their streams and waterfalls.

In addition to the Everglades, South Florida holds two relative newcomers to the national park system. Biscayne preserves a watery wilderness just south of Miami. Some 95 percent of the park lies underwater, part of it a coral reef glittering with colorful fish. A smat-tering of tiny islands and a fringe of mangrove shoreline make up the land portion. This is a park for boats. Likewise the Dry Tortugas, 70 miles off Key West. The "dry" designation was a reminder to early mariners that the islands' reefs and shoals contained no fresh water.

Far to the north, Mount Desert Island harbors the majority of Acadia National Park, where only the hardiest visitors don bathing suits. Hiking boots and snowshoes are more appropriate here, where frigid waves crash on rocky shores and old seaside villages hunker under often tempestuous Atlantic coast weather.

An entirely different ecosystem is at work in Congaree. Elevated in 2003 to national park status, this South Carolina haven of moss-draped cypress and stately herons sits between the coastal plain and the Piedmont. Regular flooding keeps the deep, dark forest and its shadowy denizens healthy. The other river-related park, Cuyahoga Valley, was bumped up in 2000 from a national recreation area. Nestled in the urban corridor between Cleveland and Akron, Cuyahoga shows that even the industrial East can lay claim to a national park. It may not have true wilderness, but this park's forested hills and bird-filled marshes provide welcome open space to city dwellers. Here you can bike or cross-country ski a towpath during the day, and take in a concert at night.

To the northwest, Isle Royale in Lake Superior is another story altogether. This is serious wilderness. One of the least visited of all national parks, Isle Royale is a remote land of thick woods populated by wolves, moose, and mosquitoes. There is no such thing as a drive-through visit to this park. Visitors boat over, then generally spend several days backpacking. Up in northern Minnesota, Voyageurs National Park

Elkhorn Reef, Biscayne National Park

features a similarly wild landscape, with loon calls echoing around pristine shorelines and bald eagles nesting on wooded islands. A maze of lakes and islands, Voyageurs protects a little-known piece of the American wilderness connecting the United States and Canada. A kayak and a pair of binoculars are the order of the day here in the warmer months. In winter you can drive onto a lake, drill a hole in the ice, and drop a fishing line.

Each of the parks in this book offers a vastly different outdoor experience. It was nearly 50 years from the establishment of the first national park, Yellowstone, to the opening of the first in the East, Acadia. Urban sprawl and highway development after World War I spurred the preservation of East Coast green spaces. The eastern and midwestern national parks now rank among the most heavily visited. From tropical shores to northern lakes, lofty peaks to subterranean caverns, these natural theme parks deliver unsurpassed thrills.

In addition to an overview and history of each park, this guide takes you through the highlights of the various areas within the park. Excursions to nearby outdoor areas follow—many of these places feature flora, fauna, and geology similar to their associated national park, and are often less crowded. There is also plenty of practical information on traveling to and within the parks. Want to know the best season for a trip? The entrance fee? The number to call for details on camping? It's all here.

In all their wonderful watery variety, the eastern and midwestern national parks greatly enrich a nation that is increasingly valuing wilderness as a measure of national success. *–John Thompson*

HOW TO USE THIS GUIDE

Welcome to the 13 national parks of the East and Midwest. Whether you are a regular visitor or a first-timer, you have a great treat in store. Each of the parks offers you fun, adventure, and—usually—enthralling splendor. What you experience will depend on where you go and what you do. But exploring an unknown land is best done with a guide, a companion who has tested the trail and learned the lore.

Our coverage of each park begins with a portrait of its natural wonders, ecological setting, history, and, often, its struggles against environmental threats. You'll see why a single step off a trail can harm fragile plants, and why visitors are detoured from certain areas that shelter wildlife. Many parks have already suffered from the impact of tourism. Be sure to leave all items—plants, rocks, artifacts—where you find them. Two of these parks have been designated United Nations World Heritage sites for their outstanding scenic and cultural wonders; five have international biosphere reserve status, signaling the distinctive qualities of their environments. Before starting off on your park exploration, use the guide to preview the parks you may want to visit. You'll notice that each park introduction is followed by the following three how-and-when sections:

How to Get There You may be able to include more than one park in your trip. The regional map in the front of the book shows them in relation to one another. Base your itinerary not so much on mileage as on time, remembering that parks often do not lie alongside interstates; park roads are usually rugged—and, in summer, crowded.

When to Go The parks of the East and Midwest are mostly year-round parks. Instead of going in midsummer, when they are hottest and often crowded, schedule your trip for spring or fall (or for June or late August) and time your arrival early on a weekday. Fall in the parks can be glorious and many of the parks bloom in spring —and off-peak vistas often coincide with a relative scarcity of visitors. Florida parks are best in winter to early spring. Consult each park chapter for details about visitor facilities.

How to Visit Don't rush through a park. Give yourself time to savor the beauty. Incredibly, the average time the typical visitor spends in a park is half a day. Often, that blur of time flashes past a windshield. No matter how long you decide to stay, spend at least part of that time in the park, not in your car. Each park's **How to Visit** section recommends a plan for visits of a half, one, two, or more days. Guide writers devised the plans and trekked every tour, but don't be afraid to explore on your own.

MAP KEY and ABBREVIATIONS

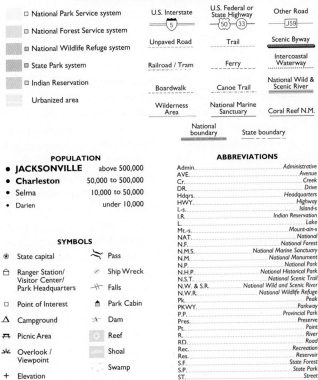

□ National Park Service system

□ National Forest Service system

□ National Wildlife Refuge system

□ State Park system

□ Indian Reservation

Urbanized area

U.S. Interstate — 5

U.S. Federal or State Highway — 50 — 33

Other Road — J59

Unpaved Road

Trail

Scenic Byway

Railroad / Tram

Ferry

Intercoastal Waterway

Boardwalk

Canoe Trail

National Wild & Scenic River

Wilderness Area

National Marine Sanctuary

Coral Reef N.M.

National boundary

State boundary

POPULATION

● **JACKSONVILLE** above 500,000

● **Charleston** 50,000 to 500,000

● Selma 10,000 to 50,000

● Darien under 10,000

SYMBOLS

⊛ State capital

⌂ Ranger Station/ Visitor Center/ Park Headquarters

□ Point of Interest

△ Campground

⊓ Picnic Area

Overlook / Viewpoint

+ Elevation

Pass

Ship Wreck

Falls

Park Cabin

Dam

Reef

Shoal

Swamp

ABBREVIATIONS

Admin.	Administrative
AVE.	Avenue
Cr.	Creek
DR.	Drive
Hdqrs.	Headquarters
HWY.	Highway
I.-s.	Island-s
I.R.	Indian Reservation
L.	Lake
Mt.-s.	Mount-ain-s
NAT.	National
N.F.	National Forest
N.M.S.	National Marine Sanctuary
N.M.	National Monument
N.P.	National Park
N.H.P.	National Historical Park
N.S.T.	National Scenic Trail
N.W. & S.R.	National Wild and Scenic River
N.W.R.	National Wildlife Refuge
Pk.	Peak
PKWY.	Parkway
P.P.	Provincial Park
Pres.	Preserve
Pt.	Point
R.	River
RD.	Road
Rec.	Recreation
Res.	Reservoir
S.F.	State Forest
S.P.	State Park
ST.	Street
TR.	Trail
WILD.	Wilderness

Other Features of the Guide

Excursions The excursions that follow each park entry take you to other natural areas in the region. If time allows, be sure to explore some of these as well. Many of the sites are much less known than the national parks and often much less crowded. The distances noted from the parks are approximate and intended for planning purposes only.

Maps The park maps and the regional map were prepared as an aid in planning your trip. For more detail on hiking trails and other facilities inside a park, contact the Park Service, phone the park itself, or visit the website. Contact the individual excursions sites at the numbers provided to learn more about them. Always use a road map when traveling and carry hiking maps when walking into the backcountry.

The maps note specially designated areas within park borders: Wilderness areas are managed to retain their primeval quality. Roads, buildings, and vehicles are not allowed in them. National preserves may allow hunting.

The following abbreviations are used in this book:

NP   National Park
NRA National Recreation Area
NF   National Forest
NM   National Monument
NWR National Wildlife Refuge
SP   State Park

Information & Activities This section, at the end of each park entry, offers detailed visitor information. Call or write the park, or visit the park's website for further details. Brochures are usually available free of charge from the parks. For a small fee you can buy a copy of the "National Park System Map and Guide" by contacting the Consumer Information Center at P.O. Box 100, Pueblo, CO 81002; or 719-948-3334. Visit the Park Service website at: http://www .nps.gov.

Entrance Fees The entrance fees listed in this book reflect fees at press time. In addition to daily or weekly fees, most parks also offer a yearly admission rate, with unlimited entries.

For $50 you can buy a National Parks Pass, which is good for a year and admits all occupants of a private vehicle to all national parks with a vehicle entrance fee. The pass does not cover parking fees where applicable.

For an additional $15 you can purchase a Golden Eagle hologram to affix to the pass for unlimited admission to U.S. Fish and Wildlife Service, Forest Service, and Bureau of Land Management sites.

People over 62 can obtain a lifetime Golden Age Passport for $10, and blind and disabled people are entitled to a lifetime Golden Access Passport for free, both of which admit all occupants of a private vehicle to all national parks and other federal sites and a discount on usage fees. These documents are available at any Park Service facility that charges entrance fees.

For further information on purchasing park passes, call 888-467-2757 or visit www.national parks.org.

Pets Generally they're not allowed on trails, in buildings, or in the backcountry. Elsewhere, they must be leashed. Specific rules are noted.

Facilities for Disabled This section of the guide explains which parts of each park, including visitor centers and trails, are accessible to visitors with disabilities.

Special Advisories

■ Do not take chances. People are killed or badly injured every year in national parks. Most casualties are caused by recklessness or inattention to clearly posted warnings.

■ Stay away from wild animals. Do not feed them. Do not try to touch them, not even raccoons or chipmunks (which can transmit diseases). Try not to surprise a bear and do not let one approach you. If one does, scare it off by yelling, clapping your hands, or banging pots. Store all your food in bear-proof containers (often available at parks); keep it out of sight in your vehicle, with windows closed and doors locked. Or suspend it at least 15 feet above ground, and 10 feet out from a post or tree trunk.

■ Guard your health. If you are not fit, don't overtax your body. Boil water that doesn't come from a park's drinking-water tap. Chemical treatment of water will not kill *Giardia,* a protozoan that causes severe diarrhea and lurks even in crystal clear streams. Heed park warnings about hypothermia and Lyme disease, which is carried by ticks, and the Hantavirus, a serious airborne virus which is transmitted by deer mice.

■ Expect RV detours. Check road regulations as you enter each park. Along stretches of many roads you will not be able to maneuver a large vehicle, especially a trailer.

Campgrounds The National Parks Reservation System (NPRS) handles advance reservations for campgrounds at the following eastern national parks: Acadia, Everglades, Mammoth Cave, Shenandoah, and Great Smoky Mountains. You can reserve a single campsite up to five months in advance by calling 800-365-2267, or by visiting http://reservations .nps.gov. Pay by credit card over the phone or Internet. Or, write to NPRS, 3 Commerce Dr., Cumberland, MD 21502. The National Recreation Reservation Service accepts reservations for many of the excursions sites affiliated with the following: Acadia, Mammoth Cave, Hot Springs, and Great Smoky Mountains National Parks, as well as numerous other Forest Service campsites. They can be reached at 877-444-6777, 877-833-6777 (TDD), or 518-885-3639 (international callers); or by visiting www.ReserveUSA.com.

Hotels, Motels, & Inns The guide lists accommodations as a service to its readers. The lists are by no means comprehensive, and listing does not imply endorsement by the National Geographic Society. The information can change without notice. Many parks keep full lists of accommodations in their areas, which they will send you on request. You can also contact local chambers of commerce and tourist offices for suggestions of other places to stay.

Resources The back of this guide lists additional resources that can be helpful: federal and state park agencies, road conditions, and other relevant phone numbers and websites *(see pp. 342–345).*

Enjoy your explorations!

Acadia

Sea and mountain meet at Acadia, where, as one presumably ambidextrous visitor wrote, "you can fish with one hand and sample blueberries from a wind-stunted bush with the other."

The name of the park probably stems from the name Giovanni Verrazano gave the region when he sailed here in 1524; the coastline reminded the explorer of Arcadia in Greece.

Most of Acadia is on Mount Desert Island, a patchwork of parkland, private property, and seaside villages that seasonally fill with what residents call "summer people." Other bits of the park are scattered on smaller islands and a peninsula.

Mount Desert Island once was a mountainous granite ridge on the edge of the mainland. Some 20,000 years ago, towering glacial ice sheets flowed over the mountains, rounding their tops, cutting passes, gouging out lake beds, and widening valleys. As the glaciers melted, the sea rose, flooding valleys and drowning the coast. The pre-glacier ridge was transformed into today's mountainous island that thrusts from the Atlantic like a lobster's claw.

Samuel de Champlain, who explored the coast in 1604, named the island L'Isle des Monts Déserts, sometimes translated as "island of barren mountains." From his ship, he probably could not see the mountains' forested slopes. The summer people rediscovered Mount Desert in the mid-19th century, built mansions they called "cottages," anchored their yachts in rock-girt harbors, and cherished the wild. To preserve it, they donated land for the park, the first east of the Mississippi. The original name, Lafayette National Park, was changed in 1929.

Dependent on donated land since its inception, the park took what it could get, skirting around private property and growing piece by piece. Acadia's real estate was so patchy that Congress did

- Eastern Maine
- 47,000 acres
- Established 1919
- Best seasons early spring, summer, and fall
- Hiking, boating, fishing, bicycling, snowshoeing, cross-country skiing, bay and island cruises, stargazing
- Information: (207) 288-3338 www.nps.gov/acad

Lighthouse, Acadia National Park

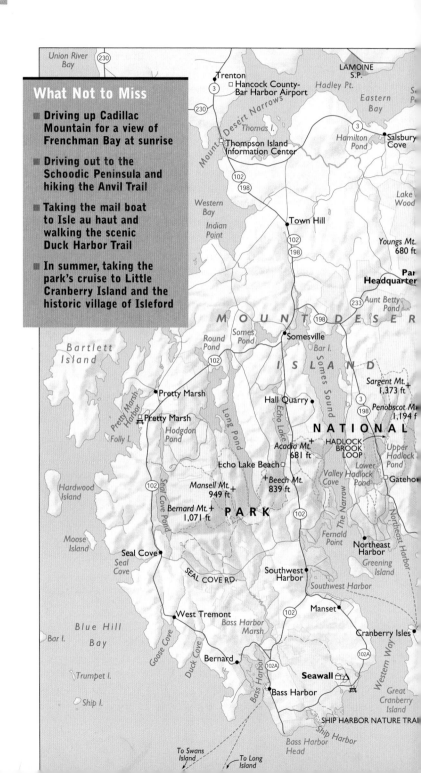

What Not to Miss

- Driving up Cadillac Mountain for a view of Frenchman Bay at sunrise

- Driving out to the Schoodic Peninsula and hiking the Anvil Trail

- Taking the mail boat to Isle au haut and walking the scenic Duck Harbor Trail

- In summer, taking the park's cruise to Little Cranberry Island and the historic village of Isleford

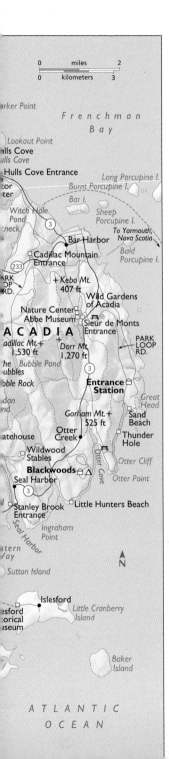

Map labels:

0 miles 2
0 kilometers 3

arker Point

F r e n c h m a n
B a y

Lookout Point
lls Cove
lls Cove

Hulls Cove Entrance

Long Porcupine I.
Burnt Porcupine I.

tor
ter

Bar I.

Witch Hole
Pond
neck

Sheep
Porcupine I.

To Yarmouth,
Nova Scotia

Bar Harbor

Cadillac Mountain
Entrance

Bald
Porcupine I.

RK
OP
RD.

233

Kebo Mt.
407 ft

Wild Gardens
of Acadia

Nature Center
Abbe Museum

Sieur de Monts
Entrance

A C A D I A

adillac Mt.
1,530 ft

Dorr Mt.
1,270 ft

PARK
LOOP
RD.

he
ubbles
bble Rock

Bubble Pond

3

dan
nd

atehouse

Entrance
Station

Great
Head

Gorham Mt.
525 ft

Otter
Creek

Sand
Beach

Thunder
Hole

Wildwood
Stables

Blackwoods

Otter Cliff

Seal Harbor

3

Otter Point

Stanley Brook
Entrance

Little Hunters Beach

Ingraham
Point

tern
ay

N

Sutton Island

Islesford

esford
orical
useum

Little Cranberry
Island

Baker
Island

A T L A N T I C
O C E A N

not set the park's official boundaries until 1986.

The sixth smallest national park, Acadia is one of the ten most visited—by almost three million people a year. Heavy traffic can produce gridlock. The Island Explorer shuttles help alleviate the problem.

How to Get There

From Ellsworth, 28 miles southeast of Bangor, follow Me. 3 south for 18 miles to Mount Desert Island, where most of the park is located; the visitor center is three miles north of Bar Harbor. Another section lies on the Schoodic Peninsula, a 1-hour drive northeast of Bar Harbor. To get to the park's islands, see **The Islands** p. 26. Airports: Bangor and Bar Harbor.

When to Go

All-year park, but main visitor center is open from mid-April through October. Expect traffic in July and August. Spectacular foliage attracts crowds in late September. Snow and ice close most park roads from December through April, but parts are open for cross-country skiing.

How to Visit

Allow at least a day for **Mount Desert Island,** with drives on the 27-mile **Park Loop Road** and the road to **Cadillac Mountain.** On a second day, enjoy an uncrowded view of the rocky coast by visiting the **Schoodic Peninsula.** If you have more time, take your pick of one of the trails or smaller islands.

EXPLORING THE PARK

Mount Desert Island: 60 miles; at least a full day

The geology of Mount Desert Island tells a complex tale, beginning some 500 million years ago when vast rivers carried sediments to the floor of an ancient sea. These layers of sand, silt, and mud accumulated at the rate of roughly an inch every century until they were thousands of feet thick. Pressure and heat fused these sediments into bedrock, which was then forced up to become an enormous mountain range; the mountains in turn were eventually worn down by erosion. Periods of intense volcanic activity and massive intrusions of magma created the beautiful fine- to coarse-grained granites that are visible throughout the park.

This dramatic geological history, combined with the powerful forces of glaciation, has left a number of open, rocky areas from which one can drink in the beauty of the Maine coast. One of the best perches of all is from **Cadillac Mountain,** a 1,530-foot-tall landmark capped with pink granite.

To get the most from a tour of the island, try the **Park Loop Road** that landscape architect Frederick Law Olmsted, Jr., helped design in the 1930s. In the summer, this means getting up very early. (On clear days, traffic is heaviest between 10 a.m. and 3 p.m.) The day before, check the time of sunrise in a local newspaper or at the visitor center. About 30 minutes before dawn, pack a picnic breakfast and a blanket, and drive from the visitor center to Cadillac Mountain. The 3.5-mile mountain road switchbacks up to a parking area.

From there, walk to the **Summit Trail,** find a niche in the rocks that faces east, and settle in on the highest point along the North Atlantic coast. Here is one of the first places where dawn touches the continental United States. After the sunrise, hunt for blueberries along the trails radiating from the summit. The blueberry season runs from late July through August. If you're here in the fall, be sure to scan the sky for hawks.

On the way down, stop at one of the eastern overlooks for a view of **Frenchman Bay,** a vast, island-dotted seascape; its name takes note of the area's early French settlers. (Another way to see the bay is on a 2-hour sea cruise; check schedules at the Municipal Pier in Bar Harbor or in the park's publication, the *Beaver Log.)*

Return to the loop road and turn right. Less than a half mile farther, bear right again (the road becomes one way), and continue

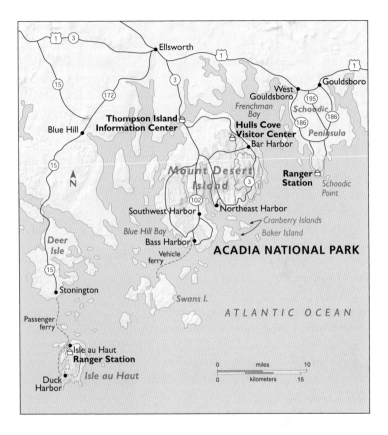

south toward the ocean. Two worthwhile stops you'll soon approach are the **Sieur de Monts Spring Nature Center** and the **Wild Gardens of Acadia.** The Bar Harbor Garden Club manages the wild gardens; they are open to the public year-round for free. Many of the island's 500 species of plants grow here.

Take a stroll on the trails near the gardens for glimpses of some of the more than 300 species of birds that are found on Mount Desert; you can pick up a list at the visitor center on Me. 3 near Bar Harbor. Yellow-bellied sapsuckers and American redstarts flit through the trees.

Farther along the road, skip **Sand Beach** for now. You may want to return to the beach later for sunbathing on the sand, much of which is made from the crushed shells of billions of marine creatures, or a very brisk swim (the summer water temperature is between 55°F and 60°F).

Not quite a mile farther, a sign marks **Thunder Hole.** Park on the right and walk down the concrete steps to the cleft in the rocks, named for the roars produced when air, trapped and squeezed by incoming surf, explodes out of a cavern. The best times to hear the thunder are at half tide with a rising sea or during a storm. Other times, you may hear only gurgles and sloshes.

Continue to the 110-foot **Otter Cliff.** Park, cross the road, and walk the shore path to **Otter Point.** Champlain's ship ran aground on a ledge near here in 1604, and he had to spend time ashore to repair the vessel. Numerous brightly colored lobster buoys bob offshore. Linger to savor the essence of the Maine coast: rocks, gulls, the tang of salt air. At Hunters Head the loop road turns away from the sea and soon becomes two-way as you head back to where you started. You'll pass **Jordan Pond,** one of many glacier-carved bodies of water on the island.

Your drive has taken you around the eastern side of the island. To explore the western side, you must drive out of park property and then back in again. Continue north on the loop road, cross the bridge, and bear right to get on Me. 233. Head west to Me. 198, then south on Me. 102 toward Southwest Harbor. Continuing south, on your left (though obscured) is **Somes Sound,** the only fjord on the U.S. Atlantic coast. On your right is **Echo Lake,** a swimming spot with a small beach.

Me. 102 passes through Southwest Harbor. Beyond, near Manset, bear left on Me. 102A, which leads to a large patch of park property. You can picnic at **Seawall,** then stretch your legs on the nearby 1.25-mile **Ship Harbor Nature Trail,** which gives a lesson in how a forest shore is knit to the tidal sea. The trail courses through some of the best bird-watching spots. Look for breeding yellow-bellied and alder flycatchers, blue-headed vireos, ruby-crowned kinglets and Swainson's thrushes. Spruce grouses occasionally are here, too, but they're rare and elusive.

A short detour off Me. 102A takes you to **Bass Harbor Head,** site of a 19th-century lighthouse. Take the road through Bass Harbor and bear left onto Me. 102 toward Tremont. Continue north for 7

Rocky coast of Mount Desert Island

miles to a tract of park called **Pretty Marsh,** a beautiful picnic spot. A short worn path leads to the rock-strewn shore. Stay on Me. 102 and retrace your route from Somesville to the visitor center.

Carriage Roads & Hikes

In 1917 John D. Rockefeller, Jr., a summer resident of Mount Desert Island, launched the building of a 57-mile network of broken stone roads for horse-drawn carriages. Convinced that the newfangled automobiles would destroy the tranquillity of the island, he banned them from the carriage roads. The roads were graced by 17 hand-built bridges, one of cobblestones and the remaining 16 of granite. Rockefeller later donated most of the road network, along with 11,000 acres of his land, to the park.

While the carriage roads are still not open to cars, they are a treasure prized by hikers, bikers, horseback riders, cross-country skiers, and anyone seeking a respite from the incessant hum of the internal combustion engine.

To introduce yourself to the carriage roads, try the 4-mile **Hadlock Brook Loop.** Park at the Me. 198 Parkman Mountain parking area just north of **Upper Hadlock Pond** and walk to the trailhead. Take the left fork east toward **Hemlock Bridge,** a gem of hand-hewn stone. Follow the rising road to another handsome span, **Waterfall Bridge,** site of a 40-foot cascade. (You can turn around here, cutting your hike to about 2 miles round-trip.) Cross the bridge and walk south for a mile to one of the network's well-marked intersections. Turn right at intersection 19, right again at intersection 18 and continue along the pond. Watch for loons and listen for their haunting call. The road crosses **Hadlock Brook Bridge** and loops back to the trailhead.

Along the edges of the road are carpets of club moss, meadowsweet, huckleberry, wintergreen, and sweet fern, a native plant that grows on drier sites from Nova Scotia to North Carolina. Builders routinely planted sweet fern along these roads in an effort to make them blend in with the natural landscape. In addition to making tasty tea, the fern's leaves were favored by Native Americans as a compress for poison ivy.

The park has more than 120 miles of hiking trails that range from easy strolls along the ocean or around ponds to steep climbs up Cadillac and other mountains. For a jaunt into history, try the **Gorge Path** that, like several other trails, has stone steps to ease the

Summer Home of the Rich & Famous

Few natural areas in America have had such strong links to the wealthy as Mount Desert Island, home of Acadia National Park. In summers stretching from roughly 1880 until the Depression, a stream of people with names like Rockefeller, Morgan, Vanderbilt, Kennedy, Ford, and Astor flowed into the area. They transformed the island from a mix of modest dwellings to a collection of some of the most elegant vacation homes in the country.

To understand how Mount Desert Island became a playground for the wealthy, we need to go back to 1844, when the artist Thomas Cole returned from a summer on the island with a fabulous array of landscape paintings. Soon other artists arrived, among them Frederic Church and Fitz Hugh Lane. Before long, friends of the artists and other social movers and shakers began flocking to the island. Most preferred to stay with area farmers and fishermen, a habit that earned them the name "rusticators."

By the late 1800s, the richest of the new arrivals were building magnificent estates. Before long, Mount Desert rivaled Newport, Rhode Island, as the center of the summer social scene. Yet, despite their rush to build, some members of the wealthy class worked to protect the island's natural areas from development.

Sandy beach, Acadia

Enjoying Acadia's shoreline

way up slopes. The flat stone steps imbedded in rising ground were built at the turn of the 20th century when development came to the island in a major way. The path begins at a parking spot on Park Loop Road near 407-foot Kebo Mountain and leads to a wooded trail. Cairns mark the trail as it follows a rocky, brook-washed ravine.

About a mile into the woods, you'll reach an intersection. Depending upon your time and stamina, you can turn around and retrace your steps back or push on to Cadillac (*see p. 18*) or **Dorr Mountain,** each a steep hike of more than 1.5 miles. The latter mountain is named after George B. Dorr, the first superintendent of Acadia. He spent 43 years and devoted some of his family's fortune to preserving the land. Views of the ocean and rocky coast are spectacular from atop either peak, thus making the trek up worth the time and effort.

Schoodic Peninsula: **100 miles; a half day**

The 45-mile drive around Frenchman Bay to the park's only mainland portion, the Schoodic Peninsula, provides several scenic views of Mount Desert Island. Beginning from Bar Harbor, take Me. 3 to US 1 south of Ellsworth and head east to West Gouldsboro. Go south via Me. 186 to Winter Harbor, then follow signs to the park entrance. From there, drive or bike the 6-mile, one-way road to **Schoodic Point.** The massive granite rocks here are laced by black diabase, the product of magma that welled up into cracks. Schoodic's displays of thundering surf usually top those of Mount Desert Island. And the audiences are much smaller; the peninsula does not draw crowds the way Mount Desert does.

A trail system explores the western section of the point, running through wetlands and forests with spurs to the ocean. The longest is the 12-mile **Anvil Trail,** which begins at the Blueberry Hill parking lot and climbs about 440 feet for views of Little Moose Island and Frenchman Bay. In this wilderness, look for moose, white-tailed deer, rabbits, porcupines, and raccoons.

The Islands: A full day each

Fragments of Acadia are on islands. Two worth visiting are Isle au Haut, about half of which is park property, and Little Cranberry Island, home to the Islesford Historical Museum. Boats serve both islands year-round. Get boat schedules from the visitor center or from the boat operators.

The trip to **Isle au Haut,** or "high island," named by Samuel de Champlain, begins at Stonington at the tip of Deer Isle, about 40 miles to the southwest of Ellsworth. To make the boat on time from Mount Desert Island, allow at least 2 hours for the drive and for finding a rare legal parking place near the harbor. Bring lunch. The mail boat takes passengers on a first-come, first-served basis. The 45-minute voyage ends at the Town Landing. In summer, the boat also stops at Duck Harbor, a park campsite and trailhead.

For a fine hike, get off at Town Landing and turn right. A short distance down the road is a ranger station. Here begins the 4-mile **Duck Harbor Trail,** which takes you through upland forest, along the shore, and past blueberry brambles (picking and eating allowed) to **Duck Harbor.** Spend the day here wandering the area's trails, enjoying the scenery of woods and water, and watching for ospreys and bald eagles.

If you'd prefer broad vistas, head to the cliffs on the southern tip of the island. But don't be in such a hurry that you miss the flora on the way: red-topped lichen called British soldiers, pitcher plants, and cranberries in early autumn.

The 2.5-mile boat ride from Northeast Harbor to **Little Cranberry Island** takes about 20 minutes in good weather; you can also catch a boat at Southwest Harbor on the opposite side of Somes Sound.

The tiny island, with rocky shores, spruce trees, and quiet country lanes, boasts 75 year-round residents, most of whom can trace their ancestry back to the 18th century. As your boat nears the picturesque village of **Isleford,** winding among bobbing lobster boats in the protected harbor, you'll spot two buildings of note: the gabled, wooden **Blue Duck Ship's Store** and, directly behind, the

Islesford Historical Museum, housed in a brick Georgian Revival building. Both structures are part of Acadia National Park. They contain turn-of-the-20th-century ship models, navigation aids, dolls and toys, photographs, tools, and other relics that tell the story of the Cranberry Isles—a cluster of five islands—and their seafaring people.

Another option for getting out on the water is to take an **Islesford Historical Cruise** *(207-276-5352. Fee, reservations required)*, a ranger-led boat tour focusing on island history. It stops at Sutton Island, and Big and Little Cranberry Islands. Meet at the municipal pier in Northeast Harbor.

Quiet harbor, Acadia National Park

INFORMATION & ACTIVITIES

Headquarters
P.O. Box 177
Bar Harbor, ME 04609
207-288-3338
www.nps.gov/acad

Visitor & Information Centers
Visitor center on Me. 3 south
of Hulls Cove, open daily mid-
April through October.
Thompson Island Information
Center on same road just
before Mount Desert Island.
Open May to mid-September.
Off-season, information at
headquarters 2.5 miles west of
Bar Harbor on Me. 233.

Seasons & Accessibility
Park open all year. In winter
visitor facilities close, and
much of the Park Loop Road is
unplowed. For recorded
weather information, call 207-
667-8910. For boats to Isle au
Haut, call 207-367-5193; for
Islesford on Little Cranberry
Island, call 207-276-5352.

Entrance Fee
$20 per vehicle for 7-day pass.

Pets
Permitted on leashes except on
swimming beaches, in public
buildings, on some trails, and
at Isle au Haut campsite.

Facilities for Disabled
Visitor center, some rest rooms,
and carriage roads are wheelchair accessible. Wildwood
Stables has two carriages
designed to hold wheelchairs.
Free guidebook available.

Things to Do
Free ranger-led activities:
nature walks, photography
workshops, stargazing, films,
slide shows. For bus tours call
207-288-3327 for National
Park tours or 207-288-9899
for Oli's Trolley. Boat cruises,
carriage rides, hiking, bicycling,
swimming, fishing, cross-
country skiing, snowshoeing,
and snowmobiling.

Special Advisories
■ Be careful on ledges and rocks
along shore; algae are slippery.
■ In spring and fall, watch out
for strong storm waves.
■ Overnight backpacking is
not allowed.

Campgrounds
Two campgrounds, 14-day lim-
its. Blackwoods open all year.
Reserve through National Parks
Reservation Service (see p. 13).
Reservations recommended
May through October; other
times first come, first served.
Fee $20 per night. Seawall open
June to early September; first

Eagle Lake, Mount Desert Island

come, first served. Fees $14-$20 per night. Showers outside park. Tent and RV sites; no hookups. Food services in park.

Hotels, Motels, & Inns
(Unless otherwise noted, rates are for two persons in a double room, high season.)

In Bar Harbor, ME 04609:
■ **Bar Harbor Inn**
Newport Dr. 207-288-3351 or 800-248-3351. 153 units. $189-$575. Pool, restaurant, bar.
■ **Bayview**
111 Eden St. 207-288-5861 or 800-356-3585. 33 units. $135-$260. Pool. Mid-May to mid-October.
■ **Best Western Inn**
452 Me. 3. 207-288-5823 or 800-528-1234. 94 units. $105-$125. AC, pool. May to late October.
■ **Cleftstone Manor**
92 Eden St. 207-288-4951. 16

units. $100-$225. Mid-April to late October.
■ **Cromwell Harbor Motel**
359 Main St. 207-288-3201. 26 units. $105-$150.
■ **Harbor Regency Holiday Inn**
123 Eden St. 207-288-9723 or 800-234-6835. 221 units. $145-$345. AC, pool, restaurant. Mid-May to late October.
■ **Wonder View Inn & Suites**
5 Eden St. 207-288-3358 or 888-439-8439. 79 units. $103-$220. Pool, restaurant. May to October.

In Northeast Harbor, ME 04662:
■ **Asticou Inn**
Me. 3 and Me. 198. 207-276-3344 or 800-258-3373. 48 units. $225-$325. Pool, restaurant. Mid-May to mid-October.
■ **Kimball Terrace Inn**
10 Huntington Rd. 207-276-3383 or 800-454-6225. 72 units. $150-$163. Pool, restaurant. Mid-May to mid-October.

In Southwest Harbor, ME 04679:
■ **Moorings Inn**
Shore Rd. 207-244-5523 or 800-596-5523. 22 units, 4 cottages. $65-$150. May to October.

For more accommodations, call the Chambers of Commerce of Bar Harbor at 207-288-5103, Northeast Harbor at 207-276-5040, or Southwest Harbor at 207-244-9264.

Excursions from Acadia

Maine's Big Sur Drive

Begins 10 miles north of Acadia

197 miles one way; one day US 1 from Ellsworth northeast to Calais is truly a road less traveled. Most tourists never get past Bar Harbor and miss the crashing surf at Acadia National Park's Schoodic Point, the tiny fishing villages that dot the coast, and the small cities a stone's throw from the Canadian border. This is the 1-day route that links them all.

Start at Ellsworth and head north on US 1 for 9 miles to the Hancock-Sullivan Bridge across Taunton Bay. Pull over after 1 mile at the **Sullivan Harbor Scenic Turnout** for views of Cadillac Mountain and Mount Desert Island. Sixteen miles east of Ellsworth, turn right on Me. 186 toward Acadia National Park's **Schoodic Point.** For the next 6 miles, the road winds along the eastern shore of Frenchman

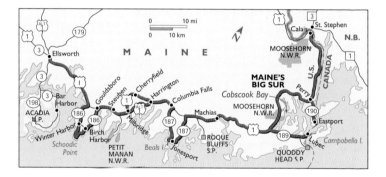

Bay to Winter Harbor Village. Less than a mile from town, turn right for a side trip to the point, which is a 2,016-acre preserve that has a 6-mile **scenic drive** along the windswept granite shores of Schoodic Peninsula, views of Mount Desert Island and Cadillac Mountain, hiking trails, and tidal pools full of life. The park road ends at the tiny fishing village of Wonsqueak Harbor.

Return to Me. 186 a few miles north at Birch Harbor. At the end, continue north again on US 1 for 2 miles, turning right to visit **Bartlett Maine Estate Winery** (*207-546-2408. Tastings May–Oct.*), where the Bartlett family has been making fruit wines since 1983.

Follow US 1 for 3 miles to reach Washington County, the "sunrise county." Once the territory of the Passamaquoddy Indians, it is larger than Delaware and earned its sobriquet by being the first place in the United States to greet the rising sun each morning. It could as easily have been called the "blueberry county"; about 30 million pounds are harvested each year.

Turn right onto Pigeon Hill Road in Steuben to visit the 6,950-acre **Petit Manan National Wildlife Refuge** *(207-546-2124),* where more than 300 types of birds—including bald eagles, peregrine falcons, and roseate terns—have been sighted. A few miles farther, at the head of Narraguagus Bay, is **Milbridge,** home to one of the world's largest blueberry-processing plants. Stay on US 1 at the junction of US 1A to visit the "blueberry capital of the world." To cut out several miles of driving, take US 1A north for 8 miles to Harrington.

Continue for 3.5 miles past Harrington to Columbia Falls; stop by the elegant **Thomas Ruggles House** *(207-483-4637. June–mid-Oct.; donation),* built for a rich lumber dealer in 1818. Just past Columbia Falls is a right turn onto Me. 187 for a 10-mile side trip to the boatbuilding and fishing communities of **Jonesport** and **Beals.** In Jonesport, look for the puffin mailbox of Capt. Barna Norton to sign on for a cruise to Machias Seal Island *(see p. 36)* or Petit Manan Island *(207-497-5933. June–Aug.; fare).* Take Me. 187 back along the shore of Chandler Bay to US 1.

It's less than 2 miles to the turnoff for **Roque Bluffs State Park** *(207-255-3475. www.state.me.us/doc/prkslnds/roque.htm. May–late-Oct.; adm. fee),* with its sandy beach and freshwater swimming pond. **Machias** (Muh-TCHAI-uhs) is just 5 miles beyond the turnoff. The town's name comes from the Native American word *mechises* for "bad little falls." For the best view of these waters, go into town and park in the lot on Me. 92. Walk onto the footbridge, suspended over the falls, foamy and reddish brown with tannin from cedar trees.

Turn right on Me. 92 just south of town to visit the **Fort O'Brien State Historic Site** *(207-726-4412. www.state.me.us/doc/prkslnds/obrien.htm. Mem. Day–Labor Day),* near where the first naval battle of the American Revolution was fought in 1775. Stroll along **Jasper Beach,** with its wave-polished pebbles of jasper and rhyolite.

About 16 miles past Machias, turn right onto Me. 189 for **Quoddy Head State Park** *(207-733-0911. May–mid-Oct.; adm. fee; see p. 38),* Lubec, and Campobello Island over the border in New Brunswick, Canada. Turn off Me. 189 after 9.5 miles to go to the park and adjacent **West Quoddy Head Light** *(light closed to public).*

Gulliver's Hole, Quoddy Head State Park

The park's steep ledges offer a terrific vantage point for the famous Bay of Fundy tides, which rise 20 to 30 feet. Perched atop a 90-foot cliff on the easternmost point of land in the United States, the candy-striped lighthouse is visible from 20 miles at sea.

Once back on Me. 189, continue toward **Lubec.** This easternmost town in the country was once home to 19 sardine factories. It's also the access point for the International Bridge to the 2,800-acre **Roosevelt Campobello International Park** *(506-752-2922. www.nps.gov/roca. Late May–mid-Oct.),* the Canadian summer home of Franklin D. Roosevelt. As you climb the hill after clearing customs, turn around and look across the Narrows, where the strongest tidal currents on the east coast flow at 15 miles per hour. Friar's Head picnic area, on the left just before the entrance to the international park, offers views of Lubec, Eastport, Cobscook Bay, and the mouth of Passamaquoddy Bay. If you're headed for East-port and want to save about 40 miles of driving, consider taking the Deer Isle Ferry, which leaves from just a few miles past the park entrance; from Deer Isle, you can take another ferry to Eastport.)

Retrace Me. 189 to US 1 and head north toward Calais. After 3 miles, the road enters the southern boundary of the **Edmunds Unit** of the **Moosehorn National Wildlife Refuge** *(207-454-7161. www.mainebirding.net/moosehorn),* a breeding ground for migratory birds and other wildlife, including the reclusive American woodcock. With the Edmunds Unit to the south, the refuge is the northernmost in a chain of migratory bird refuges that extends from Maine to Florida. Many of the unit's 6,700 acres border Cobscook Bay. When you watch the tide come in from the shores of **Cobscook Bay State Park** *(207-726-4412. www.state.me.us/doc/prks lnds/cobscook.htm. Mid-May–mid-Oct.; adm. fee; see pp. 38–39)*, it's easy to understand why the Native Americans named the bay of churning waters "boiling tides." They average 24 feet in height.

Seven miles past the park entrance, watch for the turnoff to **Cobscook Reversing Falls** in Pembroke. Tidal waters from Dennys and Whiting Bays tumble through the narrow channels in either side of Falls Island, creating reversing waterfalls.

The road to the falls is poorly marked: Turn right off US 1 onto Leighton Point Road; after 3.2 miles, turn right and continue for 1.2 miles past the Clarkside Cemetery. When the road forks, go left and continue 1.7 miles into the park. The tip of **Mahar Point** provides

Lobsters

Overwhelmed by the sheer number of lobsters off the New England coast, early settlers considered them despicable creatures, good for little more than animal food. But in the mid-1800s, lobsters began to catch on as a meal for humans. And then they went fast. Populations in southern New England were nearly wiped out in less than a century. Today, with roughly two million lobster traps off the coast of New England, a mature lobster has about a one-in-ten chance of avoiding the dinner plate. Those who manage to survive can live for decades, growing several feet long and weighing up to 40 pounds.

Lobsters have five pairs of legs, at least one of which have developed into pincers. Their flipper-like tails help them to swim both forward and backward. While lobsters are able to swim freely within 12 days of life, the crustaceans spend most of their time crawling along the ocean floor.

Lobster eaters particularly enjoy the meat found in the pincers, or claws, as well as the heavily muscled abdomen.

Live lobsters are blackish or brownish green on top, and yellowy orange, red, or blue on the bellies. They only turn red when boiled.

Lobstermen catch their prey in cages called pots that have dead fish inside for bait. Farther out at sea, trawlers are used to catch the creatures.

a fine view of the fierce white water. Watch for bald eagles, ospreys, and seals.

Halfway between the Equator and the North Pole is the town of Perry, named for Commodore Oliver H. Perry, a hero of the War of 1812. Two miles from the Perry town line, at the junction of US 1 and Me. 190, turn right onto Me. 190 for Eastport. For the first few miles the road passes by the Pleasant Point Indian Reservation, home to more than 850 Passamaquoddy Indians. It's another 5 miles to downtown Eastport. To see **Old Sow Whirlpool,** one of the world's largest, turn left onto Water Street at the end of Me. 190, pass the entrance to the Deer Isle Ferry, and continue to Dog Island at the end of the road. The whirlpool is best seen about 2 hours before high tide.

Back at the junction of US 1 and Me. 190, continue north on US 1 for 2 miles to the 45th Parallel picnic area. In 1896, the National Geographic Society erected the red granite stone that marks the halfway point. About 5 miles from here, pull over at the next rest area to view the red granite cliffs of the St. Croix River.

Between Robbinston and Calais, look for 12 small, numbered granite markers on the river side of the road. Lumberman and journalist James S. Pike put them there in 1870 to time his racehorses.

At the Calais (CAL-lus) town line, the **St. Croix Island International Historic Site** *(207-726-4412. www.nps.gov/sacr)* is named for two long coves that meet to form a cross. Samuel de Champlain landed here in 1604, making this island in the middle of the St. Croix River the site of the country's first European settlement north of St. Augustine, Florida.

Located on the bank of the St. Croix River across from St. Stephen in New Brunswick, Calais is one of the busiest ports of entry along the 3,000-mile U.S.-Canadian border. Continue north on US 1 through town for 5 miles to the 16,080-acre **Baring Unit** of the **Moosehorn Wildlife Refuge** *(207-454-7161)*. The American bald eagle has taken up residence here, a fitting sentinel at the end of this road to the border. Nesting areas line the entrance to the refuge at Charlotte Road.

■ **197 miles long; one day** ■ **Southeastern Maine** ■ **Ellsworth to Calais on US 1 and Me. 186, 187, 189, and 190** ■ **Best months April–Oct.** ■ **Road to Schoodic Point is one way.**

Atlantic Puffin

With its clownishly colorful bill, the Atlantic Puffin is more widespread in Maine waters now than it was a quarter century ago. Thanks to reintroduction efforts that began in the 1970s, puffins have returned to nest on islands from which they had been wiped out by persecution and predation.

For many years, puffin chicks were transplanted from colonies in Canada to Maine, where biologists raised them. When the birds became adults, they returned to their foster homes and began breeding on their own.

Though puffins occasionally are seen from land, they spend most of their nonbreeding lives far out at sea. There, they search for food by diving deep into the water—usually to depths of 50 feet or so, although they have been known to go as far down as 200 feet.

Masters of fishing, the birds use their wings underwater almost like flippers as they forage for food. They can collect up to a dozen small fish each trip, managing to clamp them each in turn crosswise in their bills.

Those massive bills take about five years to fully develop. During warm weather, the bills are bright orange, yellow, and blue. In the winter, they lose their intense coloration.

These appealing birds are not shy. You should be able to see them easily on a tour to Machias Seal Island (see p. 36), on the U.S.–Canadian border.

Atlantic puffin

Machias Seal Island

60 miles east of Acadia

One of Maine's most appealing icons, the Atlantic puffin nests on a few islands about 10 miles off the coast. A boat trip to Machias Seal Island has long been a reliable way to see nesting puffins; two companies specializing in this 60- to 90-minute summertime journey are Norton's Tours in Jonesport and the Bold Coast Charter in Cutler.

When the weather permits, a limited number of visitors can land on the tiny, treeless island and see puffins, as well as common eiders, common and arctic terns, razorbills, and black guillemots. Common murres are often seen in summer, though the species does not nest on the island. Stray birds blown off course during storms often rest on Machias for a few days before resuming their flights.

All the good bird-watching is done from one of the many observation blinds on Machias. Small groups of people can spend between 30 to 45 minutes inside the blinds at a time, watching and photographing the puffins that perch on the roof. The birds use the blinds as launching pads, from which they dive into the sea when they spot fish.

The island itself is the subject of a territorial dispute between the United States and Canada. The United States says Machias Island became part of the country in 1783, when Great Britain relinquished its control over the colonies. Canada claims it has had sovereignty over the island since 1621. To reinforce that claim, the Canadian government points to the facts that it has maintained a lighthouse on the island since 1832. The Canadian Wildlife Service established Machias as a migratory bird sanctuary in 1944.

Today, Canada continues to man the 60-foot lighthouse that warns ships of the treacherous shoals and infamous high tides in the Bay of Fundy. The building is closed to the public. However, visitors are free to roam around it before returning to the mainland. En route home (or to the island), watch the waters for whales, seals, and porpoises.

■ **10 acres** ■ **Northeast Maine** ■ **Boats leave from Jonesport and Cutler, Me.** ■ **Best months May–Sept.** ■ **Hiking, bird-watching, boat cruise** ■ **Fee** ■ **Contact Norton's Tours, 207-497-5933; or Bold Coast Charter Co., 207-259-4484**

Great Wass Island Preserve

 The Great Wass Archipelago consists of 68 beautiful islands that on many days are wrapped in far more fog and bluster than the mainland just a few miles away. These cool, moist conditions have created a fascinating oceanic microclimate, populating the archipelago with plants normally found much farther north in subarctic regions.

Great Wass Island Preserve contains a medley of pink granite shorelines dotted with beach-head iris, bird's-eye primrose, and, on the interior, sizable stands of jack pine that form the southern limit of the trees' range in Maine.

You'll also find open peat lands layered with sphagnum moss, cranberry, sundew, pitcher plant, and baked-apple berry. Bird-watchers will absolutely love Great Wass because it is a wonderful place to spot spruce grouse, downy and hairy woodpeckers, eastern kingbirds, Swainson's and hermit thrushes, and cedar waxwings. You might also see a multitude of warblers—including Nashville, yellow, chestnut-sided, magnolia, palm, Blackburnian, black-and-white, and black-throated green—as well as black ducks and spotted sandpipers.

The **Little Cape Point** and **Mud Hole Trails** begin at the parking area, each going to different parts of the eastern shore. If you have the time and energy (roots, rocks, and wet spots can make for slow going), by all means consider the 5-mile loop walk. Head out to the shore on the Little Cape Point Trail, passing through stands of jack pines and stopping at fine viewpoints of the coastal plateau bogs. On reaching the shore, turn left and walk north, following a series of rock cairns and markers. Be sure to take your time here, pausing along the way to explore the tidal pools. Eventually you'll reach the Mud Hole Trail, which will take you back to the parking lot through a blanket of spruce and fir.

Those even more ambitious can turn right instead of left at the shore end of the Cape Point trail, and head for the southern tip of the island at **Red Head.** Be aware that this amounts to a 9-mile trek over rather grueling, rocky terrain, though in truth it would be hard to imagine a more satisfying way to wear yourself out.

■ **1,579 acres** ■ **Southeast Maine, off Me. 187 near Jonesport**
■ **Best months May–October** ■ **Hiking, bird-watching** ■ **No pets**
■ **Contact The Nature Conservancy, 14 Maine St., Brunswick, ME 04011;**
(207) 729-5181

75 miles northeast of Acadia

Quoddy Head State Park

85 miles northeast of Acadia

You'll find a magnificent slice of the Maine coast at Quoddy Head State Park. **West Quoddy Head** is another site famous for being one of the easternmost locations in the contiguous United States. Try the walk to **Carrying Place Cove,** an inlet fringed with wildflowers. In autumn, it is the perfect place to watch migrating seabirds; in summer, look for Lincoln's sparrows and palm warblers.

Also of interest is a wonderful peat bog, the north side of which has been exposed to a height of more than a dozen feet by rain and the action of waves. This kind of cross-sectional view of a bog is so rare that the site has been designated a National Natural Landmark.

As you explore this area, keep your eyes on the water, and you may well see any number of harbor seals. They're especially visible during high tide, busy feeding on a variety of fish such as cod, flounder, herring, and rockfish. During low tide, harbor seals settle onto rocks for a bit of shut-eye, and therefore become more difficult to see. Should danger arise during these siestas, a sharp bark of alarm goes out, and they all bail off the rocks for the safety of the water. Watch Quoddy Head's waters for migrating whales, too. There is a plaque in the park that tells visitors what species they might see.

■ **481 acres** ■ **Southeast Maine, off Me. 189 near South Lubec** ■ **Best months mid-May–mid-Oct.** ■ **Hiking, bird-watching, whale-watching** ■ **Adm. fee** ■ **Contact Bureau of Parks and Lands, 106 Hogan Rd., Bangor, ME 04401; 207-733-0911 (summer), 207-941-4014 (winter)**

Cobscook Bay State Park

80 miles northeast of Acadia

Cobscook Bay State Park has the look of the Maine coast before the birth of ubiquitous outlet malls and restaurants. Far from the hubbub of the southern part of the state, you'll discover a quiet seaside retreat dominated by towering spruce trees. Whether just stopping for a picnic lunch or pitching your tent for the night, Cobscook is a good jumping-off point for further exploration of Down East Maine.

What to See and Do
You've set up camp at a site with sweeping views of Whiting Bay and realize you've forgotten to pack dinner. No problem.

Cobscook Bay

Cobscook Bay is Maine's only state park with a clamming area where visitors are allowed to dig. Bring a big pot and plan to get dirty as you try your hand (at low tide) at this popular activity. After tending to your scraped knuckles, watch the setting sun cast a pink glow over the shimmering waters as you dine on your hand-picked steamers.

If you're an early bird, scramble up **Cunningham Mountain** for views of the sun rising over secluded **Whiting Bay,** part of the larger Cobscook Bay. Leaving from Broad Cove Road, the 0.2-mile trail climbs up the granite hill. From this vantage, you may be one of the first people in the lower 48 states to see the sunrise. If you hike up in the predawn darkness, don't forget a flashlight since the path is rocky. The trail connects to a **nature trail** that follows the park's western edge through the woods.

Another path, the 0.75-mile **Anthony's Beach Trail,** meanders through the woods and along the rocky shore to a large wharf. Be sure to follow the trail blazes; it's easy to get lost.

The park's jagged shoreline and many coves lend themselves to sea kayaking. Numerous islands and small bays can be reached by small motorboat or canoe. Boat launch facilities are near the middle of the park and in the northwest corner. There are no boats for rent in the park.

Reversing Falls

The local Maliseet and Passamaquoddy Indians called the area Cobscook, or "boiling waters," for the white-capped reversing falls that are found near the park. The best time to see the falls is a couple of hours before high tide, when the incoming water is as much as 24 feet higher than at low tide. This causes the flow of water in the bay to temporarily reverse direction.

Ask the park ranger for directions and a tide chart.

More than 200 species of birds have been sighted at **Cobscook Bay,** including bald eagles. The park office has bird lists, as well as a collection of field guides available for visitors.

Camping

Cobscook Bay offers 106 tent and RV sites, with nearby shower facilities. Four secluded spots are accessible only by short trail. A couple of dozen sites are available on a first-come, first-served basis. A few sites have wooden Adirondack shelters. Reservations advised in season; call 207-287-3824 or 800-332-1501 *(Maine only. Fee.)*

Nearby Sights

The picturesque fishing village of **Lubec,** located about 10 miles east of the park, is the easternmost town in the country. Follow the signs to West Quoddy Head, guarded by a red-and-white-striped lighthouse *(closed).*

From Lubec, cross Franklin D. Roosevelt Memorial Bridge to Campobello Island in New Brunswick, Canada. The large wooden home where President Franklin D. Roosevelt's family spent many vacations now is the centerpiece of **Roosevelt Campobello International Park** *(506-752-2922. May–mid-Oct.).* The 34 rooms inside are furnished much as they were when FDR spent his summers here.

■ **888 acres** ■ **Southeast Maine** ■ **5 miles off US 1 in Dennysville**
■ **May–mid-Oct.; trails open year-round** ■ **Camping, hiking, boating, kayaking, clamming, bird-watching, whale-watching** ■ **Adm. fee** ■ **Contact the park, R.R. 1, Box 127, Dennysville, ME 04268; 207-726-4412**

Deer Isle Drive

Begins 20 miles west of Acadia

82 miles round-trip; half-day This drive is a Down East sampler, circuiting a peninsula that juts into Penobscot Bay. You'll visit historic Castine and the fishing villages of Deer Isle and Stonington, then head back through the interior to Blue Hill.

Begin in Orland at the junction of US 1 and Me. 175, near where the Penobscot River meets Penobscot Bay. Follow Me. 175 south a short way to Me. 166A, then continue south on that road for a few miles to **Castine,** home of the **Maine Maritime Academy** *(800-464-6565. www.mainemaritime.edu).* Markers around this quaint village chronicle its history, which dates back to the early 17th century. The French were the first Europeans to settle here, followed briefly by the Dutch and then the British.

At the waterfront, you can tour the academy's training vessel, the *State of Maine (800-227-8465. July–Labor Day).* The **Wilson Museum** *(Perkins St. 207-326-8753)* has a nice collection of prehistoric and Native American artifacts. Military history buffs might enjoy exploring **Fort George,** built by the British in the late 18th-century, and **Fort Madison,** earthworks created by Americans in 1811.

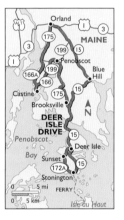

From here, go north for a few miles on Me. 166 toward Penobscot, and then north on Me. 199 for 3 miles to Me. 175, again toward Brooksville. After about 6 miles, you'll come to the Bagaduce River bridge. Stop here to see the **Reversing Falls,** a phenomenon caused by the fast-flowing tides.

Six miles beyond the falls is the **Caterpillar Hill rest area**, where you can view Deer Isle, Penobscot Bay, Camden Hills, and the Bay Islands. About a half-mile past the rest area, go south on Me. 15 and over the suspension bridge onto **Deer Isle,** the second largest island off the coast of Maine. The island's granite has been used over the years in such landmarks as Rockefeller Center in New York City.

Turn right and follow signs to Sunset, overlooking Southwest Harbor. Continue south 4 miles to Stonington Harbor, a port for charter boats and the ferry for Isle au Haut *(Isle-au-Haut Co.*

207-367-5193; no service Sun. in winter; fare).

To return to US 1, head north on Me. 15 for 20 miles to Blue Hill, which prospered during the late 1700s as a shipbuilding and trading center. Now somewhat of an artist colony, the town is best known for its pottery made from local clay. Another draw for the artistically inclined is the **Haystack Mountain School of Crafts** *(207-348-2306)* on Deer Isle, which has been here since 1961.

From Blue Hill, continue north on Me. 15 for another 12 miles to rejoin US 1 at Orland.

■ **82 miles round-trip; half-day** ■ **Scenic drive** ■ **Southeast Maine** ■ **Best months May–Oct.** ■ **Roads intersect constantly, often sharing multiple designations. Pay attention to directions.**

Rachel Carson Salt Pond Preserve

75 miles southwest of Acadia

Few people have done more to improve our relationship with the Earth than marine biologist Rachel Carson. Her decision to speak out against the wholesale use of pesticides in her 1962 book, *Silent Spring*, brought her tremendous criticism. In the end, however, her skills as a scientist and writer, reinforced by her tremendous courage, enabled her to be a catalyst for political changes that ultimately saved countless species of wildlife.

While *Silent Spring* is her best-known book, Carson wrote several other on natural history. One of her best, *The Edge of the Sea,* was researched in part here at the salt pond, which was donated to The Nature Conservancy by Helen Williams and her two sisters, Anne and Elizabeth.

After a short walk through a ribbon of seaside rose, strawberry, goldenrod, and meadowsweet, you'll find yourself at the upper edge of the tidal zone—a line marked by rough periwinkles, tortoiseshell limpets, and blue mussels. Look for Irish moss (the source of carrageenan, which is a stabilizer for everything from chocolate milk to salad dressings), as well as rockweed and knotted wrack. The bulges visible near the tops of these last two plants are actually air chambers that allow the leaves to float near the surface of the water and maximize exposure to the sun.

Some scientists use the term "ecozone" to describe an ecological niche with conditions that favor specific life-forms. What makes

Birders on boardwalk at Rachel Carson Salt Pond Preserve

the intertidal zone so exciting is that so many different niches are only a few feet apart. Some species here require constant submersion, while others are submerged only twice a day during high tide; still others may be submerged only during twice monthly spring tides.

At the center of the preserve is the **salt pond,** a wonderful spot to drop to your knees and look for dogwinkles, green sea urchins, green crabs, and smooth periwinkles. One note of caution is in order here. Many tide-pool residents are living in very precise locations, chosen for food and security; if you disturb one of the creatures here, or even move a rock, it's essential that you return it to its original location.

Those looking for more of a walk can follow a series of **trails** and old **logging roads** on the upland section of the preserve, part of a farm that is reverting to woods. Access is across Me. 32 from the pull-off.

■ 78 acres ■ Southern Maine, east of Brunswick off Me. 32 ■ Best months May–Oct. ■ Hiking, bird-watching, wildlife viewing ■ Contact The Nature Conservancy, 14 Maine St., Suite 401, Brunswick, ME 04011; 207-729-5181

Biscayne

Biscayne is a seascape in watercolor, offering gorgeous vistas on the shore and beneath the sea. Standing on the park's narrow shore, you look out upon a bay that is tranquil on the surface and teeming with life below. Aboard a glass-bottom boat, you look down and see some of that life: dazzling colored fish, fantastically shaped corals, fronds of sea grass gently waving back and forth.

Biscayne National Park is an underwater wilderness. Ninety-five percent of its 173,000 acres lie beneath sapphire water. The remaining part consists of about 50 barrier islands and a mangrove shoreline, the longest such undeveloped shore on Florida's east coast.

If local preservationists had not protested vehemently in the 1960s, the islands would have been developed like their neighbor Miami Beach. Biscayne Bay itself would have been scarred by a long causeway and gouged by a 40-foot deep channel. Thankfully, preservationists saved the day, and the area was set aside as a national monument in 1968. Twelve years later, it became a national park.

Biscayne supports a wondrous diversity of marine and bird life. Manatees float among the shallows, grazing in seagrass meadows. More than 250 species of fish make this a snorkeler's and diver's paradise. Birders can see cormorants, white ibises, snowy egrets, and brown pelicans that can spot a fish from as high as 30 feet in the air.

Crystal clear only on windless days, the waters remain quite pure. On the reefs close to shore, snorkelers can see corals, spiny lobsters, and jewel-toned tropical fish. Farther out live sea turtles, squid, rays, and barracudas.

The bay's islands keep ocean waves from battering the bay. Thus shielded, Biscayne provides sanctuary to the life within it and beauty to those who come to look beneath the surface.

- Southern Florida
- 173,000 acres
- Established 1980
- Best months mid-Dec.–mid-April for islands; late May–Aug. for reefs
- Canoeing, swimming, scuba diving, snorkeling, glass-bottom boat tours
- Information: 305-230-1144 www.nps.gov/bisc

Coral reef, Biscayne National Park

How to Get There

From Miami, take the Florida Turnpike (Fla. 821) south to Speedway Boulevard, and turn left (south). Continue 4 miles on Speedway Boulevard to North Canal Drive and turn left (east). Follow Canal Drive to the park entrance. From Homestead (about 9 miles), take Southwest 328th Street (North Canal Drive) to the park entrance at Convoy Point. Airport: Miami.

When to Go

The best time to visit the park is from mid-December to mid-April, subtropical Florida's dry season. In summer, you face the perils of mosquitoes and fast-moving thunderstorms, but seas then are generally the calmest—making them ideal for snorkeling and diving. Hurricanes are occasional.

How to Visit

Unless you have your own boat, plan to see Biscayne on a tour boat. You can look underwater on a reef cruise aboard a glass-bottom boat or swim the shallow waters on a snorkeling cruise. There are scuba cruises also to the outer reef for qualified divers. Make reservations in advance. Cruises may be canceled if there aren't enough passengers or for bad weather.

What Not to Miss

- Cruising through the park in a glass-bottom boat from Convoy Point

- Renting a kayak and exploring the mangrove bays from Dante Fascell Visitor Center

- Visiting Elliott Key and hiking along the nature trail for great views

- Taking the snorkelers' cruise and seeing the colorful corals and fish that live beneath the bay's surface

If you arrive too late for an excursion, you can get fine views from the jetty at **Convoy Point.** The concessionaire rents canoes and kayaks to anyone interested in exploring the mangroves.

Elliott and **Boca Chita Keys** offer overnight anchorages. Fishing is excellent for marlins and sailfish on the ocean side, while grouper and snapper are more likely to be found in the bay.

Boaters should be careful not to damage the coral reefs that have taken centuries to develop.

In the **Dante Fascell Visitor Center,** there's a permanent exhibit on the park's ecosystems, and audiovisual programs and ranger talks.

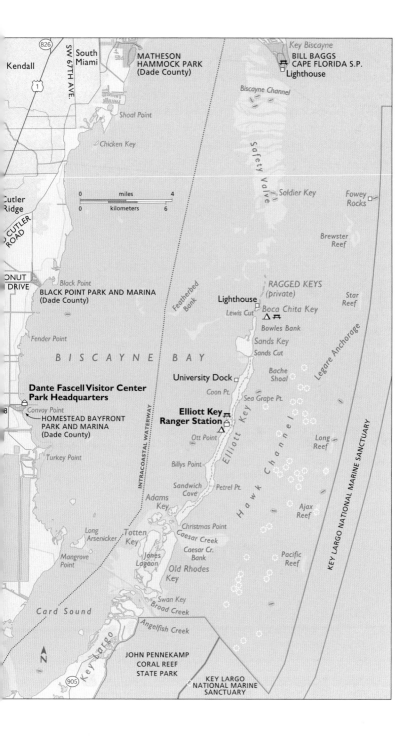

EXPLORING THE PARK

Reef Exploration: **A half day**

Depending on how intrepid you are, there are several ways to see the reef. Certified divers have the most destination options; trips for them leave on the weekends. Cruises for snorkelers leave daily and last for 3 hours. If you don't want to get wet, you can take a cruise aboard the 49-foot-long glass-bottom boat; these tours also leave daily and last for 3 hours, but are less expensive than the snorkeling cruises.

Glass-bottom boat, Biscayne Bay

Sign up for a trip to the reef well ahead of time (*see Information & Activities p. 56 for details*). Schedules vary by season. (If the weather is rough, snorkelers can explore the waters in the bay.) Boats leave from Convoy Point.

The **Intracoastal Waterway** runs through the bay; you'll see the posts with signs that bear numbers keyed to navigational charts. In one short, shallow stretch near the waterway, natural grass beds rise near the surface and are visible at low tide. Bonefish, prized by sportfishermen for their speed and strength, inhabit the grass beds.

On the snorkeling trip, the boat slips through the keys toward the reefs beyond. Here in the waters, snorkelers will see a brilliant floor show: the multicolored flash of a passing parrotfish, the sinuous glide of an angelfish, the little jungles of coral. Slowly the boat moves to another vantage point, and a new seabed show starts. Giant brain coral and mountainous star coral dominate the reefs. Sea fans and other soft corals ripple in the calm, clear water. Members of the crew help identify the vibrantly colored fish flitting around the massive coral formations.

There is nothing busier than the parrotfish, with its rainbow plumage and beak-like mouth used for grazing on the microscopic algae that grow on the coral. By nibbling and ingesting the coral constantly, the fish turns it into sand.

Some of the creatures in this underwater wonderland are perfectly named. The grunt actually grunts, surgeonfish conceal scalpel-like spines near their tails, while triggerfish have dorsal spines that resemble triggers.

Only an expert can begin to explain the curious life of the bluehead wrasse, one of a host of gaudy tropical fish you might see in the water. This branch of the wrasse family is named for its "supermale" leader; females and lesser males are not only smaller but also a different color. If the tribe loses its leader, another male takes over, growing larger and changing color to blue. If all the males are eaten by predators, then a female changes sex and takes on attributes of the supermale.

Mangrove Shore: **A quarter-mile; at least an hour**

If you have little time, no boat, and some curiosity, walk the shore around **Convoy Point,** a fine place for a picnic. If you have more time, inquire about renting a canoe or kayak to (continued on p. 52)

Underwater Florida

The warm waters that surround Florida are a paradise for underwater enthusiasts. Some use scuba equipment for exploration, but millions more use only a snorkel and mask to enjoy the beauty just beneath the waves.

That beauty is under constant threat from human pollution in the form of sewage, fertilizers, even fishing lines and trash. In 1990, 2,800 square nautical miles of ocean were set aside for the **Florida Keys National Marine Sanctuary.** Stretching from Key Largo to the Dry Tortugas, this is the second largest marine sanctuary in the United States.

Running parallel to the Keys is the only living coral reef in the continental United States; it is a haven for fish, lobsters, snails, sponges, jellyfish, and sea anemones. What surprises many is that the coral itself is alive, made up of millions of slow-growing polyps that can be as small as a pinhead (and only as big as the tip of pencil eraser). These combine to form the fantastic

shapes of the stony and soft corals, while minute plants called zooxanthellae give color to the reef.

Viewed through goggles, reefs are like a fantasy landscape. Staghorn, elkhorn, and finger corals form forests of

Elkhorn coral

Stinging coral

Surgeonfish

Staghorn coral

Parrotfish

Star coral

Spotted lobster

Brain coral

Shrimp

giant branches; star, flower, and brain corals stand out like mountain boulders. Purple sea fans and green Venus sea fans wave like leaves on trees in the current. Gaudy-colored butterfly fish flick through the subterranean woodland.

Nasty surprises lurk here, too, such as the aptly named red fire sponge that produces a burning sensation if you touch it, and stinging corals that leave the unwary itching or in pain.

Even the bleak-looking hardbottom community at the base of the reef plays a vital role in the underwater ecosystem. The sediment-covered limestone is home to soft corals, sponges, shrimp, and crabs. Take care: Boats anchors and curious divers can easily (if inadvertently) destroy this delicate fauna.

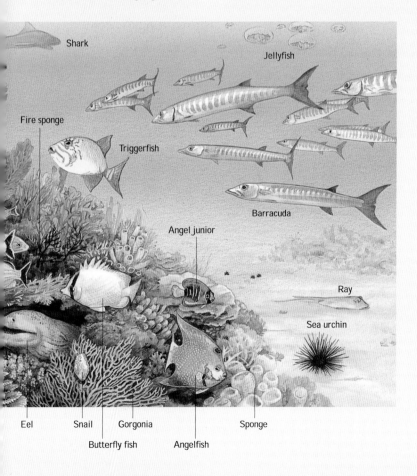

Shark

Jellyfish

Fire sponge

Triggerfish

Barracuda

Angel junior

Ray

Sea urchin

Eel   Snail   Gorgonia   Sponge

Butterfly fish   Angelfish

Mangrove forest, Biscayne National Park

explore mangrove tidal creeks. This is one of the longest continuous stretches of mangrove trees left on the east coast of Florida.

Thanks to the mangroves' ability to either block salt absorption at their roots or to secrete the salt through their leaves, the trees thrive in salty environments like the Florida Keys.

The mangroves are critical to this marine environment. They stabilize the shore, trapping their own fallen leaves and other organic material in the tangles of their stilt-like roots. In the process, they slow the waters down that flow into the bay from the land, allowing sediment to settle.

The trees attract many birds including the mangrove cuckoo and the white-crowned pigeon. Barnacles, fish, and other sea creatures cluster at the trees' half-submerged roots. The decaying mangrove leaves, rich in protein, provide food to the tiny animals at the bottom of a food chain that ends with the fisherman who eats the gray snapper caught in the bay.

The mangroves also filter damaging pollutants from the freshwater runoff into the bay. Whether you walk or paddle a boat, watch carefully for the bay animals that find food and refuge in the mangrove waterways. On a winter's day, you may see a manatee, the huge, grass-chewing "cow of the sea" that can grow up to 13 feet long and weigh as much as 3,000 pounds. Declining water-quality, destruction of seagrass beds, and speeding powerboats threaten the gentle herbivores' existence.

The scene keeps changing as each outgoing tide carries its bounty of nutrients out to sea, and each incoming tide brings in new inhabitants for the sheltering mangroves.

Island Cruise: **A half day**

Begin this outing at Convoy Point, where you'll catch a boat that takes visitors to three of the Keys in Biscayne Bay.

Geologists define a key as a formerly living coral reef that was exposed when sea level dropped about 100,000 years ago. As the waters crept up again, creating Biscayne Bay, only the tops of those reefs remained. They now form the string of barrier islands along Florida's southeastern coast.

The Miami Circle

Five miles north of the park, at the confluence of the Miami River and Biscayne Bay is the Miami Circle, a remnant of the Tequesta (pronounced te-KES-ta) Indians who inhabited South Florida centuries ago.

The 2000-year-old ruin is 38 feet in diameter. It contains 24 large holes and many smaller ones arranged in a circle, all carved in limestone. Historians speculate that the these were postholes used to support a chief's house or a village center. Archaeologists have uncovered some 150,000 artifacts at the site, including dolphin skulls, pottery shards, and stone axes.

The Tequesta were one of the first groups to make permanent villages in the area; they established hunting and fishing camps on the shore and islands now within the park. Sadly, the Tequesta vanished by the 19th century, victims of diseases brought over by European explorers, cultural disruption, and war.

The park is involved in a feasibility study to see whether the ancient stone circle should become part of Biscayne National Park.

The Keys' flora was imported, either on the wind, in the water, or through bird droppings. You'll see tropical plants here that typically are found in the Caribbean and Central America.

The cruise passes near **Caesar Creek,** named after a pirate called Black Caesar. Legend has it that Caesar was a slave in Haiti who escaped early in the 19th century. He turned to piracy, preying upon the merchant ships that were sailing to Cuba.

Pirates were just some of the many hazards seamen faced near the Keys. Narrow shipping channels, the coral reef, and treacherous weather brought many a ship to her end here. The remains of several have been cataloged within park boundaries. Federal law protects them from salvagers or souvenir collectors.

To the north is 7-mile-long **Elliott Key,** the longest in the park. In the last century, farmers and harvesters of sponges and turtles lived here. The jungle-like growth conceals the foundations of a house, old water cisterns and even the remains of a Model T Ford.

Elliott Key has primitive campsites, rest rooms, a nature trail, a swimming area, a ranger station, and what conservationists label a "road scar"—a bulldozer's legacy and a reminder of how close the island came to development.

The next island is **Sands Key,** to the north. Early Spanish mapmakers labeled this *las tetas,* which means "the breasts," a nod to the two low shell mounds created by Native Americans who hunted and fished on the Keys centuries ago.

The cruise stops on **Boca Chita,** where there is a boat dock, primitive campsites, and rest rooms, but no drinking water.

In the late 1930s, Boca Chita belonged to Mark Honeywell, an Indianan who made a fortune from thermostats. He and his wife, Olive, bought the Key in 1937 as a tropical retreat. They built a number of stone structures; the ones that still exist are the barn/garage, chapel, picnic shelter, generator building, and the 65-foot lighthouse on the northern tip. Made of Miami oolitic limestone, the ornamental **lighthouse** is open to the public when a park employee is present.

The Honeywells has elaborate parties on Boca Chita; Miami developer Carl Fisher once brought his famous elephant, Rosie, to one of the events.

After Olive Honeywell died, her husband lost interest in the property. He sold it several years later, and it eventually became part of Biscayne National Park.

Reproduction Under the Sea

When you dip your head under the water in the Florida Keys, you're entering a new realm in terms of animal reproduction. Some of the creatures below the surface can change their sex, while others can act as either a male or a female.

In the first category, there's the parrotfish. At some point in their lives, many female parrotfish undergo a hormonally induced sex change. Nobody is sure why this happens, but it may occur when there is a shortage of males.

The coral reefs themselves are created by several different kinds of sexuality. A pioneer reef begins when polyps on an existing reef create a new polyp the traditional way: The male produces sperm and fertilizes the female. However, in some corals, males and females are identical and can produce both sperm and eggs.

In either case, the coral larva, called a planula, swims through the ocean for hours or days. It latches itself onto a hard surface, and secretes limestone to form a protective shell. The planula then begins to build its own colony, reproducing asexually in a process called budding. A single planula can thus eventually multiply into a community of thousands.

Angelfish and coral, Florida Keys

INFORMATION & ACTIVITIES

Headquarters
9700 SW 328th St.
Homestead, FL 33033
305-230-1144
www.nps.gov/bisc

Visitor & Boat Information
Dante Fascell Visitor Center open daily all year. For park information, call 305-230-7275. For information and reservations for concessionaire-run glass-bottom boat, snorkeling, scuba diving, canoe trips, call 305-230-1100. Rentals available. Tours leave from Convoy Point.

Seasons & Accessibility
Open year-round. Keys (islands) can be reached by boat only. Private concessionaires operate daily, though underbooked cruises may be canceled in the off-season. Private boats allowed; boat docks available on Elliott, Adams, and Boca Chita Keys

Entrance Fees
None. $15 overnight docking fee for private boats at Elliott and Boca Chita Keys. Fees charged by concessionaire for boat trips.

Pets
Allowed on leashes no more than 6 feet long in the developed areas of Convoy Point and Elliott Key. Not permitted on boat tours.

Facilities for Disabled
Dante Fascell Visitor Center is fully accessible, as are rest rooms at Elliott Key and Boca Chita Key. Concessionaire boat tours accessible with assistance.

Things to Do
Ranger-led activities: tours in glass-bottom boat, canoe trips, island nature tours, interpretive exhibits. Also available: swimming, snorkeling, scuba diving, water skiing, boating, canoe rentals, fishing, lobstering, hiking, birding. Special events: Family Fun Fests, Saturday classes, lecture series. Offered seasonally; call for details.

Special Advisories
■ Do not touch coral or other living things on the reef. They are easily damaged; they can also inflict deep cuts and cause serious infections.
■ Mosquitoes and other insects can be a problem on the islands, particularly from April to December; carry plenty of insect repellent.

Campgrounds
Two boat-in campgrounds, both with 14-day limit. Elliott Key and Boca Chita Key open

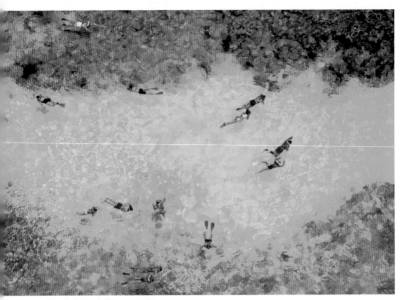
Snorkelers at Biscayne Bay

all year, first-come, first-served basis. Water at Elliott Key only. Tent sites only. $10 fee per site per night; one campsite is free with overnight docking. Group campground at Elliott Key. Fees $25 per site per night.

Hotels, Motels, & Inns
(Unless otherwise noted, rates are for two persons in a double room, high season.)

In Florida City, FL 33034:
■ Best Western Florida City
411 S. Krome Ave. 305-246-5100. 114 rooms. $109-$179. AC, pool.
■ Comfort Inn
333 SE First Ave./US 1. 305-248-4009. 123 units. $50-$250. AC, pool.

■ Knights Inn
1223 NE First Ave./US 1. 305-247-6621. 49 units, 6 with kitchenettes. $79-$169. AC, pool.

In Homestead, FL 33030:
■ Days Inn
51 S. Homestead Blvd. 305-245-1260. 100 units. $99-$139. AC, pool, restaurant.
■ Everglades Motel
605 S. Krome Ave. 305-247-4117. 14 units. $69-$109. AC, pool.

For more accommodations, contact the Homestead/Florida City Chamber of Commerce, 43 N. Krome Ave., Homestead, FL 33030. 305-247-2332.

Excursions from Biscayne

John Pennekamp Coral Reef State Park

30 miles south of Biscayne

The country's first underwater park spreads for roughly 22 miles along Key Largo and 3 miles out into the Straits of Florida, preserving a popular and beautiful piece of the Keys' coral reef. The adjacent Florida Keys National Marine Sanctuary extends protection to some of the best sections of the reef—marked by yellow buoys—resulting in a swath of clear, shallow water where multihued corals and tropical fish live unmolested.

Ninety-five percent of the park's acreage is submerged. The actual land consists of mangrove swamps and tropical hammocks that offer refuge to wading birds, mammals, and rare plants.

Wedged between reef and shore, luxuriant beds of sea grass wave in gentle currents, constituting yet another ecological community favored by manatees, sea turtles, fish, and crabs. The warm currents of the Gulf Stream and gentle trade winds keep this bountiful ecosystem a year-round haven for a diverse pool of wildlife.

The present reef took almost 7,000 years to grow to full maturity. Like the Keys, the reef is built upon the skeletons of tiny polyps. But unlike the dry rock of the islands, the reef is still alive, its thousands of polyps continuing to add to the sprawling underwater housing complex. Whips, sea fans, and plumes anchor to the hard mass, undulating in currents and providing shelter and feeding grounds for a kaleidoscopic array of crabs, sponges, shrimp, and 600 species of fish.

Before the preserve was established, it was common practice for visitors to break off pieces of the reef to take home as souvenirs. Like cave formations that take millennia to grow, the souvenirs were irreplaceable. In the late 1950s, Gilbert Voss of the Marine Institute of Miami noticed the destruction that was occurring and began working to protect the reef. His most outspoken ally, *Miami Herald* Assistant Editor John Pennekamp, lent Voss's research the power of the press. Pennekamp had played a key role in the founding of Everglades National Park, so he knew just what needed to be done. In 1960 the preserve became a reality.

The main concession building is the place to go first, to sign up for glass-bottom boat and snorkel tours (*fee*). On days of calm, clear weather, there are usually three of each tour, and they provide the easiest way to see the reef, which lies 6 to 8 miles out in the

Christ of the Deep

Graced by pillars of sunlight, the most well-known landmark in nearby Key Largo National Marine Sanctuary stands on the seafloor under 20 feet of water, its arms uplifted and its robes flowing. The 9-foot tall bronze statue of Jesus Christ is a copy of "Il Christo degli Abissi," placed

Christ of the Deep

in the Mediterranean Sea near Genoa as an inspiration to those who work or play in the ocean.

ocean. The 2.5-hour tours provide about 90 minutes of reef time. In the glass-bottom boat, you'll have a guide to point out what's what. Since the boat rolls a bit, you may get a little dizzy staring at the wonders below. If so, look up for a while at a point on the horizon, or take a breather out on deck.

Whether you see the reef wet or dry, it promises an entrancing visual feast. Schools of blue-striped grunts swing through a forest of elkhorn coral; neon-blue parrotfish nibble on coral rock for its algae; brilliant Dali-esque wrasses clean other fish for a free meal of parasites and dead skin.

Look sharply for moray eels skulking down in hidden recesses, pink plume worms decorating dark corners, and huge sponges standing like thrones in a mermaid's palace. In addition to the wonders of the natural world, you'll also probably see at least one of the many wrecked ships that litter the Straits of Florida. On some pieces of wreckage colonies of coral have begun to grow.

On the way to and from the dock, your boat will navigate the narrow mangrove channels that buffer the shoreline and provide sanctuary for creatures of the air and sea. Dolphins and manatees sometimes surface close enough for a good view. The meadows of sea grass that grow along here may not be as visually stunning as the reefs, but they do attract a sizable number of the same marine creatures that frequent the coral.

Among the few plants that flower underwater, the seagrasses help keep the water clear by trapping sediments. They also provide food and habitat for a wealth of marine life and are thus more than just a nuisance for propeller blades. From the water's surface you can see scars along the shoreline where boats have worn paths through the sea grass shoals.

Since it's illegal to harm protected sea grass, coral, or any other plants or animals, tread with care. If you plan on boating, steer for blue or green water, avoid any brown patches, and use navigation charts. On the reefs, use the park's mooring buoys instead of dropping an anchor. And don't ever stand on or handle the coral. Of all the ecosystems in the country, this is one of the most delicate.

While on shore, take a turn around the two short nature trails. The quarter-mile **Wild Tamarind Trail** provides a nice introduction to a hardwood hammock. Markers explain the historical uses of trees such as Spanish stopper (tea from its leaves was drunk as a treatment for diarrhea), Jamaica dogwood (Native Americans used the poison bark and leaves to stun fish), and soapberry (sap and orange berries make a good lather). Dawdle along this aromatic trail and marvel at the botanical variety a small tropical hammock can pack.

By the water's edge, the .25-mile **Mangrove Trail** boardwalk crosses tidal creeks to an observation platform overlooking the dense mangroves.

To learn more about this ecosystem and the creatures that live in it, you can stop by the **visitor center;** it has a 30,000-gallon saltwater aquarium full of fish, coral, anemones, and sponges. And if you have the urge, return to the concessionaire and inquire about their scuba courses and tours. They also rent fishing boats, kayaks, canoes, and diving equipment. A **canoe trail** of about 2.5 miles gives you a chance to see the mangrove wilderness up close.

After your more strenuous adventures, kick back at **Cannon Beach** on Largo Sound. For some easy snorkeling, swim out about 130 feet and take a look at the reconstructed Spanish shipwreck. You can also enjoy a quiet swim at the **Far Beach** area. There are several areas within the park where you can fish, but you'll need a saltwater license.

■ 178 nautical square miles ■ Key Largo, US 1 at Milepost 102.5 ■ Best months: Oct.–April ■ Camping, walking, guided walks, boating, canoeing, fishing, bird-watching; boat tour ■ Contact the park, P.O. Box 487, Key Largo, FL 33037; 305-451-1202. www.pennekamppark.com

Crocodile Lake National Wildlife Refuge

25 miles south of Biscayne

Had you been one of the uncounted thousands of Spanish fortune hunters shipwrecked along this coast who managed to escape being crushed between your ship's hull and the reef that tore it open, your joy at survival might have waned somewhat as you swam toward Key Largo's mangrove-tangled shore. Lurking in the pale green shallows were the Calusa, a tribe of tall men and women known to enslave castaways, and swarms of crocodiles whose main interest was feeding.

The reptiles are still here; as many as 500 winter at the Crocodile Lake National Wildlife Refuge, which lies on Largo's dreamily serene backcountry coast. The refuge's crocodile community is believed to be North America's most populous.

The refuge is closed to the public. However, if you're driving along Fla. 905 and have binoculars, you might observe the exceedingly shy lizards sunning themselves on the banks farthest from the road. Resist the impulse to wander down to the water; it is illegal to trespass, puts you in rattlesnake territory, and also destroys the ground-level nests of the migratory terns that roost along this portion of the shore.

If you have an extra hour, consider taking **Card Sound Road** to Upper Key Largo. The two-lane toll road is an interesting alternative to US 1, crossing the hardwood hammock county at Florida's southeastern tip, and rising over mile-wide Card Sound to Key Largo via a high bridge that gives a brief but unusual panorama.

In the 1950s, this tract of South Florida was slated to be the site of a new city that was advertised as "an imitation Mediterranean coastal village." However, The Nature Conservancy and the federal government bought the land from the developers, and the refuge was established in 1980.

There have been plans on the books to install an observation platform and a boardwalk through the wetland, and to develop a butterfly meadow.

■ 6,606 acres ■ North Key Largo, off Carl Sound Rd. ■ Best months: Oct.–April ■ Wildlife viewing, scenic drive ■ Contact the refuge, P.O. Box 370, Key Largo, FL 33037; 305-451-4223. http://southeast.fws.gov/CrocodileLake/

Marvelous Manatees

R ipples appear at the surface of the water, followed by a whiskered snout, a tremendous round gray head, and the wrinkled hump of a neck. The fantastic creature snorts and gives you a brief, incurious glance, then gracefully turns and disappears back into the still waters of the lagoon.

The sighting of a Florida manatee is a rare and wonderful thing. Though this subspecies of the West Indian manatee occasionally strays into other states during warm weather, the creatures generally confine themselves to the coastal waters of Florida and south Georgia. The *Trichechus manatus* can survive in fresh, brackish, or salt water, and its preferred habitat includes estuaries, bays, canals, and lazy rivers.

Feeding on sea grasses, manatees especially like water that's 3 to 7 feet deep, and this has been their undoing. Most of the deaths among manatees are caused by collisions with boats. Propellers rake their backs, and slow-moving barges crush them against the seafloor. It is an amazing fact that the majority of Florida manatees have had a run-in with a boat at some point; the lucky survivors are left with scars and deformities.

Even though manatees are seriously endangered, there is no evidence that, in Florida at least, their population was ever much larger. The 2,000 or so manatees known to exist in Florida may be the largest number that ever lived at this northern extreme of their range. If boaters observe the no-wake zones and other regulations, manatees have a fighting chance for survival.

Why should we care about the continued existence of these odd-looking creatures? They have no direct economic value. Indians hunted them for food and leather; however, they probably cannot be raised commercially because of their low reproductive rate: one calf every two to five years.

One proposal considered using them to control aquatic weeds, but it would take 3,000 manatees just to graze the 400-acre headwaters of the Crystal River. So these "sea cows" are not of much use.

Yet to see them swimming up from the murky depths is to feel a surge of gratitude that nature still has secrets, that animals this large and strange can still emerge from rivers right off highways. Besides, their value to the state as a tourist attraction is incalculable.

Manatees average about nine

West Indian manatees

feet in length and weigh about 1,000 pounds, though they can weigh up to 3,000 pounds, or about as much as a car. They use their front limbs to maneuver and feed; the body tapers back like a seal to a flat tail.

They are harmless, have acute hearing, and sometimes squeal to communicate. One observer noted that a mother and her calf, separated by a floodgate, vocalized for 3 hours until the gate opened.

They also like to play. Five manatees were seen bodysurfing at Blue Lagoon Lake for more than an hour, vocalizing and nuzzling each other between rides.

There are several places in Florida where you can go to see manatees. **Merritt Island National Wildlife Refuge** in Titusville (*321-861-0667. http://merrittisland.fws.gov/*) has a manatee observation deck. Others include **Homosassa State Wildlife Park** (*352-628-2311*), and **Everglades National Park** (*see pp. 130–145*) as well as **Bahia Honda State Park** (*see p. 123*) in the Keys.

Dagny Johnson Key Largo Hammocks State Botanical Site

30 miles south of Biscayne

There was a time when the Upper Keys were mostly a vast bristle of West Indian tropical hardwood fringed by mangrove. Where much of this perfect chaos once rustled softly in the trade winds, you can now park your RV, order up key lime pie or beer, buy bait, or stay in a motel room.

Inside Dagny Johnson Key Largo Hammocks State Botanical Site, more than 2,300 acres of the ancient scrub endure. Just north of US 1 in **North Key Largo** on the Atlantic Ocean side of the highway is the largest remaining stand of hardwood hammock and mangrove wetlands in the Keys, the verdant shoreline that Juan Ponce de León saw as he charted the islands in the early 16th century.

You can explore the preserve on your own, guided by the information brochure given out at the park entrance. Points of interest are keyed to numbered boulders along the **main trail,** which is accessible for wheelchairs as well. If you visit on a Thursday or a Sunday morning, ask about ranger-led tours that point out many of the 84 species of protected plants and animals found here; a large number of them are rare or endangered, and some of the native fruits are available for sampling.

There are 6 miles of **trails in the park,** some of which are paved and perfect for biking and inline-skating. In recent years, the park has become a haven for a sizeable variety of butterflies such as Schaus swallowtail, silver-banded hairstreak, and mangrove skippers.

The months of April and October are good ones for birders, as migratory birds tend to funnel over the Keys en route to their summer or winter homes. These birds are partially responsible for many of the tropical plants and trees in the park. They originate from seeds that the migratory animals have carried in their digestive tracts that they in turn got from the food they consumed on Caribbean islands, and in Central and South America.

■ Florida ■ 2,304 acres ■ North Key Largo, Monroe Co. Rd. 905, a quarter-mile north of US 1 ■ Best months: Oct.–May ■ Hiking, guided walks, biking, butterfly- and bird-watching ■ Contact the site, P.O. Box 487, Key Largo, FL 33037; 305-451-1202. www.floridastateparks.org/keylargohammock

Tropical Hardwood Hammocks

In the Keys, "hammock" has two meanings. It can refer to the word that people of the Caribbean used to describe a swinging bed they invented for more comfortable sleeping in their humid clime. Or it can mean a low rise or hillock on a sea coast, definition that first appeared in English among 18th-century mariners.

Along the coasts of southern Florida throughout the Everglades, and in the Florida Keys, "hammocks" refers to the latter: the dense, vine-entangled forests that geologists believe arose here about 100,000 years ago, after the Keys' coral reef foundation was left high and dry when ancient seas receded. A curious mix of plant and animal communities evolved along with them and competed with populations of hardy slash pines that thrive atop fossilized coral limestone.

The hammocks support more than 20 species of broad-leafed trees, shrubs, and vines, most of them native to the West Indies. Biologists assume their seeds were washed ashore, arrived on driftwood, or were left in the droppings of migratory birds.

Tropical hammocks sprang up as far north as Cape Canaveral

A cypress hammock

on the Atlantic shoreline, and as far west as the mouth of the Manatee River on the Gulf Coast. Most of these have been destroyed, leaving most of the remnants in the Florida Keys.

The hammocks drew their roster of animals from mainland North America, the creatures arriving in improbable ways, such as clinging to trees washed out to sea by flooding, arriving as captives of the Calusa tribe, or as tiny stowaways in their dugout canoes.

Poke around long enough in a hammock and you're likely to come nose to nose with raccoons, rough green snakes, red-bellied woodpeckers, cotton mice, and white-tailed deer.

Lignumvitae Key State Botanical Site

60 miles southwest of Biscayne

It is still possible to see what the Keys were like before agricultural and entrepeneurial ventures cut, quarried, burned, buried, paved, or otherwise made them tame. In 1970, The Nature Conservancy and the state of Florida joined forces to buy and preserve the 280-acre Lignumvitae Key and nearby Shell Island.

Situated in the calm waters of Florida Bay off Lower Matecumbe Key, Lignumvitae's fossilized coral rock supports a vibrant virgin forest of gumbo-limbo, strangler fig, poisonwood, mastic, pigeon plum, and the rare lignum vitae. Meaning "wood of life," the lignum vitae was used as a remedy for gout, syphilis, and other disorders. The wood, which can grow for more than a thousand years, is among the hardest in the world. When used in boat construction, lignum vitae routinely outlasts bronze and steel.

The trees provide a lush refuge for many wild birds. You might see such reclusive creatures as white-crowned pigeons, ospreys, double-crested cormorants, and great white herons.

Early in the last century, Miami millionaire W. J. Matheson bought the hardwood hammock. He built a four-bedroom hideaway of coral rock in 1919 and installed six cannons near the house, salvaged from the H.M.S. *Winchester* that ran aground nearby in 1665. A windmill generated power; fresh water came from a 12,000-gallon cistern that filled with rainwater.

You can see the house on the guided tours that rangers lead (*fee*). Because the island's ecosystems are delicate, visitors cannot explore the island on their own. In addition to the house, the tour includes a walk through hardwood forest so you can see the trees and some of the more than 120 species of native plants.

Be sure to wear long sleeved shirts and bug repellent; Lignum vitae is a natural subtropical environment at its most pristine, and that means swarms of hungry mosquitoes are prevalent most of the time.

Nearby **Windley Key Fossil Reef State Geological Site** (*305-664-2540*) is an interesting complement to the living coral reefs found elsewhere. One of the highest of the Upper Keys, Windley rises 18 feet above sea level. From the early 1900s to the 1960s, Windley's limestone was mined for "keystone," a popular decorative facing. The stone was shipped by rail until a hurricane in 1935 destroyed the railroad. It was then shipped up along the Overseas Highway.

A **short trail** through the quarry lets you stand inside a fossilized coral reef and marvel at its complex structure. Packed together in high walls are petrified brain corals, star corals, snails, clams, green algae, and other organisms, cemented in place by calcite sediment. Though you can't see its full thickness, the reef extends in places down to 180 feet. A side trail traverses a hammock of cactus, palms, and hardwoods.

Visiting these Keys is well worth it. You'll return with a better sense of the natural islands than many of the people who call the Keys their home.

■ **280 acres** ■ **South Florida, 1 mile west of US 1 at Milepost 78.5** ■ **Best months Nov.–April** ■ **Guided walks, canoeing, bird-watching, boat tours** ■ **Two tours a day (fee), Thursday through Monday by boat from Robbie's Marina at Milepost 77.5; 305-664-9814** ■ **Contact the site, P.O. Box 1052, Islamorada, FL 33036; 305-664-2540. www.floridastateparks.org/lignum vitaekey/default.asp**

Roots of lignum vitae

Congaree

S ay the word "swamp," and the first image that probably comes to mind is of a wet, sticky, mosquito-infested mire that few people would want to visit.

Such an image certainly might have kept some visitors away from Congaree Swamp National Monument, a 22,000-acre forest in South Carolina. Yet, after the monument gained national park status in November 2003—and dropped the "s" word from its name—the number of visitors each month has more than doubled. And the park's naturalist went from being "the loneliest ranger in town" to being, well, swamped, as he told the *New York Times.*

Technically speaking, Congaree is not a swamp, because it does not contain water throughout most of the year. The newest national park is actually floodplain forest that floods about ten times a year. Spreading northeast from the sinuous Congaree River, the land is the largest intact tract of old-growth hardwoods in the United States.

Push back the ghostly Spanish moss that drips from the bald cypresses, and you enter a lush backcountry inhabited by bobcats, wild boars, and playful river otters. Yellow-bellied sapsuckers drill holes into trees one day and return the next to feast on the sap that filled the holes. The rapid-fire series of knocks you hear is from another woodpecker, also hard at work boring holes into trees.

At night, rangers lead visitors on an "owl prowl," so they can hear the eerie screams of barred owls and see the glowing fungi that grows on the cypresses. According to local legends, the cypress tree's trademark "knees"—small, knobby wood growths that rise around the trunk's base—are really wood elves who came to life at night to dance through the forest.

Congaree was named for the Native American tribe that lived here centuries ago. They were decimated in the 18th century, victims of a smallpox epidemic that came over with European settlers.

- Central South Carolina
- 21,890 acres
- Best seasons spring and fall
- Established 2003
- Camping, hiking, canoeing, fishing, kayaking, bird-watching, wildlife viewing
- Information: 803-776-4396 www.nps.gov/cosw

Boardwalk Loop Trail, Congaree National Park

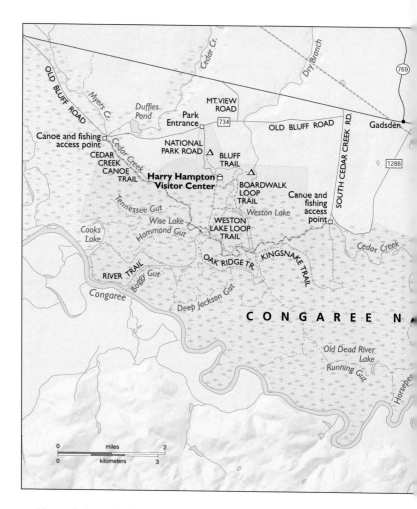

Toward the end of the next century, the country's burgeoning lumber industry moved south, with a greedy eye on Congaree's tall trees. However, the trees were so waterlogged from growing in a floodplain that they were too heavy to ship. Thus many of the old giants were saved from the ax.

Conservationists worked hard to save the rest. In 1976, Congress rewarded their efforts by setting Congaree aside as a national monument. Seven years later, it became an international biosphere reserve.

How to Get There
From Columbia, 20 miles southeast on I-77 to exit 5

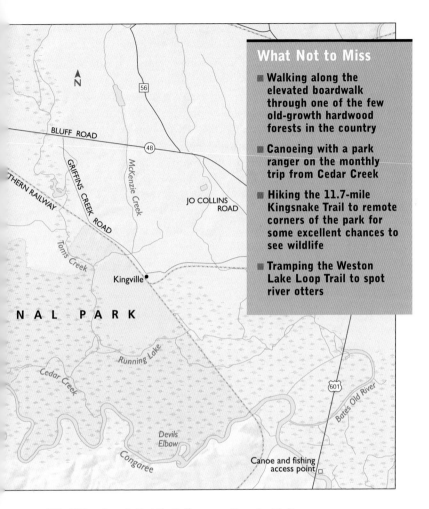

What Not to Miss

- Walking along the elevated boardwalk through one of the few old-growth hardwood forests in the country

- Canoeing with a park ranger on the monthly trip from Cedar Creek

- Hiking the 11.7-mile Kingsnake Trail to remote corners of the park for some excellent chances to see wildlife

- Tramping the Weston Lake Loop Trail to spot river otters

(Bluff Road or S.C. 48). Follow the brown-and-white signs to the park.

When to Go

All-year park. Fall is the prettiest season. Boaters find easier paddling after a rain in late winter and early spring. Call ahead after a heavy rain to see if the park is flooded.

How to Visit

Allow half a day. From the visitor center, take the **Low** and **High Boardwalk Trails** (2.4 miles total). Then do the **Weston Lake Loop Trail** (4.4 miles) around the oxbow lake. Birders like the 11.7-mile **Kingsnake Trail** into a remote part of the park.

EXPLORING THE PARK

Trails Through the Swamp: At least half a day

In this waterlogged woodland, giant loblolly pines and hardwoods rise to a canopy higher than in the Amazon rain forest. Loblolly pines rise up more than 100 feet to reach the sunlight, and some majestic old bald cypresses measure more than 25 feet in circumference, their leafy crowns shuttering the world below into a landscape of liquid echoes in shades of brown and green.

Congaree is home to some of the country's tallest trees, which are called champions. The tallest water hickory is 143 feet tall, and the park's tallest loblolly pine reaches 167 feet, as high as a 17-story building.

Logging began in swamps across the Southeast in the 1880s, and soon thereafter it focused on the old-growth bald cypress. During the next two decades all the stands within easy reach were cut, and South Carolina's floodplain forests suffered a drastic reduction. However, along the Congaree a lack of accessible waterways for removing timber and the heaviness of the constantly soaked logs helped save the irreplaceable tract.

Fierce winds from Hurricane Hugo in 1989 put a dent in the old-growth forest, toppling some of the national and state champion trees harbored here. The storm also opened up holes in the dense canopy, clearing the way for fresh growth. Dead trees, meanwhile, became homes for various birds, bats, reptiles, insects, and fungi.

About ten times a year, the floodplain is inundated, usually following dam releases and heavy rains upcountry. Sloughs and guts (narrow creeks) overflow, carrying nutrients that enrich the soil. Shallow-rooted hardwoods occasionally fall, but cypresses with far-reaching roots and supportive knees as tall as seven feet rarely topple. Animals seek higher ground, and some even find refuge on floating logs.

On a topographical map you will see very few contour lines within the park's boundaries; the elevation dips only about 20 feet from the west side to the east, so excess water can slosh all over the swamp. Yet even that slight, seemingly insignificant change of elevation produces dramatically different biological communities: At the higher, drier levels of the monument live sweet gums, cherrybark oaks, and hollies, whereas cypresses, water tupelos, and water ashes thrive at the lower, wetter levels.

Bald Cypress

Surrounded by an entourage of knobby knees in dark water, the bald cypress is a symbol of the vanishing southeastern wetlands. Throw on some swags of Spanish moss, put a heron in the water, and you have the quintessential Southern swamp backdrop.

Ranging from southern Delaware to Texas, the bald cypress spends several months of the year in watery conditions that would hurt most other trees. This adaptability gives the tree its highly valued rot-resistant wood. Over the years, cypress has been used in bridges, docks, and other structures that take heavy weathering. You can also find it in boats, pilings, fences, and decorative paneling. Fairly easy to work with, the wood is only moderately heavy and hard.

When the floodplain forests were logged in the late 19th and early 20th centuries, a lot of the old-growth bald cypresses went down. But some glorious, 500-year-old specimens measuring up to 10 feet in diameter still exist today. Most of these survivors are found in state and national preserves such as Congaree.

What are the knees for? Though no one knows for sure, the best answer is that they

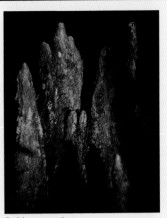

Bald cypress knees

help support the tree in the soupy ground. They may also facilitate some kind of gas exchange between the air, the water, and the mud-bound roots, similar to the finger-like roots of the black mangrove.

The cypress itself rises from a flared base with ridges that look like buttresses or rocket fins; the reddish brown to gray bark peels in long strips. Small cones are surrounded by stems of short, soft, needle-like leaves that turn from green to rusty brown in fall.

The tree is called bald because of the fact that it sheds its bark. One of four members of the redwood family native to North America, the bald cypress grows as tall as 125 feet, nowhere near its 300-foot cousins in California, but inch for inch every bit as appealing.

Stop at the visitor center for trail maps, information, and suggestions on hikes. Most people meander at least some of the 2.4-mile **Boardwalk Loop Trail,** which has interpretive markers keyed to an informational handout. As you gradually enter the floodplain forest, the vegetation changes from upland pines and hardwoods to the old-growth loblolly pines and mixed hard-woods of the swamp.

During floods, the water level can rise as high as the elevated boardwalk, or even higher. Thick vines of scuppernong grapes and climbing hydrangea hug the trunks of ancient trees, adding to the primordial atmosphere. The hairy vines belong to poison ivy, and it's worth noting that these vines and dormant stems can irritate the skin as much as the leaves.

Farther along, tupelos and cypresses grow in standing black water, stained by the tannin of decayed vegetation. A light rainfall is an especially evocative time for a walk through here—raindrops ping the reflective water, a gauzy mist blankets the forest primeval, and the birdsong seems to come from far away in time. It's little wonder that sightings of the presumed extinct ivory-billed wood-pecker surface every now and again; back in these shady depths you almost expect to find creatures from another age.

Continue down the boardwalk toward **Weston Lake.** Dwarf pal-mettos just off the walk lend a tropical accent to the surroundings. The riddled trunks of sweet gums and other trees bear the marks of

North American river otter

woodpeckers. All eight varieties of woodpeckers found in the south inhabit Congaree: pileated, downy, hairy, red-cockaded, red-bellied, red-headed, yellow-bellied sapsucker, and yellow-shafted flicker.

In summer, hummingbirds zoom for the showy orange flowers of the trumpet vine, while sparrows dart about for berries and seeds. Fallen logs lie moldering in puddles of wet vegetation. Small-scale communities are built upon the pits and mounds of overturned trees.

River otters frolic in Weston Lake, and red-bellied turtles line up on floating logs. The small oxbow lake, measuring 25 feet deep, was once a bend in the Congaree River; thousands of years ago, the river changed course—leaving the bend as a lake—and now lies 2 miles away. Near here stand dwarf forests of gnarled cypress knees; the farther you walk around to the east, the more old-growth cypress you encounter.

The boardwalk then takes you through a forest of tupelos, hollies, loblolly pines, and, above all, cypresses. Touch the rippling bell-bottom trunks of the older cypresses; their mossy surface feels like velvet. Extend the Boardwalk Loop by taking the 4.4-mile **Weston Lake Loop Trail,** which follows a cypress-tupelo slough down to Cedar Creek. In this largest of the park's creeks, you have the best chance of spotting herons and otters.

For an even longer outing, the **Oak Ridge Trail,** accessible off the Weston Lake trail, pushes farther south into the old-growth forest and makes for a 6.6-mile round-trip hike from the visitor center. If you want to walk to the river and back, plan to spend most of the day on a trek starting with the boardwalk, then taking the western sections of the Weston Lake Loop and Oak Ridge trails; the 10-mile **River Trail** takes you the rest of the way, but it will be underwater during a flood.

The 11.7-mile round-trip **Kingsnake Trail** offers further opportunities for wildlife watching and secluded exploration in the park's little-visited eastern section. The trailhead is off the Cedar Creek parking area.

The **Cedar Creek canoe trail** within Congaree slips through sunless channels of black water haunted by reclusive birds and other animals. Once a month, the park staff offers a guided trip into these mysterious parts and provides canoes for participants. Otherwise, plan to rent a canoe from one of the many outfitters in nearby Columbia.

INFORMATION & ACTIVITIES

Headquarters
100 National Park Road
Hopkins, SC 29061
803-776-4396
www.nps.gov/cosw

Visitor & Information Centers
Open daily year round. Located off S.C. 48, 1.2 miles beyond park entrance on National Park Road.

Seasons & Accessibility
Park open year-round. Call after heavy rains to see if park is flooded.

Entrance fee
There is no fee to enter the park.

Pets
Pets must be on leashes and are not allowed on the boardwalks.

Facilities for Disabled
Visitor center, rest rooms, picnic shelter, and primitive campgrounds are wheelchair accessible. So is the 2.4-mile Boardwalk Loop trail.

Things to Do
Free naturalist-led activities: nature walks and canoe tours. Environmental education and nature study. Hiking, fishing (*license required*), primitive camping, bird-watching, picnicking, canoeing, kayaking.

Overnight Backpacking
Permit required; available free from visitor centers and ranger stations.

Campsites must be at least 100 feet away from roads, trails, lakes, and flowing water.

Campgrounds
Two campgrounds and back-country camping with 14-day limits year-round. Free permits required; available at the visitor center no more than one day in advance. After Hours campsite can accommodate groups. Portable toilets, fire rings, grills, and picnic tables. The Bluff campsite also can accommodate groups; fire rings, grills, and picnic tables in open field. No open fires permitted in backcountry camping.

Hotels, Motels, & Inns
(Unless otherwise noted, rates are for two persons in a double room, high season.)

In Columbia, SC:
■ **Comfort Inn & Suites Fort Jackson Maingate**
7337 Garner's Ferry Rd. 803-695-5555. 67 units. $89-$99. AC, pool.
■ **Econo Lodge**
4486 Fort Jackson Blvd. 803-738-0510. 40 units. $55-$65. AC.

Floodplain, Congaree National Park

■ **Holiday Inn Express Columbia-Fort Jackson**
7251 Garner's Ferry Rd. 803-695-1111. 66 units. $69-$99. AC, pool.

■ **Clarion Town House Hotel**
1615 Gervais St. 803-771-8711 or 800-277-8711. 163 units. $99-$129. AC, pool, restaurant.

■ **Claussen's Inn**
2003 Greene St. 803-765-0440. 29 units. $104-$140. AC.

For other accommodations, contact the Columbia Metropolitan Convention & Visitors Bureau at 803-545-0000 or 800-264-4884.

Excursions from Congaree

Carolina Sandhills National Wildlife Refuge

75 miles northeast of Congaree

It is 200 years ago, and you are riding a horse through one of the virgin forests of longleaf pines that cover broad swaths of the South. Thousands of straight, brown-barked columns soar 120 feet or more into the sky. Yet they are spaced so far apart that you can see a mile down the avenues of trees. Great tubes of sunlight collect in warm pools on the thick, tawny wire grass of the forest floor; scattered pine straw lies underfoot. Behind the silence, a persistent breeze sweeps the woodland like the sound of a distant sea. Some of these giant pines are 400 years old and measure more than 3 feet in diameter. Panthers, bison, red wolves, and black bears roam the open forest, adding a further thrill and a hint of danger to your solitary intrusion.

Of the 90 million acres of longleaf pine forest that once graced the Southeast, only about two million are left, in severed parcels. The rest disappeared as the trees were logged; the land was either

Carolina Sandhills National Wildlife Refuge

cleared for other uses or replanted with different species, primarily slash pine. The suppression of natural fires also has contributed to the demise of longleaf pines by allowing hardwoods to move in and take over.

Situated just below the fall line between the Atlantic coastal plain and the Piedmont, Carolina Sandhills National Wildlife Refuge preserves one of the few remaining large stands of longleaf pine as well as interlaced stretches of wetlands and fields. The refuge contains a remarkable diversity of flora and fauna: more than 750 plant species, 190 bird species, 42 species of mammals, 41 of reptiles, and 25 of amphibians.

The Sandhills began millions of years ago as a delta plain formed by rivers running from the mountains and foothills, depositing sediments, and fanning out into the sea. In the past 50 million years wind and water have eroded the area into the hills you see today. Dominating the uplands are the magnificent longleaf pines, their monumental boles shooting up to crowns of sunlit needles. The needles can grow up to 18 inches long, and the cones vary from 6 to 10 inches.

Red-cockaded woodpeckers make nests high in cavities of older longleaf and loblolly pines; the birds can easily penetrate the soft, rotten wood of 80- to 100-year-old trees that have red heart disease. For protection, the woodpeckers drill holes that release a stream of pine resin, which deters snakes and other predators from climbing to the nests. Naturalists at the refuge are doing their best to save this tightly niched endangered species that is so dependent on longleaf pines for survival.

The forest itself receives a payback of sorts when the red-cockaded woodpecker moves from one cavity to another, leaving a potential home for screech owls, wood ducks, raccoons, flying squirrels, or bees.

When the refuge was established in 1939, the area was a wasteland of eroded hills, denuded of trees and devoid of much wildlife. Beavers, wild turkeys, and white-tailed deer were restocked and have since grown to healthy populations. You can see turkeys crossing roads and fields, especially on spring mornings. Red-cockaded woodpeckers nest in late spring, when neotropical songbird migration reaches its peak. On early summer evenings, listen for the nasal honk of the pine barrens tree frog, a bright green creature more often heard than seen.

The hot days of late summer are good times for spotting wild-flowers and white-tailed does with new fawns (*see sidebar p. 82*). In the fall, sharp-eyed observers have a good chance of seeing hawks and bald eagles. Ducks and Canada geese arrive in the Carolina Sandhills after the first frost. At any time of the year you have the opportunity to view the small resident population of great blue herons, particularly at the refuge's many ponds and lakes.

Start out at the refuge office, then proceed north on the 9-mile (one way) **Wildlife Drive.** The quiet road also makes for a nice bike ride. Near the refuge office, look for the large cones of longleaf pines all over the ground.

A short way up on the left, pull over for the 1-mile **Woodland Pond Trail** around Pool A, which feeds into Little Alligator Creek. A catwalk crosses the quiet stream edged by pond pine and tulip poplar, the understory bristling with thickets of titi and impenetrable stands of bamboo. Sphagnum moss, carnivorous pitcher plants, and sundews dapple the banks of the stream. Geese come honking overhead, set their wings, and glide onto the pond with a light splash.

Continue driving or cycling to the middle of the refuge, where you have your choice of ponds and lakes for fishing or bird-watching. **Tate's Trail,** a 3-mile footpath, wends alongside Martins Lake and up to Lake Bee.

Farther along, near the end of the route, pull off to the right and drive about half a mile up a sandy road to the 15-foot-tall wooden **observation tower.** You'll see prickly pear cactus growing in the dry, sandy soil around the base. From the top there are views of fields of broom sedge and tree-fringed ponds. Off in the trees, barred owls cackle, shriek, and call in a raspy voice that sounds like "Who-cooks-for-you, who-cooks-for-you-all?"

To maintain the open pine forests and fields at desired successional stages, the refuge selectively thins the woods by harvesting timber and periodically sets prescribed burns. Persimmon, sassafras, blackberry, and other shrubs and trees thrive on the edges of clearings, waiting for the opportunity to spread.

■ **45,348 acres** ■ **Northeastern South Carolina, on US 1, 4 miles north of McBee** ■ **Best months April–May, Sept.–Oct.** ■ **Hiking, biking, bird-watching** ■ **Contact the refuge, 23734 US 1, McBee, SC 29101; 843-335-8401. www.carolinasandhills.fws.gov/**

Red-cockaded Woodpecker

Since the vast pine forests of the South have been reduced to about 2 percent of their original acreage, the numbers of red-cockaded woodpeckers have likewise dwindled precipitously. Between 10,000 and 14,000 individual birds are all that stand between this endangered species and extinction.

The sound of the red-cockaded woodpecker's hammering frequently fills the woods. Males use their beaks to bore nest holes high up in the trunks of living, mature pines that typically have been afflicted with red heart disease; the bird then drills small holes around the opening. Many scientists theorize that the resulting pine pitch that oozes down the tree repels predators.

Each family group or cluster of four to nine birds requires on average 200 acres of territory. Still the very presence of the demanding birds speaks wonders for the general health of an old pine forest.

About the size of a cardinal, the red-cockaded woodpecker is distinguished by its black cap and nape, and its white cheeks. On males, a small red streak—the cockade—extends on either side of the cap from behind the eye down

Red-cockaded woodpecker

toward the white cheek patch. The bird's call is a distinctive raspy *sripp* and high-pitched *tsick*.

Breeding pairs remain together for several years, raising one brood a year. But parents don't get stuck with all the hard work. Young males from previous years stay in the area to help incubate the next season's eggs and raise the fledglings.

Young females, on the other hand, leave home to look for mates, ideally ones who already have cavity nests.

The U.S. Fish and Wildlife Service put the red-cockaded woodpecker on the endangered list in 1970.

Forty Acre Rock Heritage Preserve

85 miles north of Congaree

In the transition zone between the coastal plain and the Piedmont, oak forests intermingle with piney uplands and cool, winding creeks. Dotting this region are fissured granite outcroppings, the exposed portions of 450- to 500-million-year-old magma domes.

Forty Acre Rock is one of the outcroppings. While it only covers 14 acres, the rock supports a great abundance of plants, including about a dozen rare, threatened, or endangered species. Adapted to thin soil and dry conditions, some of these plants are found only in these specialized southeastern environments.

A figure-eight **loop trail** of about 4 miles takes you past the major biological communities in the preserve. From the parking area, head out on an old logging road that now makes for a nice, wide, needle-strewn path. Cutting trees along here once opened up niches for cottontail rabbits and red-tailed hawks, as well as indigo buntings and bright yellow prairie warblers. New growth has transformed it into an inviting home for other species such as opossums, mockingbirds, and pine warblers.

The trail then skirts a placid pond with views of the beaver dam that created it; you'll see wood ducks and, if you are very lucky, beavers swimming near their lodge. White-tailed deer frequent the

Fawns

The sight of a speckled fawn bounding along behind its mother is a sure sign that summer has arrived in the Piedmont. After about seven months of gestation, the doe drops one to three fawns, hiding them in separate patches of high grass to reduce the odds of a predator wiping out an entire litter.

For the first month of life, the fawns venture out only a few hours a day in short intervals.

They spend the rest of the time lying motionless, their spots helping to camouflage them. People who encounter a concealed fawn often assume—incorrectly—that it has been abandoned. The best thing is to leave it alone; the mother is probably nearby.

Another note of caution: Slow down when you see a single deer near the road, even if it has already passed. Deer travel in family groups, so there could be more about to jump out in front of you.

shrubs and briar patches found along the stream floodplain.

The stream below Forty Acre Rock is home to several species of diminutive fish and leopard frogs. Near a shallow cave, a small waterfall (dry in summer) makes soothing woodland music that serenades passing hikers. Emerging onto the rock itself, you have wonderful views of an upward sloping granite slab that feels almost like a high mountaintop.

If you're here in spring, you'll see the succulent diamorpha spread like tiny red beads across small pools in the rocks. By summer, the red plant has turned into a shriveled, black, seed-bearing stem. This pioneering plant is among the first to colonize the bare rock.

The endemic pool sprite is another small plant; it grows only during the brief period of late winter rains. As more soil builds up in the depressions, herbs and shrubs begin to take root, to be followed at last by scrubby red cedars and other species of trees.

Scattered all about the granite face of Forty Acre Rock are mosses and lichens, varying from the lush black rock moss to the bristly reindeer moss. Look up and you may see turkey vultures gliding over the rock or rising on warm updrafts to become distant specks in the sky. Unfortunately, though, it's not all pristine beauty up here: Over the years untold thoughtless visitors have left their marks—graffiti, fire scars, and broken glass—that detract from the natural wonders.

The trail loops back along the south side of the beaver pond through a forest of shortleaf pine and tangled honeysuckle to reach **Flat Creek.** Look carefully for the lightly speckled leaves of trout lilies, which bloom yellow in spring; Easter lily, jack-in-the-pulpit, and creeping phlox may also brighten the path as you make your way back to your car.

A new 141-acre addition on the northwest side of the preserve protects the headwaters of Flat Creek and three endangered freshwater mussels. This stately tract contains mature hardwoods, rich bottomlands, a prairie remnant, and a field of boulders.

■ **1,567 acres** ■ **North-central South Carolina, 8 miles south of Pageland on US 601** ■ **Best seasons spring and fall** ■ **Hiking, nature study** ■ **Contact South Carolina Department of Natural Resources Wildlife Diversity Section, P.O. Box 167, Columbia, SC 29202; 803-734-3894. www.dnr.state.sc.us/wild/heritage/hp/fortyar/default.htm**

Anne Springs Close Greenway

100 miles north of Congaree

Donated by a family that traces its local heritage back to the early 1800s, this jewel-like parcel of forests, lakes, and pastures offers outdoor respite from the hectic pace of nearby Charlotte, North Carolina. In 1780, British General Lord Cornwallis compared the area to an English park, and the same sense of peacefulness pervades the greenway's gentle woods and fields today. There are more than 32 miles of trails in the greenway, taking in **Steele Creek** as well as several ponds.

In addition to protecting a piece of the Steele Creek watershed, the greenway preserves a section of an old wagon route called **Nation Ford Road;** before European settlers arrived in the 18th century, the same route was a key trade artery for the Catawba Tribe.

Start out at the **nature center,** where you can touch a video screen or examine photos and mounted animals to help you identify the plants and wildlife outside. Then take the quiet 1.25-mile **Lake Haigler Nature Trail,** which loops a 30-acre lake fringed by cedars, pines, oaks, and hickories. Geese honk loudly as they swim

Flowering dogwoods, Anne Springs Close Greenway

away, and songbirds chatter in hidden perches. You may catch glimpses of white-tailed deer, raccoons, and red and gray foxes. Also secreted within the forest are opossums, beavers, and otters, but these creatures are harder to find.

In the springtime flowering dogwood trees dot the meadows with white blossoms, while bloodroot paints little snow-white dollops along the ground. All told, more than 200 species of wild-flowers bloom here in abundance, including the splashy red of wild azaleas and the pale purple of muscadine grapes.

Leading north, three **mile-long trails** cater separately to hikers, cyclists, and horseback riders. Running on or next to the old **Nation Ford Road,** these wind their way past a dairy barn built in 1946. A log cabin from the 18th century and two early 19th-century homes complement the property's natural beauty.

■ **2,000 acres** ■ **North-central South Carolina, 2 miles north of S.C. 160 off US 21 bypass** ■ **Best seasons spring, summer, and fall** ■ **Camping, hiking, horseback riding** ■ **Contact the greenway, 250 Springfield Ln., Fort Mill, SC 29716; 803-548-7252. www.leroysprings.com/greenway.html**

Hitchcock Woods

80 miles southwest of Congaree

On the edge of the ballooning town of Aiken sprawls a tract of woods and wetlands much larger than you'd expect to find so close to an urban area. The reserve began in 1939 as a gift of 1,200 acres from Thomas Hitchcock, a wealthy member of the local gentry, and his daughter Helen Clark. It now covers almost 2,000 peaceful acres and offers more than 60 miles of trails for quiet strolling and observing nature.

A crazy network of trails and bridal paths laces the woods. You can map out a good 2- to 5-mile walk, or just stroll aimlessly and enjoy the tranquillity of this remnant longleaf-pine and wiregrass habitat.

Starting in the northeast at **Memorial Gate,** you can walk along a sandy-bottomed river lined with bracken and other ferns. To the south around **Bebbington Springs** lie hills dotted with bloodroot, trailing arbutus, and other wildflowers. Quaint bridges cross small streams. You'll see oaks bearded with Spanish moss, and meadows where white-tailed deer bound past wild azaleas. Among the dozens of bird species, you may see or hear red-tailed hawks, eastern screech-owls, pileated woodpeckers, and wood thrushes.

A former game preserve, the park carries on Aiken's long-standing equestrian tradition with periodic hunts and riding events. Pedestrians are requested to announce their presence when encountering horses and carriages. Throughout Hitchcock Woods you'll notice hunt fences that Hitchcock designed. In the north section you can find the **Ridge Mile Track** that he built for training horses in the 1920s.

Just west of here, **Cathedral Aisle** is a pretty trail traversing an old railbed. The South Carolina Canal & Railroad Co. laid tracks here in 1833 to connect Charleston on the coast to Hamburg, which is now part of North Augusta. It was then the longest railroad in the world. About 20 years later, the track was abandoned.

If you're visiting between late April and early May, find the **Kalmia Trail.** The evergreen shrubs that line the narrow walk are ablaze with purple, pink, and white flowers.

■ **2,000 acres** ■ **Western South Carolina, in Aiken, off South Boundary Avenue** ■ **Best seasons spring and fall** ■ **Hiking, horseback riding, birdwatching** ■ **Contact Hitchcock Foundation, P.O. Box 1702, Aiken, SC 29802; 803-642-0528. www.hitchcockwoods.com**

Savannah River Bluffs Heritage Preserve

100 miles west of Congaree

Tucked between an interstate and North Augusta, South Carolina, this unpublicized preserve along the Savannah River champions an inordinate number of small gems native to the Piedmont-coastal plain nexus. Within these 1,076 feet of unspoiled riverfront grow several rare plants on one of the few remaining shoals in the river. One such plant, the greenish- to brownish-purple relict trillium, is on the federal endangered species list, while the white rocky shoals spider lily grows in the river and blooms briefly in late spring.

Other noteworthy species found here include the spreading

Savannah River

shrub bottlebrush buckeye, swamp privet, and the slender white-flowering herb known as false rue anemone. A 0.75-mile **loop nature trail** parallels a stream through a forest of saw palmettos and bald cypresses to reach the river.

Along the bluffs and in the water, you'll see interesting rock formations. Many historians think that Native Americans used to string nets between the rocks out in the Savannah River to create fishing weirs. The trail then follows an old logging road through the woods before turning off to return to the parking lot via a power-line right-of-way.

■ 84 acres ■ Western South Carolina, northeast of Augusta, Ga. ■ Best time: fall ■ Walking, wildlife viewing ■ Contact South Carolina Department of Natural Resources Wild Diversity Section, P.O. Box 167, Columbia, SC 29202; 803-734-3894. http://www.dnr.state.sc.us/wild/heritage/hp/savannahrb/default.htm

Cuyahoga Valley

I f there is one word that typifies Cuyahoga Valley, it might well be *surprise*. Many people are surprised by the simple fact that a national park exists in northeastern Ohio between the sprawling cities of Cleveland and Akron.

Those who explore the park find more surprises: Belying its setting in a heavily industrialized and populated region, Cuyahoga (a Native American word for "crooked") has secluded trails through rugged gorges that seem far removed from civilization, vistas of wooded hills where the urban world is out of sight, and marshes where beavers, herons, and wood ducks thrive.

Crisscrossed by roads and freeways, encompassing towns, private attractions, and city parks, Cuyahoga Valley is hardly comparable to the vast western wilderness parks. Here, visitors can ride a scenic railroad, hear a symphony concert, attend an art exhibit, play golf, or, in winter, zoom down snowy ski slopes, all within the national park boundaries.

The park's history is as unique as its potpourri of natural and man-made attractions. In the 1960s, local citizens and public officials became concerned that commercial and residential development was threatening the scenic Cuyahoga River Valley, with its villages, quiet byways, and forests. In 1974, Congress passed a bill that turned the region into a national recreation area, administered by the National Park Service. Park staff began acquiring private land within the designated 33,000 acres, as well as working out cooperative agreements with developments already in place, such as Cleveland and Summit County metropolitan park districts and Blossom Music Center, the summer home of the Cleveland Orchestra.

Over time, confusion about what a recreation area truly meant led supporters to call for full national park status, which was granted in 2000.

Today, Cuyahoga Valley National Park serves the metropolitan area in a multitude

- ■ Northern Ohio
- ■ 133,000 acres
- ■ Established 2000
- ■ Best seasons spring and fall
- ■ Hiking, fishing, biking, cross-country skiing, snow-shoeing, golfing, train rides, sledding
- ■ Information: 216-524-1497 www.nps.gov/cuva

Brandywine Falls, at Cuyahoga Valley National Park

of ways. People who live nearby find it a convenient place to jog, ride bicycles, or picnic. Children ride sleds down its hills in winter. Nature lovers find refuge in its pockets of wild greenery, home to dozens of species of birds and wildflowers. Fans of the arts watch Shakespeare and musicals at Kent State University's Porthouse Theatre. Cuyahoga Valley may not fit everyone's idea of a national park, but that doesn't tarnish the appeal of its many rewards.

How to Get There

From Cleveland, go 10 miles south on I-77. From Akron, go 5 miles north on I-77 or Ohio 8. From the east or west, I-80 (the Ohio Turnpike) bisects the park, as does I-271. Airports: Cleveland or Akron.

When to Go

Year-round park. Weekends can be crowded along the Towpath Trail from spring through fall, and especially in summer. Many activities are curtailed in winter, but downhill skiing, cross-country skiing, snowshoeing, and sledding are popular. Spring wildflowers and fall foliage make these especially colorful and appealing seasons.

What Not to Miss

- Taking a narrated ride on the vintage railroad
- Walking or biking along the Ohio and Erie Canal Towpath Trail
- Visiting Boston or Peninsula for their museums, shops, and restaurants
- Hiking in the Ledges at sunset for spectacular views
- Sojourning to any or all of three waterfalls: Brandywine, Bridal Veil, and Blue Hens

How to Visit

Stop at the **Canal Visitor Center** for an overview of canal and valley history, and information on park activities; be sure to ask about tours that rangers lead and other special events that the park offers.

Walk or bicycle a portion of the **Towpath Trail** before driving east to take in the beauty of **Tinkers Creek Gorge.** Then head south to see **Brandywine Falls,** continuing on to the towns of **Boston** and **Peninsula** for museums and exhibits.

Walk some of the scenic trails south of the Happy Days Visitor Center, especially in the area called the **Ledges.**

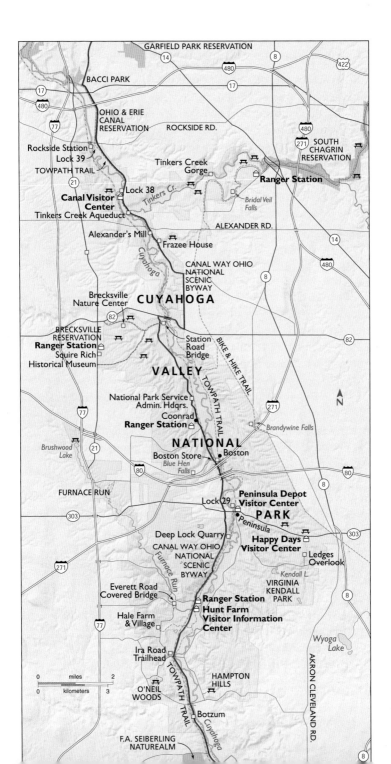

EXPLORING THE PARK

Ohio & Erie Canal Towpath Trail: Two hours to half a day

A few decades ago, placing the Cuyahoga River at the heart of a national park seemed an odd choice. After all, this was the same heavily polluted river that caught on fire in 1939 after a spark from a blow torch ignited floating debris.

The fires that continued to plague the river sporadically until 1969 did help serve a purpose. The federal government responded to this and other environmental troubles, albeit slowly, by passing the Clean Water Act and establishing the Environmental Protection Agency. And the Cuyahoga itself is far cleaner today, after extensive rehabilitation efforts. Though park personnel still don't recommend swimming or boating, the river corridor serves as a thread of life running 22 miles through the center of the park that is home to a surprising diversity of wildlife.

Between 1825 and 1832, a canal was built parallel to the river between Cleveland in the north and Portsmouth on the Ohio River in the south. The 308-mile-long canal essentially opened the territory up to the east, fostering economic growth in the Cuyahoga Valley. By 1840, Ohio had gone from teetering on the brink of bankruptcy in 1819 to becoming the third most prosperous state in the country.

The emergence of the railroads and bad management rendered the canal obsolete; it stopped functioning after a bad flood in 1913. But the adjacent towpath, where mules once trudged towing boats, has been converted into one of the area's most popular hiking and bicycling trails. Running nearly 20 miles through the park (and extending both north into Cleveland and south into Akron), the **Ohio & Erie Canal Towpath Trail** is the heart of recreational activity in the park. Passing through forests, meadows, and wetlands, the fully accessible trail invites casual walking as well as serious running or biking.

Start your visit at the **Canal Visitor Center,** which is in an early 19th-century structure that was used as a tavern, general store, and residence. The placid-looking white frame house acquired a dicey reputation; canal travelers used to call it Hell's Half Acre. You can watch a video and inspect historical displays spanning 12,000 years of valley history.

Just outside is **Lock 38,** the last operational lock within the park. This was one of 44 that allowed boats to negotiate 395 feet of elevation change as they traveled inland from Lake Erie to Akron and

The Ledges, Cuyahoga Valley National Park

vice versa. Costumed rangers and volunteers demonstrate the lock's function on summer weekends.

Slightly more than 1 mile farther along the trail is **Alexander's Mill,** near the spillway for Lock 37. Built in 1855, the mill ran successfully on waterpower until 1970. It is the last mill left in Cuyahoga County.

As you explore the towpath trail (and the rest of the Cuyahoga Valley), consider taking advantage of one of the park's partners: the **Cuyahoga Valley Scenic Railroad** *(800-468-4070. www.cvsr.com).* The engine pulls coaches circa 1940 along the river on its route from Akron to Independence, making seven stops within the park. Some trips allow hikers and bikers to follow the towpath trail as far as they wish, then board the train and return to their starting point. Themed rail trips are offered throughout the year.

Drive east along Tinkers Creek Road and Gorge Parkway into beautiful **Tinkers Creek Gorge,** a national natural landmark within the Cleveland Metroparks System. An overlook along the parkway presents a spectacular view of the wooded valley and the creek 200 feet below.

Farther east is the parking lot for **Bridal Veil Falls.** Take a short walk from here into a steep-sided valley that goes to a pretty spot where a tributary of Tinkers Creek drops over a series of sandstone ledges. It's one of about 70 waterfalls that tumble into the gorge. The shaded ravine is home to hemlocks, beeches, maples, oaks, and birches, creating an environment reminiscent of more northerly hardwood forests.

The paths that meander through the gorge compose part of 186 miles of trails in the Cuyahoga Valley, allowing short strolls just off paved roads and day-long loop hikes that course through numerous habitats and landscapes.

Brandywine Falls & the Ledges: **A full day**

Perhaps the park's most famous natural feature, Brandywine Falls cascades 60 feet down over a series of sandstone-covered shelves in the eastern part of Cuyahoga.

You reach the falls by a walkway to viewing platforms, one high and another lower, at streamside. Brandywine is striking in any season, whether in the throes of the spring's high water or frozen in the winter, when flows and icicles create a white curtain of columns and swirls.

Not quite so grand, but also exquisite and always less crowded, **Blue Hen Falls** is just minutes away on the west side of the Cuyahoga River, in an intimate valley forested in maple and beech.

Be sure to stop at the **Boston Store** in the nearby village of **Boston.** Since 1836, the charming white frame building has been a warehouse, store, post office, residence, and general gathering spot. Inside you'll enjoy a fascinating national park exhibit on the design and building of the boats that plied the Ohio & Erie Canal during its heyday as a thriving commercial corridor.

Just south, the town of **Peninsula** produced boats in its workshops that were widely regarded as the best on the canal. Today, Peninsula is a very appealing village with shops, cafés, and art galleries, as well as a bike-rental facility for those who'd like to take a spin on the adjacent towpath trail.

One of the park's must-see sites can be found southeast of Peninsula on Kendall Park Road. The main trail at **the Ledges** arcs around a small plateau, following a path beneath dramatically eroded bluffs of 320-million-year-old sandstone conglomerate. The evocative setting of tall trees, ferns, and mosses makes this a hike to be taken slowly, enjoying the chattering of red squirrels, the scolding calls of chickadees, and the infinite variety of rock shapes.

On the east side of the Ledges, venture into the tight passageways of **Ice Box Cave;** on the west, the **Ledges Overlook** is a fine spot for sunset views over wooded ridges rolling away to the horizon.

Check the park schedule during your visit for activities at the **Happy Days Visitor Center** on Ohio 303. A hub for park arts activities, the center hosts concerts, dances, lectures, and children's activities. Thanks to the park's artist-in-residence program and to active local groups, you may run across a painter or folk singer as you walk the towpath trail or visit other sites in the park at any time during the warm months.

Many visitors to the park find that the section just north of the **Ira Road Trailhead** ranks at the top. Here you'll find an extensive marsh created by beavers, which returned to the Cuyahoga Valley in the late 1970s after an absence of 140 years. Great blue herons, rose-breasted grosbeaks, and prothonotary warblers are just a few of the many birds found in this wetland, along with muskrat and white-tailed deer (best seen at dawn or dusk, like beavers). Belted kingfishers dive for prey among white water lilies, and red-winged blackbirds nest in the extensive reed beds.

For a taste of human history, **Hale Farm & Village,** on Oak Hill Road in the southwestern part of the park near Bath, is a living history museum operated by a local historical society. It is open May through October. Re-creating life in a typical mid-19th-century Cuyahoga Valley community, the village centerpiece is the farm that Jonathan Hale established early in the 1800s. Other historical buildings have been relocated here to reproduce a 19th-century village. Costumed interpreters spin thread, weave cloth, make baskets and candles, blow glass, shape iron in a blacksmith shop, and tell stories about what life was like during those times.

A short drive north, the **Everett Road covered bridge** is a re-creation of an 1870s structure that was destroyed in 1975 during a flood. Locals fought plans to replace the bridge with a more modern one for ten years.

Civilization, in the form of highways, suburbs, and commercial development, is never far away from the borders of Cuyahoga Valley National Park. Perhaps that, in a way, is the point: that such a variety of natural beauty and attractions can endure in an urban setting, and can so reward those who take time to explore it.

INFORMATION & ACTIVITIES

Headquarters
15610 Vaughn Rd.
Brecksville, OH 44141
216-524-1497
www.nps.gov/cuva

Visitor & Information Centers
Canal Visitor Center, Canal and
Hillside Roads, Valley View
open year-round. Happy Days
Visitor Center, 500 W. Streets-
boro, Peninsula, offers information on concerts and special
events. Open seasonally. Hunt
Farm Visitor Information Center, along Towpath Trail, open
seasonally. Peninsula Depot
Visitor Center serves as a welcome center for the park; hours
coincide with train schedule.

Seasons & Accessibility
Park open year-round for individual activities and scheduled
events.

Entrance Fees
Free to enter park. Some concerts, events, and programs
charge fees.

Pets
Permitted on leashes.

Facilities for Disabled
Many trails, visitor centers, historical properties, and activities
accessible. The crushed limestone of the 20-mile Ohio &
Erie Canal Towpath Trail is
fully accessible. Contact park
for detailed information on
sites and events.

Things to Do
Park personnel and volunteers
lead tours and nature walks,
while cultural events abound
spring through fall at venues
such as the Blossom Music Center, 330-920-8040, and the Porthouse Theatre, 330-929-4416.
    Summer activities: picnick-
ing, golfing, walking, fishing,
bicycling, horseback riding (*no
horse rentals inside the park*).
Winter activities: sledding
tobogganing, cross-country skiing, snowshoeing. For an easy
way to explore the park, take
the Cuyahoga Valley Scenic
Railroad, 800-468-4070.

Campgrounds
No campgrounds exist within
park, and backcountry camping
is not permitted. Contact the
visitor bureaus listed below for
a list of private campgrounds
in the area.

Hotels, Motels, & Inns
(Unless otherwise noted, rates are
for two persons in a double room,
high season.)

INSIDE THE PARK:
■ **Inn at Brandywine Falls**
8230 Brandywine Rd. Sagamore

Walking among wildflowers, Cuyahoga Valley National Park

Hills, OH 44067. 330-467-1812. 3 rooms, 3 suites. $108-$295, includes breakfast. AC.

■ **Stanford Hostel**
6093 Stanford Rd. Peninsula, OH 44264. 330-467-8711. 30 beds in historic structure. Separate dorms for men, women. $15 per night for Hosteling International members. $2 bedding rental fee.

OUTSIDE THE PARK:
■ **Holiday Inn Hudson**
240 Hines Hill Rd. Hudson, OH 44236 (near Happy Days Visitor Center). 330-653-9191. 288 units. $89-$109. AC, 2 pools, restaurant.

■ **Red Roof Inn**
6020 Quarry Ln. Independence, OH 44131 (near Canal Visitor Center). 216-447-0030. 108 units. $50-$65. AC.

For more accommodations, contact Akron/Summit Convention & Visitors Bureau at 800-245-4254 or www.visitakron-summit.org; or Convention & Visitors Bureau of Greater Cleveland at 800-321-1001 or www.travelcleveland.com.

Excursions from Cuyahoga Valley

Lake Erie Islands

80 miles northwest of Cuyahoga Valley The magic of an archipelago is that each island can be a world unto itself. The Lake Erie Islands, spaced like skipping stones north of Ohio's Marblehead Peninsula, give visitors a different look at each landfall, from vineyards to bird sanctuaries to a party scene that rivals Daytona beach during Spring Break. Whether you come to cast a line in waters or walk in the woods looking for warblers, the sight and sound of the lake is never far and always alluring.

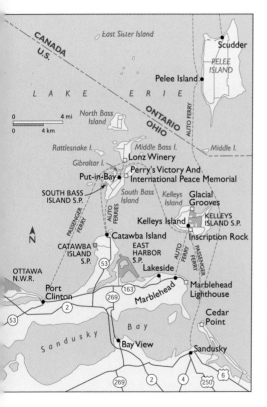

An ecological miracle, Lake Erie now teems with fish and birds only a few decades after pollution threatened to turn it into a watery tomb. Not long ago, a visibility marker dropped into the water would have become invisible almost immediately. That was the time, in the 1960s, when the lake was choked by algae.

Since then, clean water laws have stanched the worst pollution sources, and an accidentally introduced exotic species, the zebra mussel, has helped filter the water. Although there are lingering problems, Lake Erie is again producing more fish than all of the other Great Lakes combined. That means healthier water and better fishing for the hundreds of sportfishing boats that cruise Lake Erie.

Three of the islands—Kelleys, and Middle and South Bass—compose a state park. Middle Bass is known primarily for its grapes, a crop that benefits from the lake's moderating effect on temperature. The other two are the most popular for tourists. To explore the 20-some other islands in the archipelago stretching from Ohio to Ontario, you need a boat.

Ferries to **South Bass's Put-in-Bay** run frequently from Port Clinton and Catawba on the mainland. Visitors bring their cars on the ferry or rent bicycles and golf carts to tour the island, unless they get waylaid by the strip of shops and bars by the marina. That's a big draw for some of the thousands of visitors who pour off the ferry during July and August.

The more sober-minded folks head for **Perry's Victory and International Peace Memorial,** a 352-foot Doric column erected to honor Commodore Oliver Hazard Perry's bold conquest of a British fleet on Lake Erie during the War of 1812. There is no better way to see the lay of these islands than to ride the elevator to the top. From here, you can see the other islands to the north, such as the distant Pelee Island in Canadian waters. On a clear day, look to the west for West Sister Island, a federally protected refuge for nesting egrets and herons.

Then look east, to **Kelleys Island.** You won't find the big parties on Kelleys Island, and its historic winery is now a haunting ruin in the woods. Instead you'll find a small, peaceful community with abundant birds, unique coastal habitat, and glacial grooves, gashes in rocks that resemble chutes.

More than any of the other islands, Kelleys offers dramatic evidence of the past. State officials made certain that a portion of the state park was on the island to preserve the enormous grooves dug out by glaciers that moved across the surface more than 20,000 years ago. In places, the tracks are worn smooth as glass, as deep as 15 feet and as long as 400 feet.

Look for the glaciers' path at an observation point just north of the campground. You might be able to discern fossils of corals and other small creatures in the grooves.

A short bike ride across the 2,800-acre island leads to **Inscription Rock.** Native Americans carved pictographs into limestone here almost 500 years ago.

When Europeans began arriving in the area several centuries later, they too used the limestone, but in much more invasive ways. Locals, such as the brothers Datus and Irad Kelley, for whom the island was named, cut timber, quarried limestone, and built mansions, one of which still stands across Lake Shore Drive from

Inscription Rock. Quarrying activities have employed the residents of Lake Erie Islands for more than a century. However, that intrusive work has also destroyed rare glacial scars on the Kelleys Island's north end.

Nearby, along the shoreline you can find unusual plants such as the northern bog violet. Scientists use these delicate environments to monitor the lake's health. The water has cleared up, but the bottom of Lake Erie is still mired by runoff from the farms along the Ohio shoreline.

The last of the three islands in the park, **Middle Bass,** can be reached by taking ferries from the mainland and from Put-in-Bay on South Bass.

French explorers in the region called the 750-acre green spot Ile des Fleurs ("Island of Flowers"). Island of Grapes would have been a more fitting name. In 1854, a would-be vintner named Jose de Rivera bought Middle Bass, along with several others, and planted grape vines with an eye toward producing wine. Ten years later, he sold the island to Alfred Wehrle, who established Golden Eagle Wine Cellars. Golden Eagle became one of the biggest producers in the United States, and some felt the wines rivaled the finest vintages of France.

Wehrle soon had local competition from Peter Lonz, who opened his own vineyard on Middle Bass in 1884. He then bought Golden Eagle in 1926 and got through the teetotalling days of Prohibition by selling grape juice with instructions so customers could ferment the stuff at home.

All that remains of Lonz's presence is the Gothic shell of a castle-like structure built in the 1940s. It has been vacant since one of its terraces collapsed in 2000. One person was killed, and almost 80 others were hurt. You can see the remains lording over the shoreline.

Weather on the lake can be treacherous, going from placid and smooth to stormy 12-foot waves that could easily sink a small boat. But on a sunny fall day, sails fill and fishing poles bend, and island-hoppers happily lose themselves in the Lake Erie Islands.

■ **Kelleys Island: 4 sq. miles within Lake Erie Islands State Park** ■ **Lake Erie, north-central Ohio** ■ **Best seasons spring and summer** ■ **Boating, swimming, fishing, camping, hiking, ice-skating, cross-country skiing** ■ **Contact the park, Catawba Island, 4049 E. Moores Dock Rd., Port Clinton, OH 43452; 419-797-4530. www.dnr.state.oh.us/parks/parks/lakeerie.htm**

Hocking Hills State Park

160 miles southwest of Cuyahoga Valley Ask Ohioans to name the prettiest spot in the state and many will undoubtedly point you to the Hocking Hills. Surrounded by the gentle agrarian landscape of south-central Ohio, the ground suddenly folds into deep creases and high ridges, hiding cool gorges, gaping sandstone amphitheaters, moss-coated cliffs, waterfalls, and an array of other surprises.

The signature of the Hocking Hills is its dramatic formations of blackhand sandstone, named after similar rocks that are found 50 miles to the north where Native Americans used soot to inscribe the outline of a human hand into a cliff face. The area's bedrock—mostly sandstone and some shale—was created more than 300 million years ago when a shallow sea covered the region. As water rushed down from the young Appalachian Mountains in the southeast, a delta formed here, depositing layer after layer of sand and other sediment. Over millions of years, it compacted and cemented together with silica or iron oxide. Within the Hocking Hills, the sandstone lies 150 feet thick in places.

Wind and water took over next, scouring the rock to create recess caves, cliffs, overhangs, and gorges. Later, retreating glaciers stopped just 6 miles short of these hills, leaving large chunks of ice that plugged waterways and formed a bottle-shaped gorge north of

(continued on p. 104)

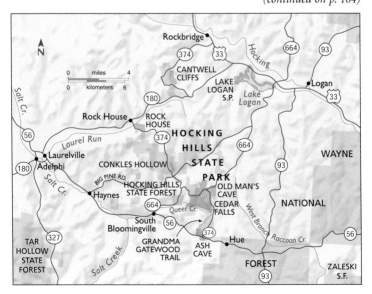

Bird-watching Sites on Lake Erie

Several adjoining sites on Lake Erie just east of Cleveland provide fine birding opportunities year-round. From Ohio Route 2 between Mentor and Painesville, take Ohio 44 north to Headlands Beach State Park and continue to the extreme eastern parking area. From here, walk northeast to **Headlands Dunes State Nature Preserve,** which can be an excellent spot to watch for migrating spring songbirds.

Spring can also bring good hawk-watching, as raptors follow the lakeshore rather than cross the water on their northward flight; merlins are fairly regular visitors in fall, as well as spring.

Walking through the dunes may scare up a migrant Common Snipe or American Woodcock. In late fall and winter, look for Northern Saw-whet Owls roosting in shrubs, and Lapland Longspurs and Snow Buntings along the beach.

Check the beach for migrant shorebirds, and the offshore waters for diving ducks. From fall through spring, continue east to the breakwater for a view of **Fairport Harbor,** where loons, grebes, ducks, and gulls congregate. This has traditionally been a good spot for rarities, from King Eider to all three jaegers to Little, Mew, and Glaucous Gulls. In late fall, scan the breakwater for the rare Purple Sandpiper. **Shipman Pond** (*via Headlands Road*) on the state park's southwestern boundary is worth a visit if you want to see wading birds and waterfowl.

Continue west on Headlands Road to **Zimmerman Trail,** part of **Mentor Marsh State Nature Preserve.** This 600-acre area is the largest reed-grass marsh in Ohio and a national natural landmark. Beech-maple and oak-hickory woodlands ring the protected area. The trail follows an old bank of the Grand River and provides access to wetlands where you may find nesting Pied-billed Grebes, Wood

American Bittern

Ducks, Virginia rails, Soras, Common Moorhens, Red-headed Woodpeckers, and Prothonotary Warblers. In migration, you might glimpse Black-crowned Night-Herons, American and Least Bitterns (the latter two are rare but regular; least may breed in the area.)

Snipe

Mentor can be home to a fine diversity of migrant songbirds in spring, with more than 250 species recorded in recent years. The visitor center is on Corduroy Road, to the southwest.

Lapland Longspur

Six miles west, warm water from a power plant in **Eastlake** attracts large numbers of gulls and flocks of waterfowl in winter. To reach it, take Erie Road north from Ohio 283 to Lake Erie. Ring-Billed and Herring are the common gull species, but a great number of

rarities have been found. Check winter flocks of Bonaparte's Gulls for the rare Little Gull that gets mixed in.

On the western side of Cleveland, another power plant just north of US 6 on the shore at **Avon Lake** provides similarly excellent gull-watching during the winter.

The harbor at the western Cleveland suburb of **Lorain** often is a haven for rare shorebirds in spring and fall. (Remember that for shorebirds, fall starts in July.) From Ohio 6 east of the Black River, drive north on Arizona Avenue, park, and walk out to the breakwater. Check the flats to the east for loons, occasional scoters, Oldsquaw, and flocks of Red-breasted Merganser from fall through spring.

King Eider

Lancaster. In the 1700s Wyandot Indians called the river that ran through the gorge *hockhocking* (bottle river), thereby giving the surrounding hills their name.

The shady, moist environment found deep in the hills' gorges mimics a much cooler climate. As a result, Canada yew, yellow birch, stately old-growth stands of hemlock, and other species normally found much farther north thrive here. This collision of climactic zones also makes for an interesting cross section of animals. Copperhead and ring-necked snakes sun on high rock ledges, while red-backed salamanders and box turtles hide on the ferny forest floor. Common mammals include the white-tailed deer, red foxes, and gray squirrels.

The park, along with **Hocking Hills State Forest** (*740-385-4402*), encompasses six units. Each one is named for its most notable attractions: Old Man's Cave, Cedar Falls, Ash Cave, Conkles Hollow, Rock House, and Cantwell Cliffs. All are within a 10-minute drive of one another.

For better or for worse, good road access makes it easy to reach the most remarkable rock formations in the Hocking Hills. To get your bearings, pick up a map and trail guide from the park office, across from Old Man's Cave on Ohio 664.

The trails within each unit tend to be no more than 1 or 2 miles long. In the state forest that surrounds and weaves among the state park units, there are more hiking and camping opportunities. Forest headquarters are on Ohio 374 near Conkles Hollow.

Ash Cave & Cedar Falls

The most dramatic unit may be Ash Cave (parking area is west of the intersection of Ohio 374 and Ohio 56). The quarter-mile trail to Ash Cave begins as a pleasant stroll along a stream shaded by pines and hemlocks, and surrounded by the blooms of trillium, jack-in-the-pulpit, and other wildflowers. As you walk northward, the walls of the gorge narrow, and then converge at a magnificent amphitheater of sandstone; a narrow waterfall plunges into a pool far below.

Follow the trail right up to the concave wall, where it arcs above you and gives you a dizzying sense of its scale. Ash Cave stretches 700 feet wide, 90 feet high, and about 100 feet deep, like a band shell. Like other recess caves in the park, the cave was formed when the softer middle layer of blackhand sandstone eroded more

The Ohio Buckeye

Aesculus glabra—the Buckeye State's namesake tree—reaches heights of 70 feet and grows wild along rich moist river banks. it produces lovely yellowish-cream flower spikes in spring, and later bears a 1- to 2-inch-diameter chestnut-shaped fruit. Native Americans called the fruit hetuck, or "eye of the buck," in reference to the light beige spot on the dark nut. They ground the nut into powder and sprinkled it in pools of water to stun fish and make them easy to harvest.

Today, the buckeye is grown mostly as a smaller ornamental variety, found in gardens through-out the central United States and parts of Europe.

quickly than the more resistant top and bottom layers. It got its name from several thousands of bushels of ashes that early Euro-pean settlers found inside. The ashes were probably the remains of bonfires that Native Americans had built over the course of hun-dreds of years.

In the early 1900s, local residents used Ash Cave as a church. The rock near the recess entrance made a nice pulpit for preachers.

Stairs to the right of the cave climb up to its rim. From here, you can follow the **Rim Trail** back to the parking area, or pick up the **Grandma Gatewood Trail** that heads north 3 miles to the next park unit, Cedar Falls. (Some maps and signs list the Grandma Gatewood Trail as the Buckeye Trail, a statewide route.)

Though you can also reach Cedar Falls by car, it seems far more appropriate to arrive by foot since this lovely grotto is among the most secluded in the park. **Queer Creek** carves chasms and basins into the sandstone before gushing over a final ledge, the most volu-minous falls within the Hocking Hills. Don't bother looking for the area's namesake cedars, though. Settlers named the spot after misidentifying the tall hemlocks.

Old Man's Cave

From Cedar Falls, the Grandma Gatewood Trail continues another 3 miles to Old Man's Cave, the park's most popular unit. Named for a hermit who lived here in the early 1800s, this area offers a lit-tle bit of everything: upper and lower waterfalls, a narrow gorge,

Hiking the Rim Trail, Hocking Hills State Park

potholes and other formations carved out by the flowing water, and the 200-foot-long cave.

The gorge is the most notable, as it cuts through the entire thickness of the blackhand sandstone. You'll follow a 300-million-year-old time line by walking the half-mile **trail** through the gorge from the upper to lower waterfalls.

Conkles Hollow

The Conkles Hollow area offers some of the best options for hikers (*Ohio 374, a few miles northwest of Old Man's Cave*). The 2.5-mile rim trail traces the edge of Conkles Hollow and allows you to peer 250 feet down into what is believed to be the deepest gorge in the state. Vistas at almost every turn take in the lush valley floor or look across the forested hills.

A small parking area on Big Pine Road, about a mile east of Conkles Hollow, serves as the trailhead for a couple of **state forest trails.** As you tramp along you'll encounter **Big Spring Hollow,** which is a horseshoe-shaped recessed cave near a 100-foot waterfall. Here you'll also see a scenic rock outcropping called **Airplane Rock,** and a double-level cave.

Cantwell Cliffs

From Conkles Hollow, Ohio 374 twists and turns for 13 miles to Cantwell Cliffs, the park's hidden jewel. The cliffs—yet another dramatic example of eroded blackhand sandstone—plunge 150 feet straight down, as if the rock was sliced away with a knife. The gorge below is a broad horseshoe-shaped glen, a peaceful world of ferns, mossy limestone walls, and trickling creeks.

The 2.5-mile **trail** leading down into the gorge should be on your must-do list. From the parking area on Ohio 374, head left at the fork in the trail and you'll soon be descending through a tight maze of slump blocks, large chunks of sandstone that have broken away from the cliff. The passage named **Fat Woman's Squeeze** gives you an idea of trail width here. The trail next passes a concave rock shelter, then crosses the floor of the gorge before climbing up the other side and looping back to the parking area.

Rock House

A half-mile **trail** off Ohio 374 leads to a recess cave that, according to local folklore, once harbored bootleggers and horse thieves. Weathering sculpted the unusual formation by widening cracks found in the softer middle layer of sandstone.

■ **2,000 acres** ■ **South-central Ohio, 50 miles southeast of Columbus**
■ **Best seasons spring, summer, and fall** ■ **Camping, hiking, fishing**
■ **Contact the park, 19852 State Route 664, Logan, OH 43138. 740-385-6841. www.hockinghillspark.com**

Dry Tortugas

In the Gulf of Mexico, about 70 nautical miles west of Key West, Florida, a 7-mile-long archipelago of seven low-lying islands forms Dry Tortugas National Park. A bird and marine life sanctuary, it harbors some of the healthiest coral reefs remaining off North American shores. Towering incongruously in the midst of this subtropical Eden is Fort Jefferson, a relic of 19th-century military strategy. The largest American coastal fort built in that century, it sprawls across Garden Key's 16 acres.

Only a minute percentage of the park's 64,701 acres are above water. The largest island is Loggerhead Key, covering 30 acres on the western end of the chain; the 19th-century lighthouse here still flashes a beacon to mariners. Moving east across about 3 miles are Garden, Bush, Long, Hospital, Middle, and East Key. The last three are little more than spits of white coral sand.

Spanish explorer Juan Ponce de León, the first European to describe the Florida peninsula, dropped anchor here in 1513. He found pellucid waters teeming with green, hawksbill, leatherback, and loggerhead turtles, and so named the islands *las tortugas,* which means "the turtles." For the next three centuries, pirates relied on the turtles for meat and eggs; they also raided the sandy nests of roosting sooty and noddy terns, more than 100,000 of which descend on Bush Key each year between March and September. By 1825, when the islands' first lighthouse began to alert sailors of surrounding reefs and shoals—a grave for more than 200 ships wrecked here since 1600—nautical charts were warning that the Tortugas were "dry," because there was no fresh water on them.

In 1846, U.S. Army strategists were concerned that hostile nations could disrupt shipping lanes in the Gulf of Mexico. So, they decided to build a 450-gun, 2,000-man fort on Garden Key. The intimidating bulk of the 50-foot-high, three-level hexagon, whose 2,000 arches

- Western Florida, Gulf of Mexico
- 64,701 acres
- Established 1992
- Best seasons spring and fall
- Camping, hiking, boating, swimming, snorkeling, bird-watching
- Information: 505-785-2232 www.nps.gov/drto

Aerial view, Dry Tortugas National Park

run half a mile around, spared it from ever having to fire a shot in anger.

During the Civil War, the Union turned the fort into a prison for deserters. It also held physician Samuel Mudd, who was convicted of conspiracy in Abraham Lincoln's murder after he set the broken leg of fugitive assassin John Wilkes Booth. He spent four years behind these walls before he was released.

Unfinished after nearly 30 years of intermittent construction, the "Gibraltar of the Gulf" succumbed in 1874 to several factors: yellow fever, hurricane damage, and the new rifled cannon that rendered its 8-foot-thick walls obsolete. It was back in action 14 years later as a Navy station; the battleship *Maine* steamed from here in 1898 to its infamous destiny in Havana's harbor 90 miles south, triggering the Spanish-American war.

In 1907, the fort was permanently abandoned. President Franklin D. Roosevelt signed the papers that made it a national monument in 1935.

How to Get There

The only way to get to Dry Tortugas is by boat or seaplane. Yankee Fleet and Sunny Days

What Not to Miss

- Taking a day trip by boat or floatplane to Garden Key
- Strolling along the fort's seawall to see great views of the Florida Keys and the Gulf of Mexico
- Snorkeling along the seawall
- Following the self-guided tour of Fort Jackson on Garden Key
- Visiting the 150-foot lighthouse on Loggerhead Key
- Watching sea lions and sea otters off the coastal strip

run regular boat service. For Yankee Fleet, call 305-294-7009 or 800-634-0939; for Sunny Days, call 305-292-6100 or 800-236-7937. For names of authorized air taxis and charter boats, call park headquarters.

Boats to the park take about 3 hours from Key West; by air, the trip takes 40 minutes.

Private boaters should refer to the National Oceanic and Atmospheric Administration's Chart 11434 ("Sombrero Key to Dry Tortugas") and Chart 11438 ("Dry Tortugas").

When to Go

The park is open all year. Temperatures range from the mid-80s to the low 50s.

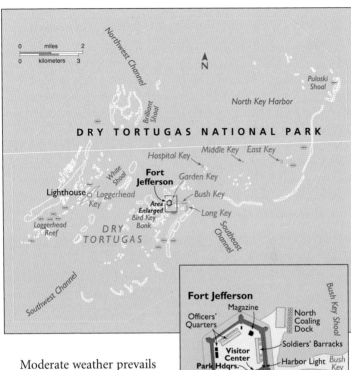

Moderate weather prevails in April and May, when visitation is at its peak. Winter is often windy with rough seas. The tropical storm or "hurricane" season lasts from June through November, when temperatures and humidity are the highest.

How to Visit

A day trip by boat or floatplane gives you an unhurried visit to **Garden Key.** You can take a self-guided walking tour of **Fort Jefferson,** stroll around the seawall, swim, and snorkel. If you're visiting between October and January, consider swimming the narrow channel to **Bush Key** to experience a true "desert island" environment. The island is closed the rest of the year to protect the nesting sites of noddy and sooty terns.

EXPLORING THE PARK

Garden Key & Fort Jefferson: **70 miles from Key West; A full day**

When you reach the park, check the announcement boards on the dock for ranger-led activities. The visitor center is just inside the fort entrance. View the self-operated video orientation program, then take a self-guided tour of Fort Jefferson's massive architecture and parade ground.

Granite spiral staircases lead to open-air gun holes atop the fort, where visitors will find splendid 360-degree views and excellent vantage points for bird-watching; bring binoculars. Early on, the Tortugas' population of terns, cormorants, gulls, boobies, plovers, pelicans, peregrine falcons, and twin-tailed frigatebirds caught the

School of fish, Dry Tortugas National Park

attention of naturalists such as John James Audubon, who sailed here from Key West in 1832 to study them.

Allow at least an hour to explore the rest of the ghostly fort. When the government broke ground on the mammoth project in 1846, many of the laborers were slaves from Key West. That continued until the Emancipation Proclamation went into effect in 1865. By then, the fort supervisors were using prisoners to do the grueling work of assembling the remote outpost with some 16 million bricks.

The planners underestimated the daunting logistics involved in building the fort. Cement, brick, stone, sand, lumber, and even water had to be imported from the mainland, sometimes from as far away as Maine. The project soon turned into an engineering fiasco. Engineers realized too late that the ground beneath the fort was made of crumbly coral rock, which began giving away under the structure's weight.

Fortunately, the fort's intimidating presence spared it from being tested in battle. Undermanned and with only one out of 450 guns in working order, the garrison pulled off an amazing bluff at the outbreak of the Civil War. A Confederate naval ship demanded that the fort surrender, to which the soldiers of Fort Garrison threatened to blow the ship out of the water. The Rebels decided not to risk a barrage and sailed away, never knowing that the only things peeking out from the gun ports were nervous Union soldiers.

Fort Jefferson's most famous inhabitant was Samuel Mudd, the Maryland doctor who treated John Wilkes Booth's leg after the actor assassinated President Abraham Lincoln. Despite the doctor's insistence that he did not know who his patient was or what he had done, Mudd was sentenced to spend his life within the fort's walls.

During a nasty outbreak of yellow fever in 1869, Mudd worked tirelessly to treat the 270 members of the 300-man garrison who got sick. Thanks to his efforts, only 38 people died, and President Andrew Johnson pardoned the doctor in 1869. His cell is in the fort, marked by a plaque.

Another famous person who spent time on Garden Key was Ernest Hemingway. The writer used to fish in the lagoon beneath the fort's mammoth guns. There is a photograph of Hemingway and his legendary editor, Maxwell Perkins, standing near the entrance. If you stand in the same spot today, nothing in that background will have changed much.

Outside the fort in the parade are the foundations of the **Officers' Quarters** and **Soldiers' Barracks.** Stroll along the fort's 0.6-mile-long **seawall** and **moat,** a sheltered habitat favored by queen conch, yellow stingray, gray snapper, sea stars, and other creatures.

It would be a shame to travel this far and not try snorkeling. The visitor center tries to keep a few goggles, flippers, and snorkels on hand to lend, but it's wiser to bring your own if you have them.

The best snorkeling from Garden Key is on the sea side of the fort's seawall, in chest-deep water covering a sandy shoal thick with sea fans, brain coral, and turtle grass. More than 440 species of fish patrol these clear waters.

Fort Jefferson, Dry Tortugas National Park

If you can enlist a companion for mutual safety, consider paddling from the campground's bathing beach along the wall, where fish tend to congregate. Watch for barracuda; although they're seldom aggressive, the fish are territorial and should be given wide berth.

If you are a confident swimmer, you can cross the narrow channel to explore **Bush Key's** primordial garden of bay cedar, sea grape, mangrove, sea oats, and prickly pear cactus. Bush is only open to visitors from October to January, however. The rest of the year it is a sanctuary for sooty and noddy terns that roost in sandy nests.

Loggerhead Key is accessible if you have a boat that can land on the beach. The park occasionally has an employee here who can let visitors into the 150-foot **lighthouse.** At least twice a season, female sea turtles climb onto the beach to lay their eggs in the sand.

INFORMATION & ACTIVITIES

Headquarters
Everglades National Park
40001 State Rd. 9336
Homestead, FL 33034
Correspondence: P.O. Box
6208, Key West, FL 33041
305-242-7700
www.nps.gov/drto

Visitor & Information Centers
Visitor center, inside Fort Jefferson, Garden Key, open daily
year round.

Seasons & Accessibility
Park open year-round. Visitation peaks in spring, when
advance reservations for boats
or planes are advised.

Only Garden Key offers
overnight stays (in campgrounds). Loggerhead and
Bush Keys available for day
use only. Bush Key is closed
from February to September
during nesting season.

Entrance Fees
$5 per person.

Pets
Permitted only in the campground and must be leashed at
all times.

Facilities for Disabled
Dock, visitor center, ground
level of fort, and Fort Jefferson
campground are accessible.

Things to Do
Occasional ranger-led activities. Self-guided walking tours
of Fort Jefferson. Also, swimming, snorkeling, wreck diving,
underwater photography, birdwatching, camping.

Special Advisories
■ Plan to bring all water, food,
fuel, and supplies. There is
no fresh water available for
campers, and no showers for
rinsing after swimming.
■ Private boats must anchor
offshore in designated areas.
There are no public boat
moorings or slips.
■ There is no public telephone
service in the Dry Tortugas.

Campgrounds
Camping is permitted only on
Garden Key, which has ten
primitive sites available. First
come, first served. 14-day limit.
Fees are $3 per person per
night. Groups of ten or more
must obtain a special permit in
advance from park headquarters. Write for reservations at
P.O. Box 6208, Key West, FL
33041; allow 30 days for
processing.

Hotels, Motels, & Inns
(Unless otherwise noted, rates for
two persons in a double room, high
season.)

Archways inside Fort Jefferson, Dry Tortugas National Park

In Key West, FL 33040:

■ **Best Western Key Ambassador Resort Inn**
3755 S. Roosevelt Blvd. 305-296-3500 or 800-432-4315. 101 units. $189-$319. AC, pool.

■ **Duval House**
815 Duval St. 305-294-1666. 28 units, 3 kitchenettes. $140-$345. AC, pool.

■ **Marquesa Hotel**
600 Fleming St. 305-292-1919. 27 units. $260-$395. AC, pool, restaurant.

■ **Westwinds**
914 Eaton St. 305-296-4440 or 800-788-4150. 22 units, 4 kitchenettes. $135-$145. AC, pool.

For other area accommodations, contact the Key West Chamber of Commerce, 402 Wall St., Key West, FL 33040. 305-294-2587 or 800-527-8539.

Excursions from Dry Tortugas

Florida Keys Drive

Florida City to Key West

126 miles one way; one day Mangrove-fringed and water-bound, the Overseas Highway (US 1) links a chain of subtropical isles that arc off the tip of Florida. Delving ever deeper into a tropical terrain, the route reveals a land of hammocks and reefs, miniature deer, and, at last, the fanciful, idiosyncratic town of Key West, your jumping off point to the Dry Tortugas.

The drive begins a mile below Florida City on the mainland, where Milepost 126 starts counting down the miles to Key West. It follows the former roadbeds and bridges of the Florida East Coast Railway, which was completed in 1912.

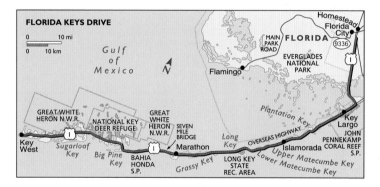

A mile beyond Lake Surprise, so named by early railroad explorers who weren't expecting to find it, the highway enters **Key Largo,** the largest and northernmost island along US 1. Bustling with activity, Key Largo contains all aspects of the Keys, from their rich tropical vegetation and opalescent waters to their billboards, dive shops, hamburger stands, and mom-and-pop motels.

At **John Pennekamp Coral Reef State Park** *(see pp. 58–60),* the first underwater state park in the United States, you can take snorkeling, diving, or glass-bottomed boats out to the lacy coral reef that parallels the Keys' Atlantic shoreline from here all the way to the Dry Tortugas.

Continuing through **Plantation Key,** where pineapple and banana plantations flourished at the turn of the 20th century, US 1 crosses Snake Creek on one of the 42 bridges that connect the Keys. At **Windley Key,** the **Theater of the Sea** *(Mile 84.5. 305-664-2431.*

www.theaterofthesea.com. Adm. fee) features sea lions, sharks, dolphins, and other sea life.

Islamorada (Spanish for "purple isle") is the only settlement on **Upper Matecumbe Key** and marks the beginning of the Middle Keys. The island's **Hurricane Memorial** *(Mile 82)* honors victims of the Labor Day hurricane of 1935. One of the most powerful ever recorded in the United States, the storm killed hundreds of people and washed out much of the railroad.

Two sites can be visited off **Lower Matecumbe Key. Lignumvitae Key State Botanical Site** (*see pp. 66–67*), an uninhabited 280-acre island, contains a rare virgin tropical hardwood forest that includes gumbo-limbo, pigeon plum, and poisonwood. At the **Indian Key State Historic Site** (*accessible via boat tours from Robbie's Marina. 305-664-4815. www.dep.state.fl.us/parks. Thurs.–Mon. Adm. fee),* you'll see the foundations of buildings and cisterns from an 1830s wrecking village, established to salvage ships that had run aground on the reef.

At the **Long Key State Recreation Area** *(Mile 67.5. 305-664-4815. www.dep.state.fl.us/parks. Adm. fee),* the swimming is poor, but beachcombers may find the rubbery egg cases left by sea turtles. The **Golden Orb Trail** here leads through a delightful mangrove-edged lagoon.

The Long Key Viaduct sweeps toward tiny Conch Key, then US 1 angles across Grassy Key and into **Marathon,** the heavily developed commercial center of the Middle Keys. Amid the

How the Keys Came to Be

In primordial times, coral reefs grew atop limestone ridges in these shallow seas. Between 120,000 to 100,000 years ago, polar ice caps enlarged and the oceans receded, dropping sea levels by 20 to 30 feet and exposing the top of the reef, which died and became a barren archipelago of fossilized coral or limestone rock. Over the millennia, waves, tides, and storms deposited seaweed, driftwood, and other organic debris, which decayed to form soil. Seeds drifted ashore or were brought in the stomachs of migrating birds. Those plants that sprouted eventually created the Keys' distinctive jungle-like tropical hammocks, virtual samplers of the West Indies' flora from which they derive.

Along US 1 in the Florida Keys

sprawl is **Crane Point Hammock** (*see p. 122*), where you'll find a thatch-palm hammock with the combined **Museum of Natural History of the Florida Keys** and **Children's Museum.**

South of Marathon, US 1 crosses the spectacular **Seven Mile Bridge.** One of the world's longest bridges, it offers sweeping views of the open Atlantic on the left and the Gulf of Mexico to the right. On the other side of the bridge, **Bahia Honda State Park** (*see p. 123*) has beaches of white sand, a rarity in the Keys. Satinwood, key spider lily, and other West Indian plants can be found along the **Silver Palm Trail.**

As the road pushes southwest, the Keys seem more isolated and less populated. Bridges become shorter, and islands begin to merge. Eagles, falcons, and red-tailed hawks like this area, and it's not uncommon to see a large osprey nest perched on a telephone pole.

Big Pine Key, unusual for its large slash pines, is the only place in the world where endangered Key deer live. Standing only 2.5 feet tall, the dainty subspecies of the Virginia white-tailed deer might be spotted if you take a 2.5-mile detour onto Key Deer Boulevard through the **National Key Deer Refuge** *(see pp. 126–127).*

For its final 30 miles, US 1 crosses one small tropical key after another until it reaches **Key West,** an eccentric tropical town nick-named the Conch Republic where the atmosphere is more Caribbean than American. Here, you can poke through the shops on Duval Street; see the southernmost point and the southernmost house at 1400 Duval St. *(private)* in the continental United States, and wander streets lined with fine Victorian homes and quaint white-frame "conch" cottages.

One of the most attractive ones is the **Ernest Hemingway Home and Museum** *(907 Whitehead St.; 305-294-1575; www.hemingway home.com; fee).* Inside the two-story house are many of the writer's furnishings. And milling about the property are about 60 cats; some are descendants of Hemingway's beloved pets.

■ **126 miles; one day** ■ **Florida City to Key West on US 1** ■ **Best seasons spring and fall**

Encounters with Dolphins

According to experts, dolphins are the only wild animals that interact with man of their own free will.

Several programs in the Florida Keys give people the chance to get to know dolphins in and out of the water. The programs teach dolphin biology and communication. Be sure to call ahead for days and times.

■ Dolphin Cove Research & Education Center, US 1, Milepost 101.9, Key Largo. 305-451-4060
■ Dolphins Plus, US 1, Milepost 99.5, Key Largo. 305-451-1993
■ Theater of the Sea, US 1, Milepost 84, Islamorada. 305-664-2431
■ Dolphin Research Center, US 1, Milepost 59, Grassy Key, Marathon. 305-289-1121

Crane Point Hammock Tropical Forest Preserve

115 miles east of Dry Tortugas

On the bay side of the highway, incongruously surrounded by Marathon's commercial clutter, is one of the Keys' most extraordinary natural places. Many of the islands once resembled this 64-acre virgin thatch palm hammock, the last of its kind in North America.

Walk the quarter-mile **loop trail** through the forest with a copy of the self-guided brochure that identifies the red mangrove, palms, and exotic hardwoods bending over you, hiding the creatures whose unseen scuffling and odd cries add a peculiar spookiness. There's much to identify here, including 160 native plants. A menagerie of creatures such as the graceful ibis stand at the brink of extinction. Along the way, look for rare tree snails, and don't miss an unusual pit gouged in the island's coral foundation by rainfall erosion, exposing fossil star and brain corals from the primordial sea that formed the Keys.

Archaeologists have uncovered a rich cache of pre-Columbian artifacts, including weapons, tools, a dugout canoe, and pottery. The oldest vessels, possibly 5,000 years old, are displayed at the adjoining **Museum of Natural History of the Florida Keys,** the islands' preeminent archive of ancient artifacts. Among the most popular of the museum's 20 major exhibits is one on the many shipwrecks that brought wealth to these isles. Bronze cannon, gold and silver from the Spanish main, and other more mundane items commemorate the anonymous fortune seekers who found only watery graves on the reefs here.

If you're traveling with young ones, set them loose inside the **Children's Museum,** an indoor-outdoor facility with interactive exhibits about Keys ecology. It should whip up their enthusiasm for a stroll along the preserve's mile-long indigenous **loop trail,** which visits the site of a long-gone Bahamian village. You'll also see the well-restored **George Adderly House,** said to be the oldest example of the Keys' quaint gingerbread conch architecture north of Key West. Its rough-textured walls are made of tabby, a mixture of limestone and crushed sea shells.

■ **64 acres** ■ **Marathon Key, US 1 at Milepost 50.5** ■ **Best seasons spring and fall** ■ **Camping, hiking, guided walks, boating, museums** ■ **Contact the preserve, 5550 Overseas Hwy., Marathon, FL 33050; 305-743-9100. www.cranepoint.org**

Bahia Honda State Park

100 miles east of Dry Tortugas Though offshore reefs shield most of the Keys from ocean waves, Bahia Honda with its wide sandy beach is a notable exception. The island hooks out into the open Atlantic at a place favorable for catching sand-carrying currents. Here you can soak up long views of glassy turquoise water, properly outlined by sand and stately rows of royal palms with long pinwheel fronds. Roseate spoonbills and other wading birds add grace notes to the tropical intermezzo.

Beach at Bahia Honda State Park

For even better views, walk out on a section of the **old railroad bridge** at the south end of the park.

Also consider taking the **Silver Palm Nature Trail** at the end of Sandspur Beach. Rimming the shore of a tidal lagoon, the trail explores some of the island's rare and lovely flora, many species of which originate in the Caribbean islands to the south of the Keys. Among the unusual plants are Jamaica morning glory, orange-flowering Geiger trees, sea lavender, white Key spider lily, and wild alamanda. Bahia Honda also contains the national champion specimens of the yellow satinwood and silver palm.

The tarpon fishing in this area is especially good. Charter fishing boats operate from here. So if you're planning on visiting, consider trying the recreation Ernest Hemingway credited with renewing his creative powers between intensive days of writing.

■ 524 acres ■ South Florida, US 1 at Milepost 37 ■ Best seasons spring and fall ■ Camping, hiking, guided walks, boating, swimming, scuba diving, fishing, biking, bird-watching, boat tours ■ Contact the park, 36850 Overseas Hwy., Big Pine Key, FL 33043; 305-872-2353. www.bahia hondapark.com

Looe Key

90 miles east of Dry Tortugas

Just south of the 720-foot-long Torch–Ramrod Bridge, Milepost 27 confirms that you've reached **Ramrod Key.** This smallish limestone knob is best known as a staging area for eager divers headed out to the reefs of Looe Key, part of the **Florida Keys National Marine Sanctuary** that is about 5 miles out in the Atlantic. The 5.3-square-mile preserve encloses the most diverse coral community in the Lower Keys, a wonderland teeming with fish and other sea creatures, with shallow depths suitable for snorkelers and scuba divers of all skill levels. Many underwater buffs rate it North America's premier dive spot.

Looe Key—not really a key but a reef—commemorates the unfortunate H.M.S. *Looe,* a British warship that foundered here in the 1700s. (Look carefully at the bottom and you might notice some of the frigate's ballast stones, their shapes at odds with the natural detritus.)

From the air, the reef sprawls darkly atop pale coral sand in the shape of a bent Y, roughly 800 yards long and 200 yards wide. Its massive accretions or spurs of pillar coral rise up from depths as great as 35 feet, nearly to the surface. Lying in sandy grooves between these great spurs are bulky, dome-shaped brain corals, patrolled by skulking lobsters and bottom-skimming sea rays. Thousands of wildly colorful fish congregate here, moving in precision-swimming schools and darting among the skinny branches of elkhorn coral. Purple sea fans sway languidly in the Gulf Stream, which surges above clusters of sponges and sea urchins. The blue-tinted scene is otherworldly.

Virtually every dive shop in the region offers half-day excursions to Looe Key daily *(8 a.m. and 1:30 p.m.),* providing all equipment. Although the water is comfortably warm, you will slowly lose body heat as you explore the reef. For many, a wet suit vest rented at nominal cost prevents the weakness, shortness of breath, and occasional nausea that some experience after an otherwise perfectly delightful hour of paddling. If you're prone to motion sickness, consider starting your medication the night before your trip.

■ 6 square nautical miles ■ South Florida, southeast of Ramrod Key (Milepost 27) ■ Best seasons spring and fall ■ Swimming, scuba diving, snorkeling ■ Contact the Florida Keys National Marine Sanctuary, P.O. Box 500368, Marathon, FL 33050; 305-292-0311. http://floridakeys.noaa.gov/

Snorkeling & Diving in the Keys

The warm water and reefs of the Florida Keys attract thousands of scuba and snorkel aficionados annually, a recreation statistically about as safe as swimming.

If you have some basic swimming skills, snorkeling is easy. It requires only a mask to see

A snorkeling discovery

underwater, a snorkel for breathing, and fins for propulsion, all of which can be rented. (Most tours also provide buoyant vests.)

Scuba diving, however, uses sophisticated equipment and requires training by qualified teachers. The best way to learn is to take lessons from a certified member of the Professional Association of Diving Instructors (PADI), the largest scuba training organization in the world. PADI Dive Center locations are listed on the Internet *(www.padi. com/Dive/getidivecenters.asp)*.

Just about anyone over the age of 12 in good health can learn to dive. You'll be asked to complete a routine medical questionnaire to see if your health requires a consultation with your physician to be sure it's safe for you to dive. Soft contact lenses don't pose a problem, but hard ones should be gas permeable.

Typically, an entry-level course begins in a pool and includes four training dives. If you'd rather try out scuba diving before committing to formal instruction, PADI offers a Discover Scuba Diving program lasting only several hours, including a shallow ocean dive supervised by an instructor after a short pool session to familiarize you with your equipment.

A beginner's PADI Open Water Diver course might consist of five or six sessions completed in 3 to 4 days, or spread over 6 weeks.

If you want to wait and see how the Keys look to you before taking a lesson, PADI-certified introductory resort courses can have you exploring the reefs in hours. They don't result in certification, but they do enable you to dive in the afternoon with an instructor following a morning of classroom and pool instruction.

National Key Deer Refuge

95 miles east of Dry Tortugas

The 8,542-acre National Key Deer Refuge on Big Pine Key was established in 1957 to protect the dwindling population of Key deer, diminutive creatures no taller than 32 inches. They're found nowhere else but in the Keys.

They are the smallest of the 28 subspecies of the Virginia white-tailed deer that have grown small over the centuries because of environmental stresses, including hurricanes, limited water and forage, and a small habitat. Their ancestors probably ranged south before the melting of the ancient Wisconsin ice age glacier, which elevated the sea level and turned what had been a tenuous peninsula into an archipelago.

Key deer bucks range from 28 inches to 32 inches to the shoulders and weigh an average of 80 pounds; the does grow to between 24 inches to 28 inches and weigh about 65 pounds. The fawns, which resemble toys, only weigh two to four pounds and leave a postage-stamp-size hoofprint.

Establishing the refuge has helped save the carefully stepping

Key deer, Big Pine Key

creatures. By 1957, hunters and poachers had reduced the herd to about 27. Today, that number has grown to about 800.

The deer are most active at dawn and dusk, and spend the rest of the day in the cool pine forests. No matter how winsome they may look as they forage along the road, do not feed them. Years of taking food from well-intentioned people has drawn the creatures to the roads. Bear this in mind as you drive across Big Pine. Observe the slow speed limit (45 miles per hour by day, 35 at night); about 70 percent of deer fatalities stem from car accidents.

To get to the refuge, turn west off the highway just south of Milepost 31 onto Key Deer Boulevard (Fla. 940), where you'll soon see a sign pointing the way. Roughly a mile and a half farther on, the road crosses Watson Boulevard. Turn left to reach refuge headquarters, where you can get a map and information on the other living things that inhabit this quiet world. In addition to the deer, the refuge is home to 21 endangered plants and animals, some of which are not found anywhere else in the world.

Look for the brochure geared to the exotic West Indian trees along the mile-long loop of the **Jack Watson Nature Trail,** which lies ahead. The trail is named for the refuge manager who campaigned successfully to ban the hunting of Key deer.

Return to the intersection and continue on Key Deer Boulevard for another 1.5 miles to an old quarry known as the **Blue Hole,** now filled with fresh groundwater and alligators of various sizes. You can leave your car and stop at the visitor center here where volunteers are on hand.

After you've gotten your fill of watching the torpid reptiles, stroll a short way to the head of the **Watson Trail.** Along the path you'll find water-filled sinkholes, and stands of thatch and silver palm rising above a riot of subtropical plants.

Return to Blue Hole and walk down Higgs Lane to the sign indicating the refuge, which lies beyond a roadside gate. From there a footpath winds through pine rocklands to **Watson's Hammock,** a hardwood forest of mostly gumbo-limbo and Jamaican dogwood rising some 50 feet to create an oasis of shade.

■ 8,542 acres ■ South Florida, Big Pine Key, at Milepost 31 on Key Deer Blvd. ■ Best seasons spring and fall ■ Hiking, bird-watching, wildlife viewing ■ Contact the refuge, 28950 Watson Blvd., Big Pine Key, FL 33043; 305-872-2239. http://nationalkeydeer.fws.gov

Great White Heron National Wildlife Refuge

85 miles east of Dry Tortugas

You probably won't see a sign announcing this federal sanctuary, home to the Keys' flying, feathered ballet troupe and the only nesting place in the United States for great white herons and the endangered white-crowned pigeon. Glance at your map, however, and you'll notice ruler-straight boundary lines embracing much of the bay side of the Lower Keys nearly to Key West.

These nearly 187,000 backcountry acres of shallow water, fringe and scrub mangrove wetlands, low hardwood hammocks, and salt

Blue heron in white phase

marsh also provide a haven for ospreys, Blue herons, Reddish egrets, Mangrove cuckoos, Black-whiskered Vireos, Green- and Blue-winged Teal, Red-breasted Mergansers, and coots. Bird-watchers consider themselves especially fortunate to record sightings of the Gawky-beautiful Roseate Spoonbill, the Ibis, and the Double-crested Cormorant, among many other uncommon species.

You can't drive to the refuge, but you can explore it by boat, and if you have the time (at least a half day) you ought to consider it. There is profoundly affecting primordial beauty here, and local fishing guides offer day trips aboard shallow-draft boats for those who simply want to observe. Within the refuge, you'll find a fertile world where native seabirds and migratory waterfowl breed, many

Protecting Key Birdlife

Red-breasted Merganser

Never leave fishing hooks and line in the wild. If your lure snags in a tree, do everything possible to retrieve it. Never discard hooked bait or fishing line by tossing it into the water.

If you hook a bird, don't let it fly away without cutting away any attached line, as it dooms the creature to entanglement and death by starvation. If a bird has swallowed a hook or is badly entangled, bring it to a rehabilitation center or call for a pick up (305-852-4486).

When cleaning fish, don't toss unwanted parts into the water, as birds can choke on them if they are larger than their usual prey.

roosting on floating nests. Once you wander into its maze of mangrove islands, you get the pleasant sense of entering a magical kingdom. And it is: this is a place where the Earth abides simply by being left alone.

If you're reasonably good at handling a canoe or kayak, it's a fairly easy paddle from Big Pine Key or the Torch Keys out into the **Content Keys,** inside refuge boundaries. If you motor out, keep your noise and speed at a minimum to avoid frightening birds from their nests or creating wakes that swamp low-lying and floating nests. Be sure to take binoculars, for within the shaded mangroves you might see the birds' dark, beady eyes fixed on you, watching your approach. You're also likely to encounter sea turtles and bottlenose dolphins. Stay about 200 feet away from the islands; causing a roosting bird to flee its nest leaves eggs or nestlings unshaded in the sun's killing glare. And since there are no facilities in the refuge, take water and food.

■ 6,207 acres (total with waters managed with state of Florida is 186,287 acres) ■ Best seasons spring and fall ■ Boating, swimming, fishing, bird-watching, wildlife viewing ■ Contact the National Key Deer Refuge, 28950 Watson Blvd., Big Pine Key, FL 33043; 305-872-2239. http://south east.fws.gov/GreatWhiteHeron.

Everglades

A short parade of visitors follows a ranger on an Everglades nature walk. For more than an hour she has shown them the living wonders in the park: butterflies and snails, alligators and fish, and bird after bird. Near the end of the walk, she gathers the visitors around her. She points to a string of nine white ibises coursing a cloudless sky.

"Imagine seeing ibis in the 1930s," she says. "That would have been a flight of about 90 birds. We are seeing only about 10 percent of the wading birds that were here then. When you get home, write your congressmen and tell them we have to save Everglades." In this threatened national park, lobbying happens on nature walks and appears in official literature.

The park is at the southern tip of Florida, a 100-mile-long subtropical wilderness of saw-grass prairie, jungle-like hammock, and mangrove swamp, running from Lake Okeechobee to Florida Bay. Water, essential to the survival of this ecosystem, once flowed south from the lake unhindered. But as the buildup of southern Florida has intensified, canals, levees, and dikes have increasingly diverted the water to land developments and agribusinesses. Vast irrigated farmlands have spread to the park's gates. The waning of the ibis carries a warning: Watery habitats in the park are shrinking because not enough water is getting to Everglades.

The park's special mission inspires the crusade to save it. Unlike parks that were established primarily to protect scenery, Everglades was created to preserve a portion of this vast ecosystem as a wildlife habitat. The park's unique mix of tropical and temperate plants and animals—including more than 700 plant and 300 bird species, as well as the endangered manatee, crocodile, and Florida panther—has prompted the United Nations to designate it an International Biosphere Reserve and World Heritage site.

- Southern Florida
- 1,508,537 acres
- Established 1947
- Best seasons winter and spring
- Hiking, canoeing, fishing (permit required), biking, wildlife viewing, boat and tram tours
- Information: 305-242-7700 www.nps.gov/ever

Ten Thousand Islands, Chokoloskee Bay

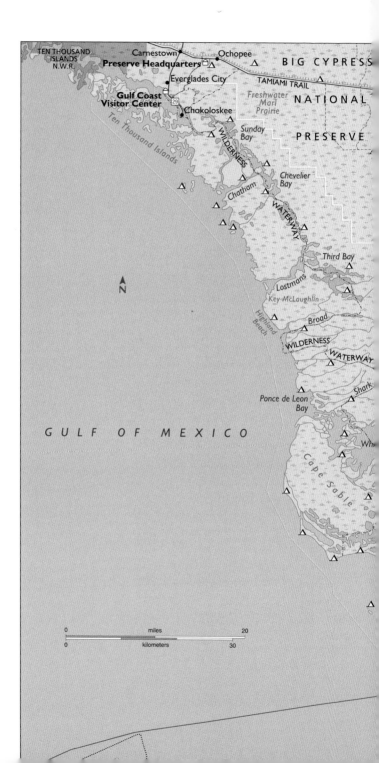

TEN THOUSAND
ISLANDS
N.W.R.

Carnestown
Preserve Headquarters

Ochopee

BIG CYPRESS

TAMIAMI TRAIL

Everglades City

**Gulf Coast
Visitor Center**

29

Chokoloskee

*Freshwater
Marl
Prairie*

NATIONAL

PRESERVE

Ten Thousand Islands

*Sunday
Bay*

WILDERNESS

*Chevelier
Bay*

Chatham

WATERWAY

Third Bay

Lostmans

Key McLaughlin

*Highland
Beach*

Broad

WILDERNESS

WATERWAY

*Ponce de Leon
Bay*

Shark

Wh

GULF OF MEXICO

Cape Sable

N

miles
0   20
0   30
kilometers

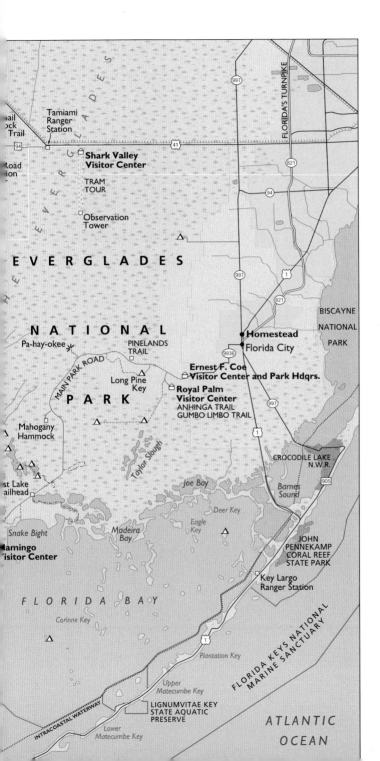

EVERGLADES

NATIONAL

PARK

Tamiami
Ranger
Station

ail
ock
Trail

Shark Valley
Visitor Center

TRAM
TOUR

Observation
Tower

Pa-hay-okee

PINELANDS
TRAIL

Long Pine
Key

Ernest F. Coe
Visitor Center and Park Hdqrs.

Royal Palm
Visitor Center
ANHINGA TRAIL
GUMBO LIMBO TRAIL

Homestead

Florida City

BISCAYNE

NATIONAL

PARK

CROCODILE LAKE
N.W.R.

Mahogany
Hammock

Joe Bay

Barnes
Sound

st Lake
ailhead

Deer Key

Eagle
Key

JOHN
PENNEKAMP
CORAL REEF
STATE PARK

Snake Bight

Madeira
Bay

lamingo
isitor Center

Key Largo
Ranger Station

FLORIDA BAY

Corinne Key

Plantation Key

FLORIDA KEYS NATIONAL
MARINE SANCTUARY

Upper
Matecumbe Key

LIGNUMVITAE KEY
STATE AQUATIC
PRESERVE

Lower
Matecumbe Key

ATLANTIC

OCEAN

INTRACOASTAL WATERWAY

MAIN PARK ROAD

The diverse forms of life in Everglades National Park, from algae to alligators, depends upon a rhythm of abundance and drought. In the wet season, a river that is inches deep and miles wide flows almost invisibly to the Gulf of Mexico. During the dry season, the park rests, awaiting the water's return. The plants and animals are a part of this rhythm. When humans change it, they put the Everglades' life at risk.

What Not to Miss

- Hiking along the scenic, 6-mile Coastal Prairie Trail to Cape Sable Beach
- Taking a boat cruise or kayaking from Flamingo to Buttonwood Canal
- Exploring the mangrove-lined bays of the gulf by taking the Ten Thousand Island boat tour from Everglades City
- Having a picnic at West Lake and enjoying the bird-watching

How to Get There

South from Miami, take US 1 or the Florida Turnpike to Florida City, then go west on Fla. 9336 (Palm Drive) to the Ernest F. Coe Visitor Center, about 50 miles from Miami. West from Miami, take US 41 (Tamiami Trail) to Shark Valley Visitor Center. From Naples, head east on US 41 to Fla. 29, then south to Everglades City. Airports: Miami and Naples.

When to Go

Everglades has two seasons: dry, which is mid-December to mid-April, and wet, which is the rest of the year. The park schedules most of its activities in the dry season because the wet season can be very uncomfortable.

How to Visit

If you can stay only 1 day, learn about Everglades ecology by taking **self-guided walks** at road turnoffs on the drive from the Ernest F. Coe Visitor Center to Flamingo. For a longer stay, make Flamingo or Everglades City your base, and time your travels to the schedules of the **boat tours.** To see the vast backcountry, you'll need a boat or canoe.

EXPLORING THE PARK

Royal Palm to Flamingo: 76 miles round-trip; a full day

The **main park road** connects the main entrance, southwest of Florida City, to Flamingo on Florida Bay. Make the drive an exploration, not a 55-mph dash. Stops at the sites suggested can be made on the way to or from Flamingo, depending upon when you want to board a concession tour boat there. Check the cruise times by calling the concessionaire *(see Information & Activities pp. 144–145).*

You can get oriented to this complex park at the **Ernest F. Coe Visitor Center.** A short film stresses environmental threats to the park and alerts you to the subtle, imperiled beauty you will be seeing. Check the schedule that is posted daily to see when rangers are leading nature walks and talks from the Royal Palm Visitor Center; there's also a schedule for boat cruises that leave from Flamingo, 38 miles away. Time your road travel each way by adjusting to the day's schedules.

Heading southwest, the flat road goes through the endless river of grass, where regal egrets poise to catch fish, and other birds dot the trees. Use a passenger as a bird spotter; simultaneous driving and bird-watching can be dangerous.

After crossing over marshy **Taylor Slough** (pronounced SLEW), turn off to the Royal Palm Visitor Center, named for the trees that

(continued on p. 138)

Snowy egrets

Walks in Everglades

To appreciate the subtlety of the various ecosystems in the Everglades, walk the well-signed trails. The dry season (Dec.–mid-April) is best for wildlife, because the summer heat drives animals into the shade and out of sight.

To follow these walks, go to the main entrance near Florida City (305-242-7700), where Fla. 9336 enters the park. The main road then winds for 38 miles through the park with lots of points of interest to see along the way.

Anhinga Trail

Begin at Royal Palm Visitor Center, 4 miles from park entrance. Half-mile; allow 30 minutes

The trail loops through a saw grass marsh, home to some 18 different grasses and flowering plants, as well as alligators and turtles. The string or swamp lily is easy to spot, with its white flowers hanging down in strands. The fruit of the pond apple tree looks like a Granny Smith apple, but it tastes of turpentine. The small, white clusters on the stalks of pickerelweed could be the eggs of the apple snail, a tasty treat for the endangered snail kite. High above in the top of a tree, a great blue heron cools off by fluttering its throat. Below, in the water, an anhinga stalks its prey. With its body submerged, the bird's head and 10-inch-long neck look like a snake cruising through the water, giving it the nickname "snakebird."

Gumbo Limbo Trail

Begin at Royal Palm Visitor Center. Half-mile; allow 30 minutes

Named for the tree with reddish bark (also called the tourist tree because it is red and peeling like a sun-burnt tourist), this trail winds through a dense hammock, or wood. The resinlike gum of the gumbo-limbo was used as a glue and as an antiseptic by both the Calusa Indians and the Spaniards. Tales are told of brewing a tea with the leaves, although the flavor of varnish made it a drink only for the desperate.

Other trees here include palms and the tamarind, whose soft bark allows the tree snail to climb up its bark. These creatures used to be collected for their colorful shells. Orchids also stand out in the dense greenery.

If you walk into a spider's web, see if the trap's owner is the golden orb weaver, recognized by the yellow head plate. The skunk-like smell? That's the white stopper bush.

American alligator, Anhinga Trail

Pinelands Trail

7 miles from park entrance. Half-mile; allow 30 minutes

Slash pine trees grow in the higher parts of the Everglades, three to seven feet above sea level. In order to thrive, they need fire to clean out the vegetation in the understory and to fertilize the minimal soil cover. In this climate, plant life recovers quickly, and dead trees provide a rich pecking ground for pileated and red-bellied woodpeckers.

The path starts in the open, moving into a thicket and then the pine forest. Flowers include the perky tickseed and the lusher looking purple blooms of the ruellia. In the summer, listen for the telltale clicking of yellow-and-black lubber grasshoppers mating.

Pa-hay-okee Overlook Trail

13 miles from park entrance. Quarter-mile; allow 15 to 30 minutes

The shortest walk provides the broadest vista. Stand on the observation platform and scan the northern horizon. The river of grass stretches as far as the eye can see. Be careful touching a sawgrass leaf, however; the edges are razor sharp.

The boardwalk leads through a hammock thick with ferns and ephiphytes. Look for huge vultures, smaller red-shouldered hawks, and herons.

And if you think you hear a pig snorting, it's probably a pig frog.

Mahogany Hammock

20 miles from park entrance. Half-mile; allow 30 minutes

The tiny periphyton, a mixture of algae and other microorganisms that live in the brown ooze below the boardwalk, are the first link in the Everglades food chain. Wading birds such as ibises, egrets, and white herons feed on them at dawn and dusk.

In the hammock, the play of light and shade through the trees looks almost familiar to those from northern climates—until they see the clamshell, cowhorn, butterfly orchids, and the strangler figs that hug their host trees to death.

dominate the area. Here you'll find two trails that couldn't be more different, despite their proximity.

You can walk the half-mile **Anhinga Trail** *(see p. 136)* on your own, but if you join a ranger-led group you'll have a better chance of spotting wildlife. The boardwalk trail skirts a shallow, freshwater slough. You almost certainly will see alligators and some fascinating birds, including the long-necked, long-beaked, black-and-white fish-spearer for which the trail is named.

The ranger adds lore to what you see. That beautiful zebra butterfly tastes terrible; a predatory bird never tries for second helpings. Those white egg sacs on that branch will hatch apple snails, the prime food of the endangered snail kite. That slim, long-snouted fish gliding through the clear water is a gar; in the dry season it can survive in a mudhole because a primitive lung allows it to breathe air. That alligator loosens the muck in lime-stone depressions called solution holes and sweeps it away with its tail; in the dry season the gator-made oasis keeps fish, frogs, snails, and birds alive—as long as they are wary of the major resident. In Everglades, unusual adaptations and delicate balances sustain the park's astonishing variety of animals and plants.

The other trail here is the half-mile **Gumbo Limbo Trail** *(see p. 136)*, named for a tree with peeling red bark. The trail takes you to a hammock *(see sidebar p. 65)*, an elevated island of tropical hardwood—including gumbo-limbos and some magnificent examples of strangler figs—in a sea of saw grass. The slight elevation keeps the ground drier, permitting the hardwoods to flourish and creating a shaded habitat for many creatures, from snakes to deer, foxes, and raccoon.

Back on the road, you'll soon notice slash pines dotting the saw grass prairie. These once covered much of South Florida's higher, drier ground. However, as Miami and other places in the region began to grow, loggers cut down many of the trees. What you see here are remnants of those vast stands.

You can make a detour 1.7 miles to **Long Pine Key,** an island of pines, saw palmettos, and hardwood hammocks; there's also a 7-mile trail that snakes through the skinny trees. Or you can take the half-mile loop in **Pinelands** farther up the road *(see p. 137)*, where interpretive signs explain the pines' dependence on fire. Without fire, hardwoods would shade out the more fire-resistant pines and take over the woodlands.

Alligators

That 10-foot-long, 300-pound lizard you see sunning itself on a log or head-slapping the water during mating season looks much the way its ancestors did 160 million years ago, when dinosaurs ruled the Earth.

Surviving into the 21st century as the largest reptiles on the continent, alligators continue to capture the imagination for their ancient history, carnivorous habits, and fearsome appearance.

If you think alligators are mindless, cold-blooded killers, think again. A mother gator builds a mud-and-grass nest up to 3 feet high, then guards her eggs for three months. She helps the hatchlings emerge, sometimes carrying them to water in her mouth.

The little ones often catch a ride on her back or head, and will stay with her for up to two years, until they are about two feet long.

Driving toward Flamingo, you can stop and take a short stroll along the boardwalk to **Pinnacle Rock,** a sample of the porous limestone that is South Florida's bedrock. At 12 miles, stop again to see dwarf cypress, trees stunted by shallow soil.

Half a mile farther is an overlook called **Pa-hay-okee,** or "grassy waters" *(see p. 137)*, the Native American name for the Everglades. A boardwalk takes you to a shaded observation stage where you can look out on a seemingly endless prairie of grassy waters. At 19.5 miles is **Mahogany Hammock,** where a boardwalk leads to the largest living mahogany tree in the United States *(see p. 137)*.

As you near the coast, the mixing of salt-water with the Everglades' fresh water becomes evident as salt-tolerant mangroves replace the saw grass, palms, and mahoganies. The mangrove-filled estuaries produce a soup rich with nutrients, the food base for a wide variety of marine life.

The best way to travel through the mangrove wilderness is by canoe, and there are several access points along the road. There are several ponds also where you might catch sight of egrets, roseate spoonbills, ibises, and herons.

If you want to picnic, there are several fine spots along the main park road, including **Paurotis Pond** *(at 24.5 miles)*, **Nine Mile Pond** *(at 26.5 miles),* and **West Lake** *(at 30.5 miles).*

The road ends in **Flamingo** on Florida Bay. Settled in the late 1800s by plume hunters, fishermen, and moonshiners, the town is now the park's southern hub. It's also the only place in the park that has a motel and restaurant.

Sign up for a boat tour in the marina ticket office near the visitor center. While you are waiting, take the self-guided, half-mile walk around the waterfront to see **Florida Bay,** a marine nursery protected by the park. Raccoons, black bears, and manatees are just some of the critters often spotted here. However, don't expect to see flamingos; they rarely appear in the town named after them.

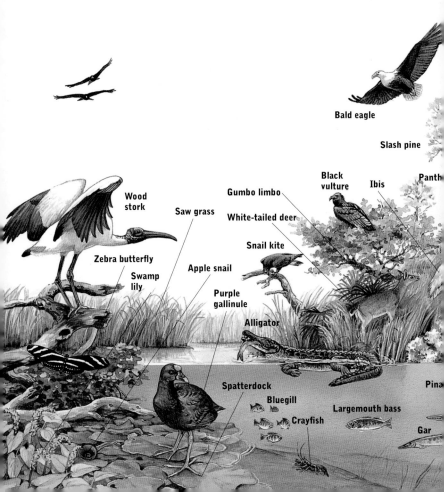

Bald eagle

Slash pine

Black vulture

Ibis

Panth

Wood stork

Gumbo limbo

White-tailed deer

Saw grass

Zebra butterfly

Snail kite

Swamp lily

Apple snail

Purple gallinule

Alligator

Spatterdock

Pina

Bluegill

Crayfish

Largemouth bass

Gar

The 2-hour, backcountry cruise begins in the marina and enters **Buttonwood Canal,** which was built in 1957. Among mangrove roots you will see along the waterway, watch for shy crocodiles that sometimes sun on the banks of the canal. The cruise crosses **Coot Bay** and enters **Whitewater Bay,** where backcountry canoeists camp on chickees, tent-size platforms raised on poles.

Osprey

Royal palm

Strangler fig

Roseate spoonbill

Brown pelican

Airplant

Barred owl

Mangrove

Great white heron

Crocodile

nap fern

Coon oysters

Mangrove snapper

Pink shrimp

Manatee

Turtle grass

Loggerhead turtle

Shark Valley to Everglades City: **49 miles one way; a full day**

The Tamiami Trail (US 41) forms part of the park's northeastern border. Stop at the Shark Valley Visitor Center at the eastern entrance. Here is a 15-mile **loop road** accessible only on foot, on bike, or, year-round, on a 2-hour, narrated tour aboard an open-sided concessionaire tram.

You will not see sharks. The valley gets its name from the Shark River because sharks gather at its mouth in the Gulf of Mexico.

But you will see alligator trails leading to hammocks in the saw grass, and you almost certainly will see the long lizards themselves. Situated at the top of the food chain, alligators act as barometers of general health in Everglades and other wetlands: A wildlife population large enough to support alligators is likely to be robust and varied.

Between 1870 and 1970, hunting alligators for their skins nearly extinguished the species as some ten million of them were killed in Florida alone. Hunting regulations and restrictions on the hide trade have brought about a recovery, though habitat loss puts increasing pressure on the alligators' numbers.

Bird-watching on the Anhinga Trail

The main service alligators provide the wetlands is to clear its channels and ponds of invading plants, creating pools that myriad animals depend on during droughts.

Alligators tend to avoid people, though small children could be mistaken for prey; hence it is best to keep your distance. When an alligator does get hungry, it will go after anything: insects, frogs, birds, turtles, other alligators, deer, even a small bear if it ventures close enough to the water that the alligator can catch it.

Veering off the loop road is a path to a 65-foot **tower** from which you can look out on the vista that became the park's name: glades that seem to go on forever. It's a marvelous place to spot turtles, alligators, and wading birds. Look for red-shouldered hawks, snail kites, northern harriers, and occasionally short-tailed hawks as they fly over the marsh.

Return to US 41 and head north into the 2,400-square-mile **Big Cypress National Preserve** *(see pp. 146–48),* part of the Everglades ecosystem. Most of the water flowing into the park comes through four floodgates that you can see north of the highway along the park boundary. At Fla. 29, turn south for Everglades City. Follow the highway through the town to the waterfront. Sign up for one of the regularly scheduled, narrated concessionaire boat tours (or you can explore by boat, canoe, or kayak on your own).

The **Ten Thousand Island** trip explores mangrove islands in the Gulf of Mexico. On the way to and from the islands, protected sea mammals—sleek bottle-nose dolphins and lumbering manatees—often pop up to look at the boat. You can usually see ospreys, pelicans, and cormorants. From a distance, the islands look like a solid stretch of low-lying green land. Close up, you see a labyrinth of thousands of waterways.

There are far fewer than 10,000 islands, but the number is unknown and ever changing. Islands form from the buildup of leaves and other organic material among the mangroves. As an island grows, storms and tidal forces may break it into fragments, which continue to grow and spread. The islands range in size from a couple of trees to several hundred acres.

The boat crosses **Chokoloskee Bay,** which shares its name with an island of shells that Native Americans built. The bay is the northern end of the 99-mile Everglades City-to-Flamingo **Wilderness Waterway,** a system of canoe trails through the park.

INFORMATION & ACTIVITIES

Headquarters
40001 State Road 9446
Homestead, FL 33034
305-242-7700
www.nps.gov/ever

Visitor & Information Centers
Ernest F. Coe Visitor Center on
Fla. 9336 at park entrance.
Royal Palm Visitor Center off
main park road a few miles
inside park entrance. Flamingo
Visitor Center on main park
road at Florida Bay may close
temporarily off-season. Shark
Valley Visitor Center at north
end of park on US 41. Gulf
Coast Visitor Center at Everglades City on Fla. 29 at northwest entrance.

Seasons & Accessibility
Park open daily year-round;
some facilities and services
limited or unavailable during
off-season, which is May to
mid-December.

Entrance Fees
$10 per car per week at main
entrance; $8 at Shark Valley; $5
per person on bike or foot.

Pets
Pets must be on leashes and are
allowed in campgrounds only.

Facilities for Disabled
All visitor centers, rest rooms,
campgrounds, and tram tours
are accessible. Several trails are
at least partly accessible. In the
backcountry, Pear Bay Chickee
is accessible.

Things to Do
Free activities led by naturalists:
nature walks and talks, hikes,
exhibits, seasonal evening programs. Also, tram tours, sightseeing boats, canoe, kayak,
houseboat, motorboat, and
bicycle rentals, fishing (license
required), crabbing, shrimping
(ask about regulations). In winter and during holidays, call to
reserve space on guided tours
and activities. Rentals and boat
tours in Flamingo: 239-695-
3101, ext. 355. Tram tour at
Shark Valley: 305-221-8455.
Boat tours and rentals at Everglades City: 239-695-2591 or
800-445-7724 in Florida.

Special Advisories
■ You'll need insect repellent
year-round, but especially
between April and December.
■ Swimming is not advised.

Overnight backpacking
Permits required; you can get
them in person no more than
24 hours before your trip at
Flamingo and Everglades City.
Fees collected mid-November
to April only. No reservations;

Anhinga chicks

first come, first served. Limits on number of people and length of stay.

Campgrounds

Three campgrounds, 14-day limit November to May; otherwise 30-day limit. $14 a night per site collected November to May only. Flamingo and Long Pine Key open all year. Reservations available mid-December to April. Reserve through National Parks Reservation Service *(see p. 13)*; rest of year, first come, first served. Cold showers at Flamingo. Tent and RV sites; no hookups. Three group campgrounds; reservations suggested during the high season. Food services in park; limited April to November.

Hotels, Motels, & Inns

(Unless otherwise noted, rates for two persons in a double room, high season.)

INSIDE THE PARK:
■ **Flamingo Lodge** (end of main park road)
1 Flamingo Lodge Hwy. 239-695-3101 or 800-600-3813. 127 units. Lodge rooms $95; cottages with kitchens $135. AC, pool, restaurant.

OUTSIDE THE PARK
In Florida City, FL 33034:
■ **Comfort Inn**
333 SE First Ave./US 1. 305-248-4009. 123 units. $59-$169. AC, pool.
■ **Coral Roc Motel**
1100 N. Krome Ave. 305-247-4010. 16 units, 4 kitchenettes. $36-$89. AC, pool.
■ **Knights Inn**
1223 NE First Ave./US 1. 305-247-6621. 49 units, 6 kitchenettes. $79-$169. AC, pool.

In Homestead, FL 33030:
■ **Days Inn**
51 S. Homestead Blvd. 305-245-1260. 100 units. $109. AC, pool, restaurant.

For other lodgings, contact the Homestead/Florida City Chamber of Commerce, 43 N. Krome Ave., Homestead, FL 33030. 305-247-2332.

Excursions from the Everglades

Big Cypress National Preserve

Adjoins the north border of Everglades Sweeping vistas of wet prairies extending to far horizons punctuated with hardwood hammocks. Soggy forests where panthers prowl softly under broadskirted cypresses that stood before Christopher Columbus was born. Mangrove thickets sheltering fish near the broken islands of the Everglades. These scenes belong to a preserve that encompasses 45 percent of the Big Cypress Swamp, the ecosystem buffering the north side of the Everglades.

Nearly the size of Yosemite National Park, the preserve covers more than 700,000 acres of prairies, sloughs, and cypress trees laden with orchids and pineapple-like bromeliads. About one-half of the remaining population of Florida panthers—numbering no more than 50—roam through here, their progress monitored with radio collars. Underpasses allow them to safely cross roadways; fences along highways, and low night-time speed limits further attempt to keep these elegant cats from extinction.

The construction of the Tamiami Trail (US 41) in 1928 made Big Cypress Swamp accessible to large numbers of people, and thus to economic exploitation. Logging and oil exploration in the 1930s and 1940s were followed by plans for draining and developing. Investors from far away bought up pieces of wetlands they knew nothing about, as a land speculation frenzy in the 1960s swept through like wildfire. Finally, plans for a major jetport—with its attendant noise and pollution—on the eastern fringe of the swamp brought together such diverse groups as conservationists, hunters, and off-road vehicle drivers to save Big Cypress.

In 1974, Big Cypress National Preserve was created as the first of its kind within the National Park Service. Preserves have looser regulations than parks. Among the varied activities allowed here are hunting, trapping, fishing, oil drilling, cattle grazing, and some off-road driving. Privately owned camps still dot the backcountry. Yet with all this apparent activity, Big Cypress remains undeveloped and attracts far fewer visitors than Everglades National Park.

Creating the preserve gave a huge advantage to the wildlife of South Florida; it protected a vast acreage through which fresh water flows from Lake Okeechobee down to the Everglades. Water does flow, albeit imperceptibly, across the swamp, at the rate of a half mile per day; the elevation drops a mere inch in that distance.

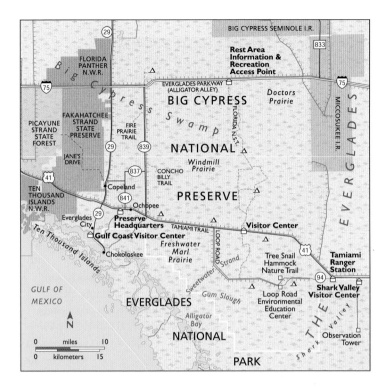

The **visitor center** 17 miles east of Ochopee has interesting exhibits and a short film to get you excited about a plunge into the preserve. You can walk out along the **Florida National Scenic Trail** *(see sidebar p. 150),* both north and south of the highway. In all, 31 miles of the Florida National Scenic Trail pass through this preserve.

Heading north, you'll see alligators in a fenced-off canal; then you skirt an airfield as you hike along fields of prairie grasses and wildflowers toward a distant line of trees. The going can get pretty muddy, especially in the wet summer season when you might find yourself up to your belt in water.

To the south are long views of sedge-filled prairie, speckled with islands of pine and cypress. Flocks of white herons and ibises sweep overhead, and the rare snail kite makes its shrill call.

Two driving tours take you into the backcountry within a leisurely morning or afternoon. The 26-mile **Loop Road** begins 4 miles west of Shark Valley and heads west (Fla. 94). The pavement ends after about 8 miles. Stop at the education center and take the short **Tree Snail Hammock Nature Trail;** look for the brilliantly striped tree snail. The passion for snail collecting a century ago grew to such a pitch that collectors would burn the hammocks to raise the snails' value. Collecting of tree snails is now illegal in South Florida.

On the western edge of the preserve, you can make a 20-mile **scenic rectangle** by heading north on Birdon Road (Fla. 841, west of Ochopee), then turning right on Fla. 837 east, and then right again to head south on Fla. 839.

Two **canoe trails** meander out into the mangrove channels of Everglades National Park. Allow 5 to 6 hours to paddle these routes, and expect to see untamed subtropical wilderness at its finest. But be sure to inquire first at the visitor center for water level and mosquito information.

■ **729,000 acres** ■ **South Florida, between Naples and Miami, 17 miles east of Ochopee** ■ **Best months Dec.–April** ■ **Camping, hiking, backpacking, canoeing, fishing, bird-watching, wildlife and wildflower viewing** ■ **Contact the preserve, HCR 61, Box 110, Ochopee, FL 34141; 239-695-2000. www.nps.gov/bicy**

Cattails, Big Cypress National Preserve

Fakahatchee Strand State Preserve

15 miles northwest of Everglades

A primitive wilderness within the Big Cypress Swamp, Fakahatchee Strand is a dense cypress forest running about 20 miles north to south and 5 miles east to west. The strand occupies a long drainage slough that formed over the centuries as water seeped into the limestone plain in the region. Organic soil filled the the sloughs, thus providing fertile ground.

Thousands of years ago, when the sea level was much lower, the watery sinkholes that dotted the land here were very important to early inhabitants. The hunter-gatherer lifestyle remained relatively unchanged until Europeans arrived in the 15th century.

Within this forbidding tangle of unchecked tropical growth lives the country's largest stand of native royal palms. Along with these tall, sleek monarchs grow a profuse variety of rare plants, including a remarkably abundant concentration of epiphytic orchids. Their eye-catching blooms decorate the trees in fantastic fashion.

Few trails penetrate the fastness of the strand, but the 2,000-foot **Big Cypress Bend Boardwalk**, 7 miles west of the junction of US 41 and Fla. 29, gives you a taste of the Fakahatchee jungle, where shaggy-limbed trees take on weird, fairy-tale shapes. Some are 6 feet in diameter and 100 feet tall.

You'll see woodpeckers and other birds illuminating the dark forest interior, alligators waiting for prey in deep water holes, and towering cypresses in the grip of strangler fig vines. The strangler figs eventually kill their host and stand as one of the dominant trees in the swamp.

South and east of Copeland, unpaved **W. J. Janes Scenic Drive** carves 11 deep miles into the interior of the forest (and continues into **Picayune Strand State Forest**). Thick walls of trees flank the road. Pull over at one of the sidetracks and get out for a short walk. Egrets and ibises trumpet in the swampy recesses, and the trail winds on, disappearing into a world of natural wonders humans rarely see.

■ 75,000 acres ■ South Florida, west of Copeland between US 41 and Fla. 29 ■ Best months Nov.—May ■ Hiking, walking, guided walks, canoeing, fishing, biking, bird-watching, wildlife viewing ■ Contact the preserve, P.O. Box 548, Copeland, FL 33926; 239-695-4593. www.florida stateparks.org/fakahatcheestrand/ default.asp

Florida National Scenic Trail

When real estate broker Jim Kern set out to hike the 160 miles from the Tamiami Trail to Highlands Hammock State Park in 1966, he could not have fore-seen how his efforts would ulti-mately pay off. Publicizing the state's lack of trails, Kern's hike was the beginning of a system that now includes more than 1,000 miles of them. Though the Forest Service originally doubted anyone would want to hike in Florida, the Florida National Scenic Trail today passes through all three of Florida's national forests, as well as many of its parks, refuges, state forests, and wilderness areas. Simply put, people do want to hike in Florida.

When finished, the trail will run 1,300 miles from Big Cypress in the south to Gulf Islands National Seashore in the panhandle.

Starting in the subtropical wilds of Big Cypress country, the trail winds among old cypresses decked with bromeliads and orchids. It then courses around Lake Okeechobee and heads across central Florida's palm and oak hammocks, lakes, and springs. In the western part of the state, the pathway takes on hilly forests and secluded rivers.

Palms and longleaf pines

Building the trails and keep-ing them cleared—a constant labor in Florida's vegetation-friendly climate—is the job of the thousands of volunteers who see the need for greenways amidst Florida's growing asphalt corridors.

The best time to hike is in the dry season, from October to March. You'll need a hat, sun-screen, insect repellent, binocu-lars, a good bird book, and water. Signs mark officially certified sections of the trail. In some cases the trail crosses private land, which may not yet be open to the general public.

For information and maps, contact the Florida Trail Association, 5415 S.W. 13th St., Gainesville, FL 32608. 352-378-8823 or 877-HIKE-FLA (445-3352). www.florida-trail.org.

Corkscrew Swamp Sanctuary

50 miles northwest of Everglades

One of the largest and most acclaimed sanctuaries of the National Audubon Society, this extensive parcel in the northwest corner of the Everglades ecosystem protects the largest remaining stand of uncut, mature bald cypress on the North American continent. Within Corkscrew Swamp's bald cypress cathedral, magisterial trees hundreds of years old climb 130 feet in the air, tufted with mosses and air plants that flourish in the swamp's humid environment. Called bald because of their bare look in winter *(see sidebar p. 73)*, the cypresses rise imposingly from quiet waters that support an astonishing profusion of life.

The undisturbed tranquillity of Corkscrew Swamp also serves as a safe haven and rookery for great egrets and endangered wood storks. Hundreds of other species find refuge here as well, including alligators, Florida black bears, otters, white-tailed deer, and red-bellied turtles.

Pileated woodpeckers flash like rubies in the trees above ponds where turtles glide among ferns and water lettuce. An orb weaver's web shimmers in early morning light, tuned to the faintest touch of a passing insect. A green lizard slips along the boardwalk, while an egret fans its wings far back in the trees. On a half-submerged log near the boardwalk, a little blue heron is stepping gracefully along, its beak pivoting side to side as the bird stares into the water. With a sudden splash, the bird plunges its beak into the water and comes up with a crayfish or a small frog. These ancient rituals continue day after day in a primordial landscape that, but for the boardwalk, has changed little over the millennia.

Among the favorites of the 200 bird species recorded here are secretive limpkins, colorful painted buntings, and 2-foot-tall barred owls. Warblers and yellow-billed cuckoos begin passing through in fall, and swallow-tailed kites arrive from South America by mid-February. With the lowest water levels in late March and early April comes the highest concentration of fish and the easiest meals for wading birds. Mornings in the sanctuary are particularly busy as hundreds of birds partake of the bountiful seafood buffet.

Wood stork nesting season generally runs from December to March. The only stork species that hatches its offspring in the United States, wood storks build their nests in trees. During the breeding season, a pair of these large, long-legged birds can consume as much as 440 pounds of fish, which they catch by wading

A wood stork and its chicks, Corkscrew Swamp Sanctuary

through shallow water with their bills open; when a fish hits, the bill snaps shut. Records show that the year 2002 wood stork nesting season was excellent, with 3,162 fledglings compared with none in 2001.

The Audubon Society had its origins at the turn of the century when a few people began protesting the slaughter of birds for plumes to decorate women's hats. By 1912, a warden was working in the swamp to guard egrets and other birds. Some 40 years later, the society acquired the land.

However, the sanctuary's future is tied to the fate of a 4,000-acre tract of wetlands and pasture within the Corkscrew watershed to the west. Several local species are declining in number, and their continued survival or irrevocable demise may be settled within the next few decades. Located 30 miles from downtown Naples, the sanctuary that once was remote is now much closer to civilization.

Known far and wide as a birder's paradise, Corkscrew Swamp attracts large numbers of serious bird-watchers armed with tripods, high-powered lenses, and other gear. These visitors tend to be a quiet, reverential lot. So even if the parking lot is crowded, the sanctuary still feels like a sanctuary.

Start in the **Blair Audubon Center,** where you will find several exhibits to help visitors better understand the swamp's ecology as well as identify its multitude of winged denizens. A 2.25-mile **boardwalk** snakes out into the sanctuary, passing first through pine woods and a slice of wet prairie, edged with saw grass and dainty purple asters.

The walk then enters the cypress strand and stays there for most of its length. There are plenty of cul-de-sacs and benches for quiet communing. Highlights include the wide views at the central marsh and the plentiful wildlife at the **Lettuce Lakes.** Volunteers are often on hand if you want to identify a plant or animal. If you're interested in slogging out beyond the boardwalk to see what the swamp really feels like, inquire about special **guided walks.**

There are reminders throughout the sanctuary of how humanity and nature can help each other, from the tropical hardwood boardwalk that requires no chemical treatment to the environmentally sensitive rest rooms. Called "living machines," the latter are self-contained water-treatment systems well worth a visit. They use sunlight, bacteria, fish, and green plants to decompose waste material and recycle water.

■ **11,000 acres** ■ **South Florida, 30 miles northwest of Naples off I-75** ■ **Best months Nov.–May** ■ **Hiking, walking, bird-watching, wildlife and wildflower viewing** ■ **Contact the sanctuary, 375 Sanctuary Road West, Naples, FL 34120; 239-348-9151. www.audubon.org/local/sanctuary/ corkscrew/**

Kissimmee Prairie Preserve State Park

110 miles north of Everglades

One of the newest and most remote preserves in Florida spreads over a treeless prairie north of Lake Okeechobee. This vast tract, the largest remaining piece of dry prairie in the world, opens from horizon to flat horizon in a tawny tumble of wire grass, herbs, and low shrubs. Florida grasshopper sparrows flit among hammocks. Sandhill cranes stalk the sloughs along the Kissimmee River. Crested caracaras ride thermals in search of prey. These and other endangered species find refuge here in an ecosystem that can hold more than 40 plant species in a square meter.

Though much of the region's dry prairie was converted to vegetable farms, and citrus and pine groves as early as the mid 19th-century, cattlemen here were content to use controlled burns to keep the prairie open for their livestock, thus preserving it the way lightning had for millennia. Fires kept forests from encroaching upon the open grasslands.

Ironically, the Army Air Corps helped prevent development by using the prairie during World War II as a B-17 training base and bombing range. In fact, signs at the visitor kiosk warn hikers about the possibility of encountering unexploded bombs and artillery shells. Bear in mind that the preserve has been carefully scoured and the chances of finding old ordnance are very slim.

Kissimmee Prairie remains wild to the core. Acquired by the state in 1997, the preserve is undergoing some development, but it will be minimal. To get there, you still travel 6 miles of unpaved road (off Fla. 724). Future plans call for another unpaved road to lead nearly half the length of the 8-mile **Military Grade Trail** to a visitor center. The rest is wide open.

Bikers and horseback riders especially enjoy exploring the backcountry scrub and marshlands. The 7-mile **Peavine Trail** heads straight north across the preserve, offering many possibilities for side trails as well as open-country rambling.

Animals you may spot include river otters, box turtles, eastern indigo snakes (nonpoisonous), wild turkeys, bobcats, and Florida scrubjay. Gopher tortoises often lumber across the trail. These brown-shelled land turtles can live more than 40 years. Their 10-foot-deep burrows provide refuge for snakes, frogs, and other animals during fires or storms. Hunters and loss of habitat have hurt the tortoise population badly. Scientists estimate that about 30 percent of their original population now exists in the southeast.

But thanks to Kissimmee Prairie and **Myakka River State Park** *(see pp. 158–161)* to the west, large chunks of Florida prairie remain intact for the benefit of those native species that depend upon it. For humans, its value lies in its slow, aesthetic appeal. Take a walk knee-deep in autumn wildflowers. Listen for the harsh cackle of the caracara or stand under a broad sky engulfed in a sea of whispering grasses.

■ 54,000 acres ■ South Florida, 4 miles northwest of Okeechobee via US 441 and Fla. 724 ■ Best months Sept.–April ■ Roads may close due to high water ■ Camping, hiking, backpacking, fishing, biking, bird-watching, guided walks ■ Contact the preserve, 33104 NW 192nd Ave., Okeechobee, FL 34972; 863-462-5360. www.floridastateparks.org/kissimmeeprairie/

Airboat on Lake Kissimmee

Highlands Hammock State Park

100 miles north of Everglades

One of the four original state parks in Florida, Highlands Hammock started out in 1935 as a grassroots effort to save a scenic hardwood hammock from being turned into farmland. The Civilian Conservation Corps set up camp and went to work building bridges, roads, and water-control structures; their well-constructed facilities remain today. The park preserves a gloriously deep and dark virgin forest of giant live oaks, laurel oaks, cabbage palms, sweet gums, and red maples. Surrounding the hammock are pine woods, a cypress swamp, scrub, and marsh, all of which shelter an abundance of birds, aquatic species, and other wildlife.

The ranger station and developed area of this thoughtfully planned park lie about a mile inside the park boundary. Pick up a

J. N. "Ding" Darling National Wildlife Refuge

While sun worshippers and shell hunters flock to the sandy beaches on Sanibel Island's gulf shore, bird lovers head for the other side of this 12-mile-long barrier island. Along Pine Island Sound is the 6,000-acre Jay Norwood "Ding" Darling National Wildlife Refuge *(239-472-1100)*. Darling was a Pulitzer Prize–winning cartoonist who won the plaudits of conservationists for his campaigns to protect wildlife.

Established in 1945, this safe haven provides a home to nearly 300 species of birds, 50 types of reptiles, and some 30 of mammals. Follow the 5-mile, one-way **Wildlife Drive** from the visitor center and loop through the refuge. From fall to spring, look for yellow-throated warblers and white pelicans; in spring and summer, look for black-whiskered vireos. You'll probably see red-shouldered hawks, often sitting on a dead tree trunk by the road, and the endangered wood stork. Only the eagle-eyed will be able to pick out the shy mangrove cuckoo.

One of the finest sights in Florida is a shell-pink roseate spoonbill feeding in the morning and evening. Hike out along **Indigo Trail** to see the birds at Cross Dike, or rent a canoe to paddle into the mangrove swamps. Check with the rangers at the Center for Education to see which species are "at home" in the refuge.

map at the ranger station and visit the nearby **Civilian Conservation Corps museum,** which has good exhibits on the New Deal-era organization.

The **park road** courses through a historic orange grove to begin a 3-mile loop. You can pull over at various places along the way to take short, but rewarding, nature trails out into the hammock.

You shouldn't miss the **Cypress Swamp Trail,** a

Little blue heron

leisurely 20- to 30-minute stroll on a narrow boardwalk around a floodplain creek where still waters reflect tall trees draped with Spanish moss. Swamp lilies and blue pickerelweed add subtle splashes of color. In addition to the impressive cypresses, you're almost certain to see alligators lurking at the water's edge, and herons and egrets flapping or squawking among the trees. Other birds commonly spotted here and elsewhere in the park are white ibises, red-tailed hawks, barred owls, and various warblers.

Highlands Hammock has canopy trees typical of the temperate southeast, yet the understory looks more like a tropical forest. The half-mile **Young Hammock Trail** on the north side of the park wends through an immature section of the hammock, while the half-mile **Ancient Hammock Trail** on the south explores an older part. You'll find an abundance of cabbage palm (Sabal palmettos); Florida's state tree got its common name because when the heart is cooked, it tastes somewhat like cabbage.

The park road makes an excellent bike loop. You can rent bicycles at the ranger station and park them at the trailheads.

■ 8,133 acres ■ South Florida, 6 miles west of Sebring on Fla. 634
■ Best months Nov.–April ■ Camping, hiking, backpacking, walking, guided walks, biking, mountain biking, bird-watching ■ Contact the park, 5931 Hammock Rd., Sebring, FL 33872; 863-386-6094. www.floridastate parks.org/highlandshammock/default.asp

Myakka River State Park

100 miles northwest of Everglades

One of Florida's oldest and largest state parks spreads along the gentle Myakka River for 12 miles, present-ing a wonderfully varied landscape of marsh-fringed lakes, oak and palm hammocks, pines, and palmetto prairies. As you drive the park road, deep woods lie to your right, while to your left are open views of marshes and **Upper Myakka Lake.** Deer, bobcats, and wild turkeys find good cover in the hammocks; alliga-tors, turtles, and wading birds sometimes make appearances out in the wetlands to the left.

The state bought the land in 1934. For the next seven years, the Civilian Conservation Corps, U.S. Army, and National Park Service worked together to develop the park. It opened in 1942.

Myakka River State Park preserves one of Florida's most diverse natural areas. In 1985 the state legislature declared the Myakka a State Wild and Scenic River, giving special protection status to a 34-mile section and making it one of only three rivers in the state so designated. South of the highway sprawls the 7,500-acre wilderness preserve, a portion of the park completely unspoiled by any development.

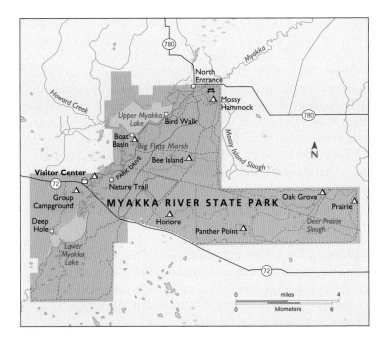

Unwelcome Guests

Myakka River State Park is one of many places in South Florida where you may spot or hear a feral hog snorting around in the underbrush. Some of these large, tusked creatures are descendants of pigs that Spanish explorers brought over; others escaped or were released from domestic swine stocks. They all breed rapidly and upset a park's ecological balance by rooting up native plants, disturbing the soil, and competing with—or eating— indigenous wildlife. A quarter of their diet consists of amphibians, small rodents, and birds and their eggs

To maintain the natural ecosystem, the park service periodically removes them. Though they're generally afraid of humans, they can be unpredictable. It's best to keep a safe distance from them.

Myakka is a big park, and even though it's very popular—particularly on weekends—you can find a quiet corner without going to much trouble. You'll be handed a brochure and a tour schedule at the entrance gate. If you want more specific information, stop at the visitor center. If you need more details on tours and rentals, you'll get plenty of help down at the Boat Basin.

Park Drive winds 7 serpentine miles along the edge of the river and lake. The drive is itself a major attraction, affording fine views of the marshes and hammocks, and offering plenty of pull-offs for further study. Most drivers travel below the 25-mph limit. Just after the road crosses the river, pull over to the right for an **unmarked fisherman's trail.** This sandy path under rattling cabbage palms and moss-hung oaks follows the river downstream about a mile back toward the highway. Few people seem to be aware of this lovely trail that offers good views of the peaceful river and wetlands.

A bit farther down the road is a 1-mile **nature loop.** The trail explores a pretty section of open forest, and interpretive markers provide interesting commentary on local flora and fauna. Along this walk, you'll discover the **Myakka Canopy Walkway.** Suspended 25 feet above the ground, the boardwalk extends 85 feet through the treetops to a 74-foot tower with views of the "high frontier."

As you continue down the road, you'll see several places along the right to pull off for more hiking. The trails, nearly 40 miles total, loop out under dense hammocks and across dry prairies. You can walk out as far as you like, but to really get into the wilderness you'll need to backpack.

The busiest area in the park is the Boat Basin, which is about 3.5 miles from the entrance. Sign up here for the popular airboat tours *(fee)* and tram safaris *(fee)* that run several times a day. The 70-passenger boats cruise around **Lake Myakka** for about an hour, while a guide outlines the ecological scene. The trams carry up to 50 passengers through the forested areas and provide a running narration. To help you explore on your own, the Boat Basin rents canoes and kayaks, and the store sells picnic, fishing *(license required),* and camping supplies. An invasion of hydrilla, an exotic weed, has reduced fish catches somewhat, but you can paddle quietly along the edges of the lake or downstream and observe alligators and long-legged birds.

A good alternative is to rent a bike here and pedal up to the north entrance (3.5 miles). The road is flat and scenic, and traffic is light. After about 2 miles, pull left for the **bird walk,** a boardwalk out to a viewing platform in the grassy marshes. Panels here help you put names to the birds you see, such as great blue herons, snowy egrets, roseate spoonbills, and various ducks.

Further Adventures

Deer Prairie Slough lies far to the east, its groves of giant maple and oak forming a high ceiling for a lush garden of ferns and subtropical plants. But since it's almost 7 miles one way from the trailhead, only hardy backpackers and bikers see it.

If you don't want to camp out, you can still experience primitive Florida by heading across the highway to the **Myakka River Wilderness Preserve.** More than a quarter of the park's total acreage lies in this sanctuary of marshes and hammocks around **Lower Myakka Lake.** A limited number of visitors are allowed in each day; register at the ranger station (entrance gate) and drive over to the parking area. A dirt track leads 1.5 miles to the lake; from here it's another half mile to **Deep Hole,** a 140-foot-deep hole that frequent anglers like.

Camping and Lodging
The park has 76 tent or RV sites, with showers. The majority are available by reservation. There is a camping fee.

For slightly more civilized accommodations, there are also five log cabins that members of the Civilian Conservation Corps built in the 1930s.

■ **37,000 acres** ■ **South Florida, 9 miles east of I-75 on State Rd. 72**
■ **Boat and tram tours, hiking, bird-watching, fishing, biking** ■ **Contact the park, 132076 State Rd. 72, Sarasota, FL 34241; 941-361-6511. www.florida stateparks.org/myakkariver**

Sunset over the Myakka River

Great Smoky Mountains

The fact invariably stated about Great Smoky is that it is the nation's busiest park, drawing more than nine million visitors a year, more than twice the number of any other national park. Most of the millions see the park from a mountain-skimming scenic highway that, on a typical weekend day during the summer, draws 60,000 people, bumper-to-bumper.

Luckily, there is plenty of park, thinly laced by 384 miles of mountain roads. Relatively few visitors walk on any of the 800 miles of trails, because most people prefer to stay in their cars.

Covering 800 square miles of mountainous terrain, the park preserves the world's best examples of deciduous forest and a matchless variety of plants and animals. Because it contains so many types of eastern forest vegetation—much of it old growth— the park has been designated an International Biosphere Reserve.

The Smoky Mountains are among the oldest on Earth. Ice Age glaciers stopped their southward journey just short of these mountains, which became a junction of southern and northern flora. Amid the woodland and craggy peaks bloom more than 1,500 species of flowering plants, some found only here. Shrubs take over in places, creating tree-free zones called heath balds, laurel slicks (because of the shiny leaves), or just plain hells (because they are so hard to get through).

The tangle of brush and trees forms a close-packed array of leaves. The water and hydrocarbons they exude produce the filmy "smoke" that gives the mountains their name. In recent years, air pollution has added microscopic sulfate particles to the haze, cutting visibility back about 60 percent since the 1950s. The pollution has also affected the park's red spruce stand—the southern Appalachians' largest.

- Western North Carolina and eastern Tennessee
- 521,495 acres
- Established 1934
- Best seasons spring and fall (traffic can be heavy in summer and fall)
- Hiking, biking, fishing, horseback riding, auto tours
- Information: 865-436-1200 www.nps.gov/grsm

A spruce on Clingmans Dome, Great Smoky Mountains National Park

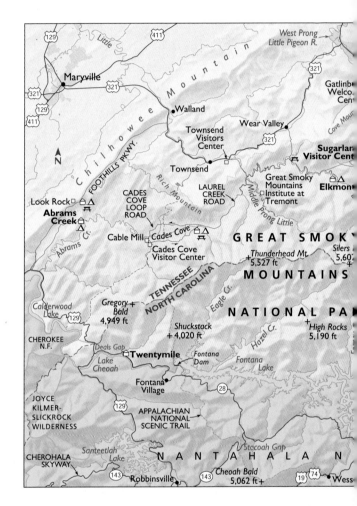

How to Get There

From Knoxville, Tenn. (about 25 miles away), take I-40 to Tenn. 66, then US 441 to Gatlinburg entrance. From Asheville, N.C. (about 40 miles away), take I-40 west to US 19, then US 441 to park's southern entrance near Cherokee, N.C. For a scenic, low-speed approach, take the 469-mile Blue Ridge Parkway that connects Virginia's Shenandoah National Park to Great Smoky. Airports: Knoxville, Tenn., and Asheville, N.C.

When to Go

All-year park. In summer and in fall (when spectacular foliage draws huge crowds), plan to

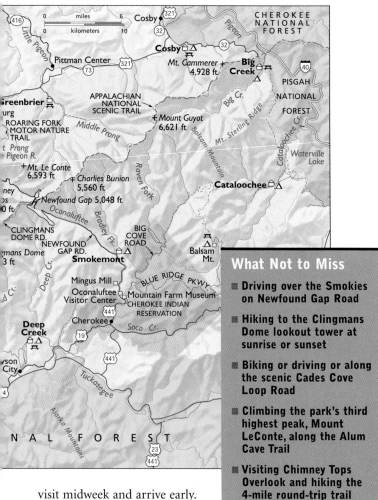

What Not to Miss

- Driving over the Smokies on Newfound Gap Road

- Hiking to the Clingmans Dome lookout tower at sunrise or sunset

- Biking or driving or along the scenic Cades Cove Loop Road

- Climbing the park's third highest peak, Mount LeConte, along the Alum Cave Trail

- Visiting Chimney Tops Overlook and hiking the 4-mile round-trip trail

visit midweek and arrive early. Visitor centers open year-round.

How to Visit

On a 1-day visit, take the **Newfound Gap Road** to **Clingmans Dome,** so you will get the best overview of the park from the highest point. The best second-day activity is the **Cades Cove loop road,** a chance to drive or cycle through pioneer history. For a longer stay, focus on the self-guided nature trails and drives, which get you away from the crowds and show you the flora and fauna.

EXPLORING THE PARK

Newfound Gap Road to Clingmans Dome:

40 to 45 miles; a half to full day

Newfound Gap Road begins at 2,000 feet and ascends to 5,048 feet. It connects the two major visitor centers, Sugarlands and Oconaluftee. Passing from lowland hardwood timber to high-altitude spruce-fir forests, the road gives you a vertical trip that is ecologically equivalent to a journey from Georgia to Canada.

Be prepared for rain on almost any day. A clear day below can be a day of mist and fog on high.

From Sugarlands, stop after 5 miles at **Chimneys,** a fine picnic spot. Stretch your legs on the 0.75-mile self-guided **Cove Hardwood Nature Trail.** Then return to the car for a short drive to the **Chimney Tops Overlooks,** which offer views of the double summits the Cherokee called *Duniskwal-guni* (forked antlers).

Here you can extend your stop with a hike on the steep, 4-mile, round-trip **Chimney Tops Trail** through an old-growth forest and up 1,335 feet to the sheer cliffs named the Chimneys. Depending on your time and stamina, you can get out of the car at the next overlook and hike the steep trail to **Alum Cave Bluffs,** site of a 19th-century commercial alum mine and reputedly a source of saltpeter used in gunpowder during the Civil War. The trail begins with an easy 1.3-mile trail along a tree-bordered creek to **Arch Rock,** a tunnel made by eons of erosion. The trees include towering 200-year-old eastern hemlocks. This is a magnificent spot for a spring wildflower hike serenaded by the songs of nesting warblers. You can return to your car or continue on a steep 0.9-mile ascent to the bluffs.

Back in the car, continue to **Newfound Gap** (5,048 feet), through which runs the Tennessee-North Carolina state line and a long leg of the Appalachian Trail. From the overlook here, on a clear day you can see Mount LeConte (6,593 feet) and your next stop, **Clingmans Dome.** The 7-mile **Clingmans Dome Road** veers sharply off here and winds through a forest of spruce firs to a parking lot.

There begins a steep half-mile trail ending at a spiral ramp. It leads to a lookout tower at the top of the 6,643-foot dome, the highest point in the park. Here you get either a panoramic view or a sense of floating on a sea of churning clouds.

Retrace the route to Sugarlands or, depending on time and destination, continue on to Oconaluftee Visitor Center. The **Mountain**

Calling All Species

How many plant and animal species exist in Great Smoky Mountains National Park?

That's a question more than 200 scientists are trying to determine in a ground-breaking effort called the All Taxa Biodiversity Inventory. The project began late in 1997. Scientists chose to work in Great Smoky because of the park's unusually rich blend of animals and plants.

All Taxa could take years to compile. Only about 14,000 species have been identified to date, and taxonomists estimate the park could contain 100,000 life-forms (not including bacteria and viruses).

Having a complete biological map of an area such as the Great Smokies would give scientists an unprecedented opportunity to study plant and animal dynamics, range, behavior, and extinction patterns.

Farm Museum, a cluster of farm buildings gathered from their original locations within the park, is adjacent to the visitor center. From spring through October, park employees dressed as pioneers demonstrate how farm implements work. Also between spring and October, at **Mingus Mill,** a miller explains how cornmeal and flour would have been produced on an ingenious water-run turbine.

Cades Cove Loop Road: 11 miles; at least a half day

Follow Little River and Laurel Creek Roads for 25 miles from Sugarlands Visitor Center to Cades Cove Loop Road.

Before 1819, Cades Cove was part of the Cherokee Nation. Then, European settlers from North Carolina, Virginia, and other parts of Tennessee began trickling into the broad, high valley in search of affordable farmland. By 1850, more than 680 people were living there.

They left behind structures that evolved into an open-air museum along the paved, 11-mile, one-way road. Official sites are well-marked. Yet, you may find yourself making unofficial stops to admire the quietude, watch white-tailed deer bound across the valley, or see black bears feed on acorns or wild grapes.

The first stop is **John Oliver Place,** site 3. The small cabin was built with split-wood shingles and hand-hewn logs. Stand on the porch and look down the long, green-carpeted valley that drew the family to what was the edge of the American world in 1826.

Some visitors skip site 4, **Primitive Baptist Church,** because it lies on a two-way dirt road off the loop road. Don't miss it. Organized in 1827, the simple, white-frame church guards a small graveyard. Time has worn the names off many of the headstones, but you can still read a few. The church shut down during the Civil War because, according to a letter from a member, "we was Union people and the Rebels was too strong here in Cades Cove."

Methodist Church, site 5, had a door for men and another for women and children. During services, the separation was enforced in the pews by a barrier.

Just past the church is **Hyatt Lane,** an old road out of Cades Cove and now a shortcut that slices off a big piece of the tour. Stay on the loop road and continue to **Missionary Baptist Church,** site 7, that was formed in 1839 by expelled members of the Primitive Baptist Church. Because the congregation split between Union and Confederate sympathizers, this church also closed during the Civil War.

Continue on the road, past **Rich Mountain Road,** site 8. Save this for another day, if you can. The gravel road laid over a Native American trail climbs Rich Mountain and provides a spectacular backward glance at Cades Cove before exiting the park. Also requiring more time is the **Cooper Road Trail,** site 9,

Staghorn sumac

an old wagon road that is now a 13-mile hiking trail ending outside the park.

Ahead on the right is a short, two-way road to the next stops, **Abrams Falls,** site 10, and **Elijah Oliver Place,** site 11. If you take this offshoot, you reach a parking lot and a choice: a 2-hour, 2.5-mile hike up to stunning Abrams Falls, or a half-mile hike to another rustic farmstead owned by early settler Elijah Oliver. The latter features a smokehouse, springhouse, and corn crib.

Continue your drive along the loop road to the next offshoot, which leads to **John Cable Mill,** site 12, where millers ground corn meal. Here, the Cades Cove Visitor Center displays artifacts and pictures depicting life in Cades Cove that help visitors connect intellectually and emotionally with the people who called this serene valley their home.

The other buildings—a blacksmith shop, a large cantilever barn, a smokehouse—were imported from elsewhere in the park. Check schedules posted in the center to see when costumed employees are giving demonstrations.

Just beyond the mill area is **Parson Branch Road,** which can take you out of the park and the 21st century. The narrow, twisty, one-way dirt road *(sometimes closed by weather)* was carved out of wilderness about 1838; the 8-mile trip to US 129 can take an hour.

If you stay on the loop road instead, your next stop will be **Tipton Place,** site 17. Built by Hamp Tipton shortly after the Civil War, it later became the home of a blacksmith, who ran his shop nearby.

Drive on to the last stop, **Carter Shields Cabin,** site 18. Log cabins like this would be succeeded by board houses, which arrived with lumbering in the early 1900s.

Hikes & drives

The self-guided nature trails operate on an honor system. Visitors drop 50 cents into a rack and pluck out a leaflet that's keyed to numbered stops.

Balsam Mountain Trail is the easiest climbing trail in the park, a 1.5-mile loop from Balsam Mountain Campground. The trail gives you a short lesson in the identification of trees and, especially in spring, wildflowers. **Laurel Falls Trail** is paved. The 2.5-mile round-trip trail, which starts on Little River Road near Elkmont, winds through thickets of mountain laurel and rhododendron to one of the park's many waterfalls.

Black Bears

Behold the bear of the Appalachian Mountains. It shambles along, carrying its 100- to 400-pound bulk through the forests. Then, smelling honey high up, the 3-foot-high black bear rears on its hind legs, extending its height to as much as 6 feet, and reaches its claws to the bee's nest. The bear rips away the bark and feasts on the honey, the honeycomb, even the bees and their larvae.

Black bear

Later in the day it tears open a rotting log, filled with such tasty snacks as crickets, ants, beetles, and grubs. In the evening it finds a good trout stream and waits patiently. A big one swims by; the bear pins it to a rock with a quick paw.

Bears mate in June and early July. Cubs are born in midwinter, usually two per year; they sometimes nurse for a whole year.

In the fall, bears load up on food. With the onset of winter, they find a good cave or hollow tree and go into hibernation. What happens then makes for good research projects. A few days before the big sleep, the creatures eat only roughage, which goes through their systems to form anal plugs up to a foot long that prevent excretion in the den.

One of the fascinating things about hibernation is that while the bear burns up to 4,000 calories a day, it suffers no loss of calcium or bone mass. No other mammal seems to be able to lie still for four months and come out in such good shape.

Although black bears face increasing threats from habitat loss, the southern Appalachians still have a sizable population. Some 1,800 live in the Great Smoky Mountains National Park, with several hundred more inhabiting the surrounding forests.

Black bears have rarely hurt people, unless they feel threatened or have become used to human food. Feeding bears can make them more aggressive. Such bears then have to be relocated or killed.

Great Smoky Mountains National Park in the fall

For a longer stay in the park, try some of the more rugged trails. The most rewarding hike is to 6,593-foot-high **Mount LeConte,** the park's third highest peak. The shortest way up also is the steepest, via the **Alum Cave Trail** that starts at Newfound Gap Road *(see Newfound Gap Road tour, p. 166)*. Here begins a 5-mile climb to the summit of LeConte. At one point, the trail skirts a cliff face so sheer that hikers must grasp a cable to make their way up.

For the motorist, there also are self-guided nature trails using roads. The **Roaring Fork Motor Nature Trail,** 4 miles from Gatlinburg off Cherokee Orchard Road, is a curvy, one-way road running for 5 miles. About a mile before the trail begins, you'll see the **Noah "Bud" Ogle Place** on your right. A 0.75-mile path takes you around the farm's remaining buildings.

At the **Roaring Fork trail,** take the self-guiding booklet that suggests scenic stops. The road climbs a hill that provides a splendid view of Sugarland and Cove mountains. And on the roadside is an old-growth hemlock forest. The moldering chestnut logs are sad reminders of the blight that struck the one-time forest king and decimated its numbers in the early part of the 20th century *(see sidebar, p. 188)*.

INFORMATION & ACTIVITIES

Headquarters
107 Park Headquarters Rd.
Gatlinburg, TN 37738
865-436-1200
www.nps.gov/grsm

Visitor & Information Centers
Open daily year round: Sugar-
lands, on US 441 south of
Gatlinburg, Tenn., entrance;
Oconaluftee, on US 441 north
of Cherokee, N.C., entrance;
Cades Cove Visitor Center, near
Townsend, Tenn., entrance;
enter off US 321 east of
Townsend.

Seasons & Accessibility
Park open year-round. The
road to Clingmans Dome and
some unpaved roads close in
winter.

Entrance Fees
There are no fees to enter the
park, but there are some activities that require a fee.

Pets
Pets are allowed, but they must
be on leashes at all times.

Facilities for Disabled
Visitor centers and rest rooms
are wheelchair accessible. The
Sugarlands Valley Nature Trail
(a quarter-mile south of Sugarlands Visitor Center) was cus-
tom-built for visitors with
visual or mobility impairments.
Clingmans Dome and Laurel
Falls Trails are paved but steep;
negotiable with assistance only.
Free brochure.

Things to Do
Free naturalist-led activities:
nature walks (day and evening), children's and campfire
programs, pioneer exhibits
and demonstrations, slide
talks. Also annual festivals,
auto tape tour, hiking, bicycling, fishing (permit required), horseback riding
(several stables in park).

Overnight Backpacking
Permit required; available free
from visitor centers and ranger
stations. You can reserve
rationed sites and shelters up
to 30 days in advance; call
865-436-1231.

Campgrounds
Ten campgrounds, most with a
7-day limit mid-May through
October; other times 14-day
limit. Cades Cove and Smoke-
mont open all year; Elkmont
open April through October.
Reservations required mid-May
through October; available
through National Parks Reservation Service (see p. 13).

Other campgrounds open
mid-March through October,

first come, first served. Fees $12 to $17 per night. No showers. Tent and RV sites; no hookups. Seven group campgrounds; reservations recommended.

Contact park's headquarters for more information.

Hotels, Motels, & Inns

(Unless otherwise noted, rates are for two persons in a double room, high season.)

INSIDE THE PARK:

■ **LeConte Lodge** (atop Mount LeConte; access by hiking trail) 250 Apple Valley Rd. Sevierville, TN 37862. 865-429-5704. 10 cabins, no electricity, shared bathrooms. $163, includes two meals. Open late March to late November.

OUTSIDE THE PARK
In Bryson City, NC 28713:

■ **Hemlock Inn** (on Galbraith Creek Rd., off US 19) P.O. Box 2350. 828-488-2885. 25 units. $144-$195, includes two meals. Restaurant. Open mid-April through October.

In Cherokee, NC 28719:

■ **Best Western Great Smokies Inn** (US 441 and Acquoni Rd.) P.O. Box 1809. 828-497-2020 or 800-528-1234. 152 units. $89. AC, pool, restaurant.

■ **Holiday Inn Cherokee** (US 19 South) P.O. Box 1929. 828-497-9181.

154 units. $99-$130. AC, 2 pools, restaurant.

In Fontana Dam, NC 28733:

■ **Historic Fontana Village Resort** Route 28, P.O. Box 68. 828-498-2211 or 800-849-2258. 90 rooms, $79; 120 cottages with kitchens, $89-$229. AC, 3 pools, 2 restaurants.

In Gatlinburg, TN 37738:

■ **Buckhorn Inn** 2140 Tudor Mountain Rd. 865-436-4668. 9 rooms, 7 cottages, 2 guesthouses. $115-$250. AC, restaurant.

■ **Gillette Motel** 235 Historic Nature Trail, P.O. Box 231. 865-436-5601 or 800-437-0815. 80 units. $75-$95. AC, pool.

■ **Holiday Inn of Gatlinburg** 520 Historic Nature Trail, P.O. Box 1130. 865-436-9201 or 800-435-9201. 400 units. $119-$129. AC, 3 pools, restaurant.

■ **Park Vista Hotel** 705 Cherokee Orchard Rd. P.O. Box 30. 865-436-9211 or 800-421-7275. 312 units. $109-$149. AC, pool, restaurant.

For other accommodations in Gatlinburg, call the Chamber of Commerce at 865-436-4178 or 800-822-1998.

Excursions from Great Smoky

Cherokee National Forest

30 miles northeast of Great Smoky

Spread across ten counties, the Cherokee National Forest belongs to an extensive system of Appalachian woodlands that extends into the Carolinas and Georgia. Thick carpets of poplar, oak, hemlock, and pine roll over the mountainous geography, interrupted by deep ravines, cool streams, and tumbling waterfalls. Above 4,000 feet grow forests of small spruce and fir, remnants of the cold-climate landscape that retreated north after the last ice age, some 10,000 years ago.

Also on high mountaintops, rhododendron gardens and grassy balds flourish, creating microhabitats where both northern and southern plant species live. Other specialized niches are created around rock outcrops, beech-maple woods, mountain bogs, the sprayed cliffs of waterfalls, and the backed-up water in beaver ponds. In fact, although these special communities account for only a small portion of the forest acreage, they are home to 75 percent of Cherokee's rare plant and animal species.

Statistics in the forest are impressive: 262 species of birds, 70 species of mammals, 715 miles of trails, 200 recreation sites, and 12 boating areas spread out over almost 1,000 square miles.

In the springtime, the lilting songs of warblers and vireos ring through the forest as the birds arrive from farther south and begin setting up house for the summer. Dogwoods and apple trees are

Bald Mountains, Cherokee National Forest

bursting into bloom. The forest floors are strewn with bouquets of trout lilies, wild geraniums, dwarf crested irises, and woodland bluets. Summer brings out the rhododendrons and a host of other flowers; hummingbirds sip on jewelweed and bee balm, while black bears find mates and enjoy long days filled with blackberries and blueberries. With the return of autumn, broad-winged hawks and other raptors cruise high overhead. Dogwoods, maples, sweetgum, sumac, and sourwood start decking the hillsides in tones of gold and russet. White-tailed deer are in rut; hibernating animals gather food throughout the day. In the cold, hard frosts of January, bear cubs are born in warm dens, and by February, maples and spice-bushes are already braving the chill with new blooms.

■ **640,000 acres** ■ **Eastern Tennessee in two segments along the state line, divided by Great Smoky Mountains National Park** ■ **Best seasons spring and fall** ■ **Camping, hiking, white-water rafting, swimming, mountain biking, horseback riding, wildlife viewing** ■ **Contact the national forest, 2800 N. Ocoee St., Cleveland, TN 37312; 423-476-9700.** www.southernregion.fs.fed.us/cherokee/

Nantahala National Forest

50 miles southwest of Great Smoky

The Cherokee called the forbiddingly rugged southwest corner of North Carolina *nantahala,* which means "land of the noonday sun," because its gorges were so deep the sun could reach them only at midday. Today the state's largest national forest covers much of that same lushly forested, mountainous countryside. Nantahala's ten rivers, three wilderness areas, scores of waterfalls, and miles of trails make this a good place in which to lose yourself.

If you visit only one waterfall in the forest, make a point of seeing **Whitewater Falls** (*off N.C. 281 9 miles south of Sapphire. Parking fee*). Many waterfalls claim to be the highest in the east, depending upon how you measure them; certainly this series of cascades, totaling 411 vertical feet, is one of the highest and most beautiful.

Just over the South Carolina state line, the **lower Whitewater Falls** make a similarly impressive 400-foot descent. Here on the Blue Ridge escarpment, the mountains make a precipitous drop to the Piedmont, leaving a legacy of glorious waterfalls. A **short trail** takes you to two overlooks of the upper falls and of Lake Jocassee in South Carolina. The constant spray has created a miniature rain forest of moisture-loving ferns, fungi, mosses, and salamanders. In spring look for the white blooms of Solomon's seal, nodding like little lanterns from slender stems.

A hemlock in Nantahala National Forest

For a more extensive workout, you can pick up the **Foothills Trail,** an 85-mile path that passes through here.

Another forest high point is the 5,324-foot-tall **Wayah Bald,** which is accessible by car. Take US 64 west of Franklin 3 miles, then turn right on N.C. 1310 for about 10 miles. Make a right on FR 69 for 4.5 miles. A short paved trail leads to an old Civilian Conservation Corps fire tower that you can climb for views of the Great Smokies to the north and the rippling mountains of Georgia to the south. The Appalachian Trail passes by here, heading north to the Smoky Mountains, and south to Georgia.

The most untouched area of the forest lies in the northwest, where the **Joyce Kilmer Memorial Forest** harbors a magnificent stand of old-growth poplars, hemlocks, and oaks, several of which are almost 450 years old and measure more than 20 feet around and 100 feet tall.

It's entirely appropriate that the forest was named in honor of Joyce Kilmer, author of the poem "Trees" ("I think that I shall never see a poem lovely as a tree"). Walking in this shadowy forest of giants is a rare privilege. In spring giant chickweed, Canadian violet, and trout lilies knit a light counterpoint to the tall trees. An easy 2-mile, figure-eight trail takes you into a virgin hardwood cove, where old trees have kept understory growth to a minimum.

■ **531,000 acres** ■ **Southwestern North Carolina** ■ **Best seasons spring and fall** ■ **Camping, hiking, canoeing, swimming, fishing** ■ **Contact Forest Supervisor's Office, Federal Building, Post and Otis Sts., P.O. Box 2750, Asheville, NC 28802; 828-257-4200. www.cs.unca.edu/nfsnc/**

Mount Mitchell State Park

70 miles east of Great Smoky

The air atop **Mount Mitchell** is so cool that you'd think you were in southern Canada. The plants and animals certainly do; the microclimate here supports life rarely seen anywhere else in the South. And the views on clear days are among the greatest anywhere in the nation, especially if you've hiked to the top. Whether you walk or drive up the highest peak east of South Dakota's Black Hills, you'll be glad you did.

Mitchell belongs to the Black Mountains. In a mere 15 miles, the range holds six of the ten highest peaks in the East.

For a long time, New Hampshire's Mount Washington was presumed to be the highest in the east. Dr. Elisha Mitchell, a science professor from the University of North Carolina, believed the Black Mountains were, and he made three visits to the range in 1835. His calculations, based on barometric pressure readings, proved his point. Mitchell showed that one peak was almost 400 feet higher than Mount Washington. His estimate was only 12 feet short of the official height of 6,684 feet recognized today.

In 1857, when a former student disputed his claim, Mitchell went back to the mountains with his instruments. He fell from a 40-foot cliff over a waterfall to his death. The following year the mountain was named for him; he lies buried on the peak.

It would be nice to report that the forest on the peak is healthy. Unfortunately, a tiny insect called the balsam woolly adelgid (*see sidebar, p. 299*) is damaging many of the Fraser firs and red spruces. Further weakening the trees' resistance, polluted rain and clouds on the mountain are sometimes as acidic as vinegar. Ice storms and high winds, often in excess of 100 miles per hour, prune out trees that would normally be strong enough to survive.

Your first stop here should be the museum that's off the parking lot, where there are exhibits on the mountain's unique geology, flora, and fauna. Among bird species generally found in Canada and New England, dark-eyed (slate-colored) juncos and red crossbills breed this far south, thanks to the extreme altitude.

■ 1,727 acres ■ Western North Carolina, 3 miles off Blue Ridge Parkway Milepost 355 in Pisgah National Forest ■ Best seasons summer and fall ■ Hiking, camping, nature observation, museum, bird-watching ■ Contact the park, 2388 N.C. 128, Burnsville, NC 28714; 828-675-4611. www.ils.unc.edu/parkproject/visit/momi/home.html

Pisgah National Forest

60 miles
east of
Great Smoky

A vast treasury of forested highlands, Pisgah sprawls across almost 800 square miles of the Unaka and Blue Ridge mountain chains, encompassing hundreds of miles of trails and some 120 miles of the scenic **Blue Ridge Parkway.** Within the forest's two segments are 20 peaks topping 6,000 feet. The famous **Appalachian Trail** skirts Pisgah's northwest boundary, and 37 miles of the **Forest Heritage National Scenic Byway** (US 276) runs through the forest between Brevard and Waynesville. Throughout the forest, you can find thundering waterfalls, towering rock cliffs, and plenty of breathtaking mountaintop views.

Mount Pisgah itself supposedly was named by a Scots-Irish Presbyterian minister and Indian fighter after the mountain upon which Moses spotted the promised land. Combined with the adjoining 531,000-acre Nantahala National Forest *(see pp. 175–76)* just south and the 640,000-acre Cherokee National Forest in Tennessee *(see pp. 174–75),* the Pisgah holds a tremendous portion of the remaining southern Appalachian forest.

Starting on the northern end of the forest at Blowing Rock, the **Moses H. Cone** and **Julian Price Memorial Parks** compose about 8,000 acres laced with carriage trails running through hemlocks, maples, and white pines.

One of the prettiest of the trails in the Cone park is the 1-mile loop around **Trout Lake;** you can then head up **Rich Mountain** for fine views of the Blue Ridge. Ginseng grows up here, highly valued for the reputed healing power of its roots; also be on the lookout in spring and summer for white trilliums, violets, and wild geraniums. The Blackburnian and black-throated blue warblers—the former has a brilliant orange throat, the latter a white belly and dark blue wings—inhabit these woods near the southern extreme of their range.

Despite its commercial fanfare, privately owned **Grandfather Mountain** *(2 miles north of Linville on US 221. 828-733-4337. Adm fee.)* is well worth the price of admission for its stunning views, trail network, and mile-high swinging bridge. The rough-cut 5,964-foot peak was named by early settlers for the bearded-patriarch profile visible from the north. The Cherokee called it *Tanawha,* meaning "hawk" or "eagle." In the fall, broad-winged hawks migrate through the area and make an especially thrilling sight from the naked ramparts of this rugged mountain. The site also serves as an environmental habitats for bears, cougars, otters, and deer. You can drive to the top or hike the 13.5-mile **Tanawha Trail,** accessible at Milepost 305.5 on the Blue Ridge Parkway.

Grandfather Mountain is the high point in the Blue Ridge. Erosion-resistant quartzite, exposed after an older rock layer wore away millions of years ago, makes up the bulk of the massif. Dark gray outcrops offer excellent vantage points for long views of mountains and ridges and for studying soaring birds.

If you're driving at night on the parkway between Blowing Rock and Linville, stop at a pullover on the east side—**Lost Cove Cliffs** is a good bet—and see if you can spot the mysterious **Brown Mountain Lights.** On clear moonless nights, glowing stars seem to rise from Brown Mountain, 8 miles east. The brightness slowly increases, then the lights fade, and the cycle begins again.

A researcher from the U.S. Geological Survey studied the phenomenon in 1922. He concluded that headlights from cars and trains were likely being magnified by the varying atmospheric densities across the Catawba Valley.

Just south, **Linville Gorge** ranks as one of the most pristine, magnificent wilderness areas in the southern Appalachians. Dropping from high on Grandfather Mountain, the Linville River slashes down through the towering quartzite walls of the gorge. Over the millennia, the river has chiseled a 12-mile-long chasm of twisting rapids and craggy cliffs more than 600 feet high.

Linville Falls is the easiest area of the gorge to reach, located off the parkway at Milepost 316. Take the trail left of the visitor center a half mile to an overlook. From here, you can watch the tremendous volume of water gushing from the 50-foot upper falls into a huge rectangular basin; the water then plummets from a cut in the rock another 60 feet to the lower falls. All around are high walls, stone towers, and the constant washing rhythm of the river.

Though you can't see all the upper falls from this vantage, you have a wonderful view of the upper basin, which looks like a swimming pool carved from solid rock. You might be tempted to take a dip in the lower pool at the end of the trail (.6 mile away), but it's against park rules. Wait for the wilderness area downriver (southeast), where you can do as you want. While here, though, you should check out the trails on the other side, which lead to

Looking Glass Rock, Pisgah National Forest

several great overlooks. Figure on walking about 4 miles if you cover all the trails.

At the aptly named **Table Rock,** several trails walk the bluff edge where the forest service protects the endangered mountain golden heather and the threatened Hellers blazing star. Endangered peregrine falcons nest in the gorge and can be seen soaring the heights in spring or fall.

A final not-to-be-missed sight, **Looking Glass Rock** *(US 276, 8 miles north of Brevard)* is one of the largest granite monoliths in the southern Appalachians. Shooting up 400 feet from the surrounding forest, the domed face has long been a magnet to rock climbers. There are trails along the base, and you can visit the refreshing **Looking Glass Falls** just off the highway.

■ 505,000 acres ■ Western North Carolina ■ Best seasons spring and fall ■ Camping, hiking, backpacking, fishing, wildflower viewing ■ Contact national forest, Federal Building, 160A Zillicoa St., Asheville, NC 28804; 828-257-4200. www.cs.unca.edu/nfsnc/

Roan Mountain State Park

90 miles northeast of Great Smoky

Snuggled into the north side of the 6,286-foot peak, the verdant park has more than 1,500 species of native plants and trees, 180 species of wildflowers, 15 miles of trails, and a great variety of songbirds and other wildlife.

One local story claims that Daniel Boone visited the mountain on a roan horse, for which the mountain was then named. In another legend, the name stems from the native rowan tree *(see sidebar, p. 182)*. Or perhaps it's the dark red color of the mountain's flora: rhododendrons in June, ash berries in September. Among the 18th- and 19th-century botanists to study the mountain were Andre Michaux, John Fraser, and Asa Gray; they reported on such new plants as the Catawba rhododendron, Fraser fir, and Grays lily.

Roan Mountain became a popular vacation spot in 1877, when Gen. Thomas Wilder built a 20-room inn on the top. Business was so good that he replaced the inn with the 166-room Cloudland Hotel eight years later. Visitors patient enough to endure a long, jolting carriage ride over the narrow trail to the summit were rewarded with grand views of the mountains all around.

Wilder also had bought 7,000 acres of land in the area, which he mined for iron ore. By 1900, the ore was pretty well gone and so was Wilder; he sold out and moved on. The hotel was abandoned, and then taken apart. Mature balsam (Fraser) fir and red spruce were chopped down; even the rhododendrons were dug out and sold to nurseries. By 1939 just about all the salable timber had been picked over.

But nature found a way to come back. The natural rhododendron gardens revived, and the U.S. Forest Service watched over the surrounding spruce and Fraser fir. Now, the gardens are part of Pisgah National Forest *(see pp. 178–180)*. Though the park and the base of the mountain lie in Tennessee, the gardens at the top are just over the line in North Carolina.

Whether you approach **Roan Mountain** from the Blue Ridge Parkway in North Carolina or I-81 in Tennessee, you have about 35 twisty miles of driving.

At the visitor center, pick up a trail map. Out back, sample the outdoor offerings on the 1-mile **Cloudland Nature Trail.** In May, the purple-tinted showy orchis, a small orchid, is in full bloom. Also keep your eyes peeled for the three-petaled, pure white trillium. A

Roan Mysteries

Roan is a mountain of some mystery, starting with its name. Some say it's a derivation of rowan, a tree found on the mountain; others say that Daniel Boone rode a roan horse on the mountain while exploring the frontier.

Another enigma is the source of the eerie natural music sometimes heard on the mountain. Scientists speculate that electrically charged air currents brush each other near the summit, filling the air with the sound of buzzing bees.

connecting trail of less than a half mile wanders past a waterwheel on the Doe River and the site of an 1800s ore mine.

It's a 10-mile drive from here to the top. But before you leave the park, stop off for another trail. The 2-mile **Raven Rock Overlook** makes a nice, steep, switchbacking loop through rhododendrons, hemlocks, and yellow buckeye. At .6 mile there's a rock outcrop that affords fine views of the mountains west.

Head up the mountain, and at Carver's Gap, just over the state line, turn right to reach the parking area for the **Rhododendron Gardens** *(adm. fee)*. Grassy balds and heath gardens punctuate the 5-mile ridgeline between the gap and Roan High Bluff, the mountain's high point.

If you are here in mid-June, you'll be treated to the sight and scent of 600 acres of rhododendrons in full red and purple glory. Trails loop through the natural gardens, pausing here and there for distant views of the rippling smoky blue mountains to the south. The elevation provides cool air on the hottest days, and the stands of sturdy little spruce and hemlock offer their own gardens of mosses and ferns and wildflowers.

The half-mile trail from the end of the road out to **Roan High Bluff** leads to a vista of long, low mountains to the west and the green valley around the little town of Buladean, North Carolina, far below.

■ 2,006 acres ■ Eastern Tennessee, 1 mile south of town of Roan Mountain ■ Best time: blooms peak in mid-June ■ Camping, hiking, cross-country skiing, fishing, swimming ■ Contact the park, 1015 Hwy. 143, Roan Mountain, TN 37687; 423-772-0190. www.tennessee.gov/environment/parks/parks/roanmtn/

Mountain Bridge Wilderness Area

75 miles southeast of Great Smoky

Tucked into South Carolina's mountainous northwest corner and linked by trails, Caesars Head and adjacent Jones Gap State Parks were combined into Mountain Bridge Wilderness Area in 1996. This is where the Blue Ridge suddenly drops 2,000 feet to South Carolina's piedmont, forming a high rock escarpment that gives wonderful views of the foothills to the south. Low-lying Jones Gap embraces the Middle Saluda River Valley, home to more than 400 plant species, while Caesars Head spreads over the highlands, its granite outcrop namesake somewhat resembling the Roman emperor's profile.

One of the earliest settlers here, planter and merchant Benjamin Hagood, bought 500 acres before the Civil War. Hagood herded livestock up the mountain in spring and stayed in his cabin until fall. Another pioneer, Solomon Jones, reputedly laid out a road in the 1840s without surveying instruments, relying instead on his instincts for contours and grades. The Jones Gap toll road went from River Falls to Caesars Head and on to Cedar Mountain, North Carolina.

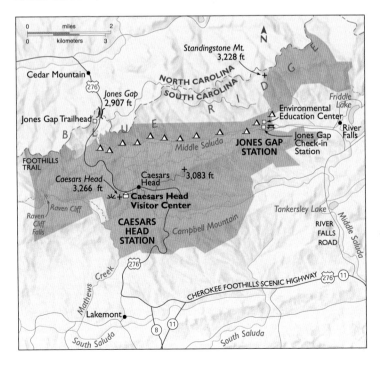

Bird-watching, Caesars Head

From the 1860s to the early 1900s, the road got plenty of use from the guests of a Caesars Head resort hotel. People came from as far away as China for the view, as well as dining, tennis, and swimming.

Only the views remain; the hotel burned in 1954, and the old dance hall is now a private club.

If you want to look up at towering cliffs, go to **Jones Gap;** for views out from the cliffs, drive up the twisty road to **Caesars Head.**

From the Jones Gap hiker station, a footbridge crosses the Middle Saluda and leads to a wide, shady picnic area and the pools of the old **Cleveland Fish Hatchery,** which operated here from 1931 to 1963. The rainbow, brook, and brown trout swimming in the pools provide a visual sample of what you might catch in the streams (*fishing license required*). Look up from here to the forested mountains and steep rock walls that rise more than 1,500 feet.

Walk to the **Environmental Education Center,** a stone-and-log building that was the hatchery superintendent's house. Among the many trails from here, **Hospital Rock Trail** zigzags up Standingstone Mountain and east around to Friddle Lake (4.4 miles one way). It's a tough 1.2 miles up to **Hospital Rock** itself, a 30-foot-long shelter where Confederates stashed medical supplies.

From the visitor center at the Caesars Head station, it's a short scramble to the overlook atop the promontory. The panorama takes in **Table Rock** and its reservoir to the southwest.

If you have time for only one hike, park at the trailhead for **Raven Cliff Falls,** a moderately difficult walk of 2 miles (one way). The worthwhile effort brings you to a series of cascades that plummet a total of 420 feet down a narrow valley.

■ 10,813 acres ■ South Carolina, northwest of Greenville, off US 276
■ Best seasons spring and fall ■ Hiking, fishing ■ Contact the wilderness area at 8155 Greer Hwy., Cleveland, SC 29635; 864-836-6115. www.discover southcarolina.com/stateparks

Devils Fork State Park

80 miles southeast of Great Smoky

One of the half dozen attractive parks strung along the **Cherokee Foothills Scenic Highway** (S.C. 11), Devils Fork State Park nestles along the southwestern shore of scenic Lake Jocassee, a 7,565-acre reservoir created by the Duke Energy Co. in 1973 to generate hydroelectric power. The name Devils Fork has been applied to this area since at least 1780, perhaps in reference to the confluence of Corbin, Howard, and Limber Pole creeks.

Stop at the park headquarters for information and a trail map. Then you can take the easy 1.5-mile **Oconee Bell Nature Trail** through a mixed forest of pines, oaks, and hickories. More than 90 percent of the world's rare Oconee bell wildflowers grow here, blooming in February or March with white petals and yolk-yellow centers.

For a bit more exercise, pick up the 3.5-mile **Bear Cove Trail** at the picnic area. The shaded route passes through mixed forest and offers good views of the lake and surrounding hills. Among the wildflowers you can see along the path are jack-in-the-pulpits, yellow trout lilies, showy white bloodroots, and violets. You have a good chance of spotting white-tailed deer and wild turkeys.

The deep, clear waters of **Lake Jocassee** are perfect for boating, fishing, and swimming. The 75-mile shoreline has quiet nooks and coves, where you can have a picnic in total seclusion. It is the only lake in the state that has trophy trout and smallmouth bass.

The park encompasses the **Jocassee Gorges,** a vast tract of land that was ripe for development. The state's Department of Natural Resources bought the land, a farsighted measure that placed 33,000 acres of mountain land under permanent protection as a wildlife management area.

Serene pleasures, such as primitive camping and hiking, await the dedicated visitor. More than 20 miles of the scenic **Foothills Trail** course through the expansive acreage, which includes the 2,500-foot-high Jumping Off Rock and its fine views over Lake Jocassee and into the mountains of North Carolina.

■ 622 acres ■ South Carolina, 5 miles northeast of Salem off S.C. 11
■ Best seasons spring and summer ■ Hiking, boating, swimming, fishing, wildlife viewing, wildflower viewing ■ Contact the park, 161 Holcombe Circle, Salem, SC 29676; 864-944-2639. www.southcarolinaparks.com

Chattahoochee National Forest

50 miles southwest of Great Smoky

Splashed across Georgia's green and mountainous north, this vast forest holds a treasury of southern Appalachian natural history.

Cool streams tumble from rocky gorges, cutting steep defiles and gathering momentum as they plunge into rivers lined with hemlock and oak. Trout-filled lakes dot the highlands like sparkling beads. In the fall the hills turn gold and scarlet, succeeded by a chilly winter and spring's impressive display. Tender new leaves and buds begin to clothe the bare limbs; blushes of redbud and orange-tinted maple appear. Brilliant wildflowers begin blooming low on dormant meadows and beside trails and creeks.

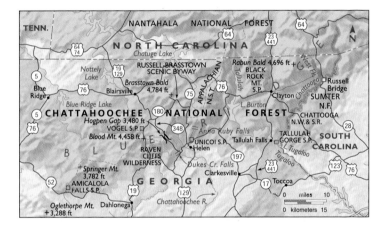

The brilliant burst of pink azalea and mountain laurel announce the long, warm days of summer. Vireos and warblers return to the forest, and the liquid flute of the wood thrush resounds once again deep in the heart of the woods.

The healthy forest you see today was not always so verdant and wild. A gold rush originating near Dahlonega drew thousands of white settlers in the 1830s, displacing the Cherokee who had been here for centuries. When the rush ended, the miners moved on; farmers stayed and began working the land. They often planted on steep slopes, failed to rotate crops, relied too much on burning, and did not plant cover crops in winter. Pretty soon they too sold out and left.

Skunked

Two species of skunks that live in the park, the striped and eastern spotted, may be its most elegant looking inhabitants. Their black-and-white coats make them stand out. Thanks to their more notorious attribute, their scent, they have little need for camouflage.

When threatened, the skunk faces its enemy and raises its tail. Sometimes, this warning step is cut, and the skunk adopts a shoot-first policy: It pivots around and sprays a stream of yellow musk from its anal glands. A striped skunk (the slightly larger of the two species) can spray up to 15 feet away, with the mist carrying an additional 30 feet. The smell itself is detectable for a mile or more.

Although the skunk can shoot five or six rounds of musk, one is usually enough. A single jet of this remarkably potent liquid equals only about one-fifth of a teaspoon.

A hit to the eye causes intense pain and temporary blindness. Tomato juice and ammonia are the best agents for removing the overpowering smell. It may sound incredible, but some commercial perfumes are made by deodorizing the oily musk and using it as a base.

In the 1880s timber companies came in and spent the next 40 years or so taking out just about everything the forest had to give. A charred, eroding land of stumps and gullies remained when the federal government made the area a national forest in 1936. The Civilian Conservation Corps and others began replanting trees to restore the forest.

Today black bears, deer, turkeys, raccoons, hawks—in all, more than 500 species of animals—find shelter in the Chattahoochee. More than 500 miles of trails, ten sizable lakes, 1,770 miles of trout streams, numerous waterfalls, scenic roads, state parks, and the Chattooga National Wild and Scenic river give visitors ample opportunity to explore.

The **Chattooga River** flows wild for 50 undammed miles, twisting through narrow passages, frothing up in constant rapids and flumes, swishing past boulders as big as trucks, and occasionally slowing down to form deep pools. The first 10 miles pass through dense forests and old fields in North Carolina; the river then becomes the boundary line between Georgia and South Carolina, turning its way down to Lake Tugaloo, just north of Tallulah Falls and the gorge.

The river made an indelible impression on the American public in the 1972 movie *Deliverance,* which was about a canoe trip that became a test of survival. Running the river by canoe, kayak, raft, or inner tube has become ever more popular over the years. Rapids ranging all the way up to Class VI offer challenges for all skill levels.

If you prefer walking, there are more than 50 miles of trails along the river. At the Russell Bridge (Ga. 28), you can pick up the **Bartram** and **Chattooga River Trails,** which together travel north about 4 miles on the South Carolina side of the river before Bartram splits to the east. Southward, the trails run 10 miles along the Georgia side to Sandy Ford, where Bartram heads west. The southerly route passes more rapids, but either direction gives you a taste of the Chattooga's cool, ferny coves and steep, rocky ridges.

The easiest place for a quick look at some exciting white water is just off the US 76 bridge. A short trail on the South Carolina

American Chestnuts

Once the king of the forest, the great American chestnut so dominated eastern woodlands that one in four trees was a chestnut. It grew to more than 100 feet tall, its nuts provided food for wildlife, and its wood was used for cabins, fence posts, and tool handles.

In 1904 an Asian fungus hit chestnuts in New York City. Within a span of 20 years the blight had ravaged trees in a 1,000-mile radius. Two decades later, the chestnut was virtually eliminated from the forest.

Yet the American chestnut has not completely vanished. Saplings still sprout from the stumps of long-dead chestnuts, sometimes growing to a height of 20 feet before succumbing to the blight. Researchers have had some success in crossing the American chestnut with Asian species to produce a blight-resistant hybrid suitable as an ornamental shade tree and nut provider. Though they may never again dominate the forest, these chestnut trees carry on the genetic inheritance of their forerunners.

side takes you to **Bull Sluice,** a Class V rapid that few paddlers attempt. To the north, the river constricts to a 15-foot-wide channel, then screams around a blind curve to the Sluice. To the south is a hazardous series of Class IV rapids. The 7 miles from here to the lake are a minefield of undercut rocks, standing waves, steep drops, and swirling eddies, all of which are off-limits to all but the best boaters.

Russell-Brasstown Scenic Byway

This 38-mile loop begins in the tourist center of Helen, rolls through the forest and ascends Georgia's highest peak.

Take Ga. 75 north from Helen. In 5 miles you can pull over on the right side for a stop at **Andrews Cove,** by the cool, clear waters of Andrews Creek. You can picnic here or hike a 2-mile trail that follows a logging road up to the **Appalachian Trail.**

Continue north, forking west at Ga. 180. In a few miles, look on the right for the spur road that climbs **Brasstown Bald,** the state's highest point. From the parking lot *(fee)* near the top, you'll need to get out and either take a shuttle *(operating seasonally)* or walk a strenuous half-mile trail to the tip-top. If you come on a clear day—preferably in spring or fall—the view from the 4,784-foot summit is gorgeous. There is an excellent visitor center up here *(706-896-2556),* and you have access to a number of worthwhile hiking trails.

Back on the road, continue west on Ga. 180 through the undulating countryside, passing picturesque farmsteads and homes, then turn left (south) on the **Richard B. Russell Scenic Highway** or Ga. 348. The road climbs to 3,480-foot **Hogpen Gap** on the Blue Ridge Divide. Water flowing west of here drains into the Tennessee River, and then to the Mississippi; to the east, streams join with the Chattahoochee, which weaves its way south to the Gulf of Mexico through Florida.

Stay with Ga. 348, pulling to the right for a superb overlook of the 9,113-acre **Raven Cliffs Wilderness** and the sleeping bear profile of **Yonah Mountain** to the south. You then descend toward Helen again.

In 4.5 miles, the parking lot for **Dukes Creek Falls** *(fee)* lies on the right. A mile-long trail takes you close to the 300-foot-high falls; you can get a pretty good look from the platform just of the parking lot.

In about another 2 miles, turn right onto Ga. 75A for the 5,555-acre **Smithgall Woods-Dukes Creek Conservation Area** *(706-878-3087)*, which has 4 miles of woodsy hiking trails, and another 20 miles of trails for bikers and walkers. From here it's 3 miles back to Helen.

■ **749,680 acres** ■ **North Georgia** ■ **Best seasons spring and summer** ■ **Camping, hiking, whitewater rafting, canoeing, fishing, ATV trails, horseback riding** ■ **Contact the national forest, 1755 Cleveland Hwy., Gainesville, GA 30501; 770-297-3000. www.fs.fed.us/conf/welcome.htm**

Tallulah Gorge State Park

50 miles
south of
Great Smoky

A stream that drops as sharply as the Tallulah River does can do a lot of landscaping over thousands of years. In less than a mile it plunges 500 feet, sawing its way through dense quartzite and leaving a legacy of rock formations and cascades.

One definition for the Indian word *tallulah* is "unfinished," and since the river does not level out, its business as a land shaper also remains unfinished. As you stand on the edge of the 2-mile-long Tallulah Gorge and peer down nearly 1,000 feet to the river, it's as though you were looking back in time, to the earliest rock layers.

The human history, by contrast, is relatively brief. A few decades before the Civil War, the first white sightseers began coming to look at the gorge. By the late 19th century, the town of Tallulah Falls boasted 20 hotels, making it one of the most popular resorts in the South. Against the protests of early environmentalists, a dam was installed above the falls in 1912 to generate electricity for Atlanta and other towns.

The gorge's novelty wore off, and the resorts lost their customers. By 1921 fires had virtually wiped the town off the map. For years, the area remained almost empty of tourists. Then *Deliverance* and other movies portrayed a place of untamed and dangerous beauty. Georgia Power Company leased acreage to the Georgia Department of Natural Resources in 1992, thus creating a new state park.

If you're traveling north, follow signs to the right for the **Jane Hurt Yarn Interpretive Center.** There's a 70-seat theater that shows a must-see 15-minute film with dramatic footage of rock climbers and kayakers. Also check out the bird-watching center outfitted with binoculars and information sheets to help you identify the birds you might see.

Ladore Falls, Tallulah Gorge

Outside, a short trail takes you to the North Rim. The 0.75-mile **North Rim Trail** is nice and flat, with several awe-inspiring overlooks. The dam is to the west. Five weekends a year *(in April and November)* the power company releases enough water to turn the river into a roiling cauldron suitable for expert kayaking. For those who prefer more peaceful waters, the 63-acre **Tallulah Falls Lake** has a beach with a guarded swimming area.

Hiking both the North and South rims gives you an appreciation for Tallulah's magnitude. This 3-mile walk begins at the interpretive center. Follow the North Rim Trail to the left to Station One; take in the views of the gorge and **Oceana** and **Bridal Veil Waterfalls.** The sun dries out the cliffs on this south-exposed side, leaving a harsh environment where only a few hardy oaks and pines dwarfed to bonsai shapes can grow.

Now take the trail west toward the dam, stopping at various overlooks. When you reach the dam, you'll need to take the stairway up to the US 441 bridge. Cross it, and you're on the **South Rim.** Fewer people visit this side, but some of the best views are here.

Between Stations 7 and 8, you will pass **Hurricane Falls Trail,** one of two descents into the gorge. This is a strenuous hike, and you'll need a permit to take it.

■ **3,000 acres** ■ **Northern Georgia, in Tallulah Falls off US 441** ■ **Best seasons spring and summer** ■ **Hiking, bird-watching, biking, swimming, tennis** ■ **Contact the park, P.O. Box 248, Tallulah Falls, GA 30573; 706-754-7970.** www.gastateparks.org/info/tallulah

Obed Wild and Scenic River

75 miles northwest of Great Smoky

Settlers avoided the rugged canyon country of the Obed River system, because it wasn't much good for farming and was too far from centers of commerce. However, the timber and mining industries did not practice the same reticence. They probed every hidden pocket of Tennessee wilderness in the early 1900s.

Yet even for these industries, this Cumberland Plateau backwater proved to be too off the beaten track; when a flood washed out the Nemo railroad bridge in 1929, nobody bothered to rebuild it. Too bad for the town, but so much the better for the wild character of the land.

It all began about 360 million years ago when a shallow sea covered the area. Compressed layers of sediment became limestone, shale, coal, and sandstone, which were then raised by plate tectonics. Here on the southeast part of the plateau, the layers were raised to a rolling plateau nearly 1,500 feet above sea level. Rivers and streams were the main sculptors of the topography you see now.

The Obed Wild and Scenic River covers about 45 miles of four streams: Clear Creek, Obed River, Daddys Creek, and Emory River. Daddys Creek joins the Obed on the south, and Clear Creek joins it farther down on the north; the combined waters then flow east, hooking up with the Emory River.

The streams have gouged out gorges 500 feet deep lined with magnificent sandstone bluffs. The big width of the gorges, though, creates an effect that is more peaceful than breathtaking, an effect that can sometimes cause inexperienced river runners to discount the "wild" part of wild and scenic.

Floating and river running are best between December and April, when the rivers are full enough to generate white water. Rapids vary from Class II to Class IV, with some of the most exciting paddling on **Clear Creek** between Lily Bridge and the junction with Obed River. Below this junction are some good rapids as well with names like **Canoe Hole** and **Widow Maker.** Winding country roads lead to several access points, making it possible to run sections varying in length from 4 to 34 miles. You can camp along the river, as long as you're not on private land still within park boundaries; signs should indicate what is and isn't public land.

Among the plenty of fine swimming holes, one of the easiest to reach is at **Nemo Bridge,** about 6 miles southwest of Wartburg on Catoosa Road and named after the old railroad bridge. A rocky beach lines a wide section of the **Emory River** here, where you can wade in over slippery rocks, then swim. The cooler water lower down feels especially wonderful on a hot day. Visibility is good enough that if you use a mask, you can probably catch a glimpse of some of the turtles, big bass, and catfish that live here.

Cross the bridge and park in the camping area to access the Obed section of the **Cumberland Trail.** Walk as far as you like along this 14.2-mile section that runs from Nemo to the Devils Breakfast Table Trailhead on Daddys Creek. The first mile or so is a gentle walk up the bluffs in a forest of second- and third-growth oak, hickory, beech, maple, and pine. In cooler damper areas hemlocks provide welcome shade, and in the spring azalea, laurel, and white-flowering rosebay rhododendron light up the understory with blooms.

■ **45 miles long** ■ **Eastern Tennessee, 20 miles NW of Oak Ridge** ■ **Best seasons spring and summer; Dec.–April for river running** ■ **Camping, hiking, whitewater rafting, canoeing, kayaking** ■ **Contact the park service, P.O. Box 429, Wartburg, TN 37887; 423-346-6294. www.nps.gov/obed/**

Freshwater Mussels

You don't have to go to the ocean to find shellfish. Native Americans appreciated the value of freshwater mussels, using them for food, scraping tools, and ornaments.

One-third of the world's freshwater mussels live in the United States; the greatest diversity of those are in the Tennessee River drainage of which the Obed River is a part.

Of the 100 species in this area, 36 are threatened or endangered. Dams have caused silt to form in the river, and that can smother mussels. The declining number of fish, which act as hosts for immature mussels, also threatens the mussel population. Pollution, poaching, and competition from the non-native zebra mussel all pitch in to spell danger for our freshwater mussels. They still have economic value: crushed shells are used in seeding cultured pearls. Beyond that, their extreme sensitivity to water quality makes them key indicators of a river's health.

Forest Mushrooms

Most of the hundreds of species of mushrooms found in the Southeast are innocuous if not edible. Some, such as artist's fungus and shaggy mane, are quite beautiful. But there also are some that are poisonous.

If you plan to do any mushroom hunting, you should familiarize yourself with these species.

The mushroom kingdom's most notorious family, the amanita, have such a benign appearance that they are often mistaken for edible mushrooms. They have caused more deaths than any other kind. The amanitas grow about half a hand high, have an umbrella-shaped cap with gills, and often have a ring around the stalk.

The aptly named destroying angel is pure white color and can be found in oak and pine woods, especially after heavy summer rains. A white-stippled orange cap gives the fly agaric a cartoonish appearance. Chewing a small amount causes hallucinations; too much can kill.

The most lethal of all mushrooms, *A. phalloides*, or death cap, is distinguishable by its grayish green to pale white color; it grows commonly in fertile soil under deciduous trees in summer

Destroying angel mushroom

and fall. Cooking or drying the death cap does not destroy toxins; there is no known antitoxin.

What would happen if you ate half a cap? For the first several hours, nothing. Then you would begin to feel sick to your stomach. After two or three days of vomiting and diarrhea, your condition would improve somewhat; meanwhile, your liver and kidneys would start to fail.

After a week in the hospital, which could involve convulsions, coma, the need for a liver transplant, and massive doses of penicillin and other drugs, you might live, but probably with some permanent impairment. Advances in medical treatment in the last few decades have increased the survival rate from a mere 10 percent to about 75 percent.

Fall Creek Falls State Resort Park

100 miles west of Great Smoky Sitting in the middle of a great triangle formed by Nashville, Knoxville, and Chattanooga, Fall Creek Falls gets more visitors than any of Tennessee's state parks. But it's also the biggest park, and it's so far out in the boondocks that you won't feel a bit pressed. Here on the western edge of the Cumberland Plateau, streams have opened up huge gorges and left dramatic waterfalls, including the 256-foot namesake falls, one of the highest east of the Rockies. Along the rim of Cane Creek Gorge are some of the most breathtaking vistas in the state.

Ancient sand dunes, swamps, and tidal plains were compressed over the last 400 million years into the rock layers you see in the gorge today. When the plateau rose, the streams knifed down and westward, joining Cane Creek. The three large waterfalls in the park were created when soft shale eroded the layers of resistant sandstone underneath, leaving a ledge from which water could

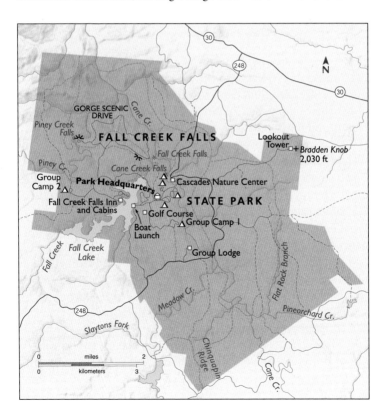

Cane Creek Falls, Fall Creek Falls State Park

plummet. The area was heavily logged in the early 1920s; the Civilian Conservation Corps came in the 1930s and planted trees and put in bridges and trails. Today, a luxuriant second-growth forest of hemlock, tulip poplar, hickory, and oak has again covered the plateau and filled in the gorge.

About one-third of the park has been developed, giving you the option of adding tennis, golf, and lodging to your agenda. That leaves more than 14,000 acres of wild woodlands for exploring. Pick up park maps at the information center, then head to the **nature center** to bone up on local geology, flora, and fauna. From here, there's a network of trails that leads to several of the park's highlights.

Take the suspension bridge over Cane Creek and swing out on the easygoing **Woodland Trail** for the quickest way to the falls. In less than a mile, you'll be standing on a high ledge enjoying the classic view down on **Fall Creek Falls.** The water cascades over a curved wall into a tremendous pool. In winter, the falls freeze into a beautiful 256-foot ice sculpture with columns and stalactites two stories tall; a faint trickle under the ice means the creek is still moving, its chilly spray riming the nearby vegetation with sleeves of ice.

If you're not up for the walk, you can drive around to the same overlook. But if you want to explore the base of the falls, your only option is to walk. The half-mile **trail** down is steep, but well worth the trouble. The deeper you drop into the gorge, the cooler and darker it becomes, the sandstone cliffs towering higher and higher above. At the plunge pool, a steady blast of mist keeps mosses and ferns green and rewards hikers on hot days. Notice the surrounding virgin forest of tall feathery hemlocks and stately yellow (tulip) poplars, the latter with big leaves that turn yellow in autumn.

Head back up and across the creek. For some scenic variety on the way back, branch left onto the **Gorge Trail.** A bit longer than Woodland, this trail offers several fine overlooks of the falls from the opposite side and others of **Cane Creek Gorge.** Your total distance to and from the nature center will be just less than 3 miles.

On the other side of the nature center you can pick up another nice walk, the 4.6-mile **Paw Paw Trail** that loops through the woods and pauses for views of **Cane Creek Falls** and Fall Creek Falls. Backpackers take to the 33 miles of trails that burrow through the forest on the park's eastern side

A 6-mile **scenic drive** courses through the park's northwestern corner. After a stop at the falls, there are pullovers for various views of the gorge. As you stare into the mile-wide gorge, with the roar of wind and water swirling up from 600 feet below, try to get a handle on 325 million years of history. Way at the bottom of the gorge are the earliest layers, the limestones that were once the shores of a sea. Fossils of ferns found along the gorge floor attest to the existence of ancient lagoons and swamps.

Up on the bluffs the dark shales and sienna-colored sandstones are burnished gold in the low light of sunset. Look for hawks and turkey vultures soaring above and in the great void of space out front.

Continuing on around the drive, you come to an overlook on **Piney Creek.** Short paths here take you to the quietly impressive **Piney Creek Falls,** an 85-foot cascade, and a bridge overlooking the upper part of the creek.

■ **21,135 acres** ■ **Eastern Tennessee, 14 miles northwest of Pikeville**
■ **Best seasons spring and fall** ■ **Camping, backpacking, hiking, swimming, biking** ■ **Contact the park, 209 Village Camp Rd., Pikeville, TN 37367; 423-881-3297. www.tennessee.gov/environment/parks/parks/FallCreekFalls**

Hot Springs

Most national parks cover hundreds of thousands of acres, are far from city streets, and keep natural resources away from commercial users. Not Hot Springs. The smallest national park is centered in a city that has made an industry out of tapping and dispensing the park's major resource: mineral-rich waters of hot springs.

The heart of this peculiar park is Central Avenue, the main street of Hot Springs, Arkansas. Rising above Central Avenue is Hot Springs Mountain, from which the waters flow. The mountain's lower western side once was coated with tufa, a milky-colored, porous rock formed of minerals deposited from the hot springs' constant cascade.

When Hot Springs prospered as a health spa in the mid-19th century, promoters diverted the springs into the bathhouses on Central Avenue. They also prettified the mountain slope by covering it with tons of dirt and planting grass and shrubs.

The park calls itself the oldest area in the National Park System because in 1832—40 years before Yellowstone became the first national park—President Andrew Jackson set aside thehot springs as a special reservation. It became a national parkin 1921. By then Hot Springs had long been famous as a spa where people "took the waters," seeking relief from bunions, rheumatism, and other afflictions. Some of the more famous guests included William Jennings Bryan, Al Capone, Babe Ruth, and President Franklin Delano Roosevelt.

The park preserves the springs' recharge zone (slopes where rain and snow soak into the ground), and the discharge zone, which contains 47 springs that belong to the park.

Each day about 850,000 gallons of water—at 143°F—flow from the springs into a complex piping and reservoir system. This supplies water to commercial baths and to park-maintained "jug

■ Central Arkansas

■ 5,550 acres

■ Established 1921

■ Year-round

■ Camping, hiking, horseback riding, bathhouse tours, thermal baths

■ Information: 501-624-2701 www.nps.gov/hosp

Quapaw Baths, Hot Springs National Park

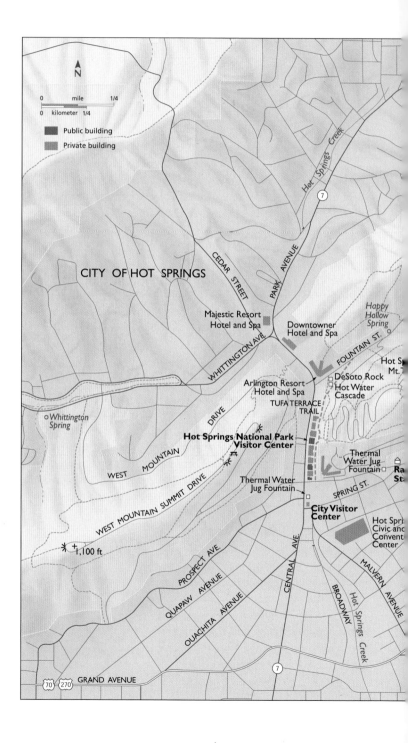

N

| 0 | mile | 1/4 |
| 0 | kilometer | 1/4 |

■ Public building
■ Private building

CITY OF HOT SPRINGS

CEDAR STREET

PARK AVENUE

Hot Springs Creek

7

Majestic Resort
Hot and Spa

Downtowner
Hotel and Spa

Happy
Hollow
Spring

WHITTINGTON AVE.

FOUNTAIN ST.

Hot S
Mt. T

Arlington Resort
Hotel and Spa

DeSoto Rock
Hot Water
Cascade

TUFA TERRACE
TRAIL

DRIVE

Whittington
Spring

Hot Springs National Park
Visitor Center

Thermal
Water Jug
Fountain

Ra
St

WEST MOUNTAIN

Thermal Water
Jug Fountain

SPRING ST.

City Visitor
Center

WEST MOUNTAIN SUMMIT DRIVE

Hot Spri
Civic and
Convent
Center

1,100 ft

PROSPECT AVE.

CENTRAL AVE.

MALVERN AVENUE

QUAPAW AVENUE

BROADWAY

Hot Springs Creek

OUACHITA AVENUE

7

70 270 GRAND AVENUE

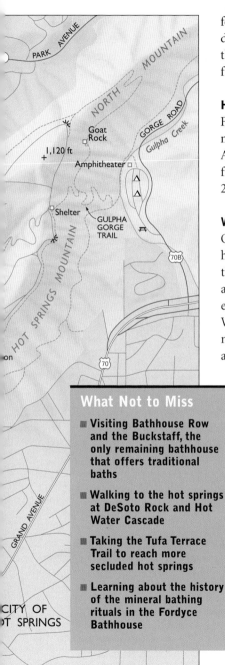

fountains," where people flock daily to fill containers with the fresh-tasting, chemical-free water.

How to Get There
From Little Rock, about 55 miles west on I-30, US 70, and Ark. 7; from the south, Ark. 7; from the west, US 70 or US 270. Airport: Little Rock.

When to Go
Open all year. Summers are hot, and July is crowded. Try the late fall, when mountains around Hot Springs are covered with spectacular foliage. Winter is usually short and mild; four-petaled bluets appear in February.

How to Visit
Walk **Central Avenue's Bathhouse Row,** then continue north to explore Hot Springs on the genteel trails of an urban hillside. To see a more rugged side of the park, hike the woodland trails of **Gulpha Gorge.**

What Not to Miss

- Visiting Bathhouse Row and the Buckstaff, the only remaining bathhouse that offers traditional baths

- Walking to the hot springs at DeSoto Rock and Hot Water Cascade

- Taking the Tufa Terrace Trail to reach more secluded hot springs

- Learning about the history of the mineral bathing rituals in the Fordyce Bathhouse

EXPLORING THE PARK

Bathhouse Row: 4 city blocks; 2 hours

In the 1830s, Hot Springs was a decidedly unposh place where Americans could take mineral baths in or near log cabins.

Fast-forward about 90 years. Elegant buildings of stucco and brick lined a stretch of Central Avenue dubbed "Bathhouse Row." The springs had been walled up and covered for protection. Visitors walked through landscaped gardens in the now-urbane spa town, completely cultural with its own opera house.

By 1985, only one of those old bathhouses—the **Buckstaff**—was still going (and continues to this day). The mineral bath business began declining in the 1960s, as medical science's faith in hot springs faded.

You can still enjoy the mystique of taking the waters. First visit the **Hot Springs National Park Visitor Center** (in the former Fordyce Bathhouse), a restored "temple of health and beauty" adorned with stained-glass windows and statuary. In rooms full of gleaming plumbing and luxurious tubs, you walk through a museum of the ritual, which in its full form involved 3 weeks of daily baths and massage. (Some hotels also have baths; ask for information at the visitor center.)

Hot Springs: half mile; 2 hours

At the foot of the mountain (*the corner of Central Avenue and Fountain Street*) look for **DeSoto Rock,** a huge boulder that commemorates both the Native Americans who named this "place of the hot waters" and the Spanish explorer Hernando De Soto. He and his party supposedly bathed in the waters in 1541, beginning a tourist tradition. Visit the hot spring pool next to DeSoto Rock. Here you can see and touch the very hot water.

Next head up the trail adjacent to the **Hot Water Cascade,** created in 1982. The water flowing here began its journey some 4,000 years ago when it fell as rain and seeped through fractures. Heated deep in the Earth, the water returns through the faults in the rock of the mountain in a year or two.

The tufa created by the cascade's splashing waters is building up at the rate of an eighth of an inch a year. The brilliant blue-green algae is the only plant species that can survive in the hot waters. So can ostracods, crustaceans as big as grains of sand.

Near the Hot Water Cascade is the **Tufa Terrace Trail,** which takes you by many concealed springs. To get there, cross the Grand Promenade, a landscaped brick walkway that runs behind the bathhouses. The walkway, which took 30 years to build and landscape, serves as a pleasant transition between the formal architecture of the bathhouses and the trails of the wooded hillside.

The springs are sealed off—and thus kept sterile—by locked green bunkers that jut out of the lawns carpeting the slope. When some of the hillside springs were open, men and women discreetly took turns soaking their feet at one of them; at another, people cooked eggs. To see more of the famous hot water bubbling out of the earth, follow the trail to **Open Springs** behind the **Maurice Bathhouse.** The two springs flow into a collecting pool, where you can safely feel the water.

Gulpha Gorge:

1.6 miles round-trip; 2 hours

To find the more traditional terrain of a national park, head north on Ark. 7 out of Hot Springs and turn right onto US 70B for Gulpha Gorge Campground about 3 miles from town. Near the amphitheater pick up the **Gulpha Gorge Trail,** which crosses Gulpha Creek on stepping-stones and courses through a woodland rich in dogwood and redbud. In spring and early summer wildflowers flank the trail.

In less than a mile the trail intersects with another up to **Goat Rock,** a fine overlook for viewing the mountains around Hot Springs.

In nearby quarries, Native Americans once mined novaculite for making arrowheads and spearpoints; now called Arkansas stone, novaculite is used as a whetstone.

Spring water fountain

INFORMATION & ACTIVITIES

Headquarters
P.O. Box 1860
Hot Springs, AR 71902
501-624-3383, ext. 620
www.nps.gov/hosp

Visitor & Information Centers
Hot Springs National Park
Visitor Center in the middle
of Bathhouse Row. Open daily.
For information, call 501-624-
3383, ext. 640.

Seasons & Accessibility
Park open year-round. Bathing
facilities open generally Monday through Saturday all year.

Entrance Fees
None, but fees charged for the
thermal baths run by concessionaires.

Pets
Not allowed in buildings;
otherwise permitted on leashes.

Facilities for Disabled
Visitor center is fully accessible
to wheelchairs; the Thermal
Feature and the Bathhouse
Row Tours are partially
accessible.

Things to Do
Free naturalist-led activities:
hikes and bathhouse tours.
Also available: audiovisual and
interpretive exhibits, hiking,
horseback riding; six bathing
facilities offering thermal
baths, whirlpools, steam
cabinets, hot packs, and
massages.

Special Advisory
Bathing in thermal waters is
not recommended for people
with certain ailments; consult
your doctor if in doubt.

Camping
One campground, Gulpha
Gorge, with 14-day limit.
Open all year on first-come,
first-served basis. Fees $10
per night. No showers.
Tent and RV sites; no
hookups.

Hotels, Motels, & Inns
(Unless otherwise noted, rates for
two people in a double room, high
season.)

In Hot Springs, AR:
■ **Arlington Resort Hotel & Spa**
239 Central Ave., 71901. 501-
623-7771 or 800-643-1502.
481 units. $78-$295. AC, 2
pools, 3 restaurants.

■ **Austin Hotel**
305 Malvern Ave., 71901. 501-
623-6600 or 800-445-8667.
200 units. $90-$95. AC, pool,
restaurant.

■ **Knights Inn**
1871 E. Grand Ave., 71901.
501-624-4436 or 800-238-4891.

Hot Springs' famous waters

50 units. $50-$96. AC, pool, restaurant.

■ **Lake Hamilton Resort**
2803 Albert Pike, 71914. 501-767-8606. 99 units. $84-$150. AC, pool, restaurant.

■ **SunBay Resort**
4810 Central Ave., 71913. 501-525-4691 or 800-468-0055. 130 condos. $99-$249. AC, 3 pools, restaurant.

■ **Williams House Bed & Breakfast Inn**
420 Quapaw Ave., 71901. 501-624-4275 or 800-756-4635. 7 units. $99-$189, includes breakfast. AC.

For additional accommodations, write or call the Hot Springs Convention & Visitors Bureau, Box 6000, Hot Springs, AR 71902. 501-321-2277 or 800-543-2284. www.hot springs.org.

Excursions from Hot Springs

Hot Springs to Harrison Drive

160 miles; one day Over forested hills and through friendly mountain towns, Ark. 7 curves and rolls south to north in the rugged highlands of western Arkansas. Along the way, the road passes fine rural scenery, a national park, two national forests, several state parks, and a national river. In addition to these, expect to find plenty of down-home hospitality in the cafés and craft shops that line the road.

The drive begins in Hot Springs, the boyhood home of former President Bill Clinton. As it cuts through town, Ark. 7 becomes Central Avenue and passes a block of lush landscaping that graces a row of elegant bathhouses that date back to the late 19th century.

The Renaissance Revival-style **Fordyce Bathhouse** (1915) now serves as the visitor center for Hot Springs National Park. Established in 1832 by President Andrew Jackson as a special national reservation, the park considers itself the oldest holding in the national park system. The city of Hot Springs encompasses part of the park.

For a grand view of the city and surroundings, turn right on Fountain Street and drive up twisting Hot Springs Mountain Drive to **Hot Springs Mountain Tower** *(501-623-6035. Adm. fee).*

Returning to Ark. 7, head north past a stretch of small motels and Victorian houses that soon becomes a 5-mile blur of flea markets, mobile homes, and billboards. After leaving this behind, the highway travels up a tree-lined valley that heralds the natural beauty to come. After 7 miles, turn left at the small town of Fountain Lake and continue on Ark. 7 another 6 miles to **Mountain Valley,** where the famous spring water is bottled.

Just north of town, you can drive 7 miles west on Glazypeau Road, then north on Ark. 227 to **Lake Ouachita** (pronounced WASH-ih-taw) **State Park** *(501-767-9366. www.arkansasstate parks.com).* The park is nestled at the edge of the state's largest man-made lake; 975 miles of shoreline encompass 48,000 acres.

After the tiny town of Jessieville, Ark. 7 enters **Ouachita National**

Forest *(see pp. 210–213)*, 1.8 million acres in the Ouachita Mountains that run east to west. The **ranger station** on the left has exhibits, information, and a short interpretive trail.

The road now begins winding up and down hills, presenting glorious views of low mountains and deep hollows. For the next 15 almost uninhabited miles you see gentle slopes of pines and hardwoods, steep rock walls, and the worn Ouachita Mountains, which look their finest in the dazzling hues of autumn.

At Milepost 42, cross the Fourche La Fave River and turn left into **Quarry Cove Park** to see the impressive **Nimrod Dam** and **Lake.** Completed in 1942 for flood control, the 97-foot-high dam stretches 1,012 feet across the lake's east end. The resulting miles of shoreline offer excellent opportunities for fishing, swimming, and waterskiing.

Beyond, Ark. 7 weaves uphill from the river and soon opens to views of the lake and surrounding hills. By the time you reach Ola, the woods alternate with soothing pastures and green farm fields. For the next few miles the air is redolent of pine woods and cured hams. In addition to hams, numerous wayside shops sell handmade quilts, pottery, honey, jams, and furniture.

In the small town of Centerville you can detour 16 miles east on Ark. 154 to lovely **Petit Jean State Park** *(501-727-5441. www.arkansas stateparks.com)*, which features dramatic overlooks, 95-foot-high Cedar Falls, and a lodge. After returning to Centerville, follow the byway past wide fields of soybean and grain that extend to the distant mountains.

Eight miles north is the historic river port of **Dardanelle.** Take a left at the sign for Dardanelle Powerhouse and Riverview Park, a worthwhile 1.5-mile digression that leads to excellent views of the mighty Arkansas River and Lake Dardanelle Dam, with its towering spillways. **Lake Dardanelle State Park** *(501-967-5516. www.arkansas stateparks.com)* lies just to the northwest of town on Ark. 22. A 7-mile excursion west on Ark. 155 takes you up a zigzagging road to **Mount Nebo State Park** *(501-229-3655. www.arkansasstate parks.com)*, where you'll be rewarded with wonderful views of the Arkansas River Valley.

As you cross the Arkansas River at the north end of Dardanelle, you'll see the prominent grain elevators at the Port of Dardanelle, where barges dock to load shipments of locally grown soybeans and grains.

North of here, the byway passes through Russellville before returning to the uncluttered vistas of hill country. After a gradual climb up through fields and forested hills, you arrive in the small town of Dover, where you can check out the abundance of local crafts and antiques, many sold from people's homes.

Five miles beyond, the drive enters **Ozark National Forest** *(501-968-2354. www.fs.fed.us/oonf/ozark, see pp. 218–20)*, whose steep-flanked mountains look more rugged than the Ouachitas to the south. Oak and hickory predominate in the 1.2 million acres of forest. Views grow more spectacular as you travel north, and a sign warns that the road is "crooked and steep next 36 miles."

Bending through a gently sloping forest, you pass signs announcing **Booger Hollow,** a tongue-in-cheek hillbilly trading post. Along with cheap souvenirs, it sells real crafts, sorghum, smoked ham, and other backwoods fare.

About 10 miles farther on, you pass through the village of **Pelsor,** where the **Hankins General Store** has been around since 1922; inside you can get a Moon Pie and catch some warmth around the pot-bellied stove. Just north of town, the forest opens to marvelous views in all directions. Stop at one of the pullouts or at the access to the 165-mile-long **Ozark Highlands Trail,** a mile beyond Pelsor.

After 9 miles, you reach the quaint highland village of **Cowell,** with its little church and pond. Past this, the drive offers more fabulous views of the valley and rumpled ridge to the west.

Three miles north of Cowell, go a mile west on Ark. 16, then northwest on Co. Rd. NE28—paved with gravel—3 miles to **Alum Cove Natural Bridge,** a fascinating 130-foot-long rock span.

Back on Ark. 7, for the next several miles you twist along the side of Judea Mountain through meadows, hollows, and coves. If you want to savor the spectacular scenery and some country cooking, stop at **Cliff House Inn** *(870-446-2292)* that hangs over the edge of the Ozarks' deepest canyon.

Just north, the byway enters Jasper, a gateway to the **Buffalo National River** *(see pp. 220–23)*. The town has craft shops, cafés, motels, and river outfitters. As you cross the Little Buffalo River on the way out of town, notice the exposed limestone and sandstone walls.

The road continues through the Boston Mountains (part of the Ozarks) before descending once again, this time down to the Buffalo National River.

Lake Ouachita

Before crossing the bridge here, stop for information at Pruitt Ranger Station *(870-446-5373. Mid-March–Sept.)*. Designated as a national river in 1972, this wilderness protects such animals as bobcats, minks, and bears.

Five miles north of the river near Harrison is **Mystic Caverns,** where you can walk through two large caves; one, **Crystal Dome,** soars as high as an eight-story building.

Beyond here, the road smoothes out, and the hills flatten into green pastures where horses and cattle graze beside barns.

Soon you come to the drive's end in the resort town of Harrison, "crossroads of the Ozarks." Here, next to the local high school, a little-known piece of the past survives: **Baker Prairie,** a remnant of the vanishing tallgrass prairie that once blanketed much of the country's midsection. For information on it, visit the Tourist Information Center *(870-741-3343)* on US 65 north.

■ **160 miles; one day** ■ **Hot Springs to Harrison, Ark, 7** ■ **Spring through fall. Peak fall foliage times vary.**

Ouachita National Forest

30 miles north of Hot Springs

The largest national forest in the country, Ouachita covers 1.8 million acres. Originally called the Arkansas National Forest, it was later renamed after a Native American word meaning "good hunting ground."

At the heart of the national forest, the Ouachita Mountains comprises long, east-west-running ridgelines, squeezed up through folding and faulting more than 200 million years ago. Sandstone and other underlying rocks formed mainly of silica (the basic material of quartz) eroded to create a sandy soil that was well suited for pine trees. Today, the trees dominate much of the forest.

Loggers have used the Ouachitas extensively; timber companies own large tracts of the land. Environmentalists once criticized the government for the degree of clear-cutting it allowed. But in recent years, more of an effort has gone toward managing public lands in a more environmentally friendly way.

This is an environment worth protecting, too. The mountains' east-west orientation creates distinct ecological niches, with north slopes significantly cooler and wetter than those to the south. Diverse geology and the Ouachitas' great age contribute to a complex ecosystem that's home to dozens of rare, endemic species of

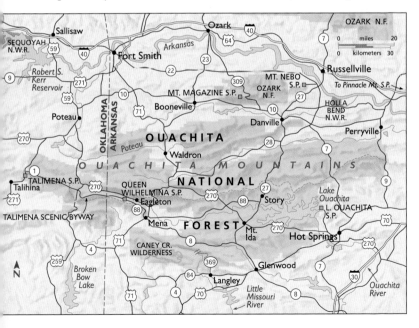

plants and animals. Endangered fish such as the leopard darter and the Ouachita Mountain shiner swim in rocky streams. A few colonies of the endangered red-cockaded woodpeckers survive in mature pinewoods. Salamanders live in moist woods on mountain slopes. So ecologically valuable are the Ouachitas that The Nature Conservancy designated them as one of the world's Last Great Places in 1995.

You must have a national forest map to explore the Ouachita Mountains. The forest's great size and maze of unpaved roads make it easy to get disoriented, so stop by a ranger station and buy a map. You can also talk to Forest Service personnel about road conditions, check on current hunting seasons *(fall and spring are times to be most cautious),* and get brochures on the forest's wilderness and recreation areas.

Ouachita National Recreation Trail

Few people have the time or energy to hike the entire length of the Ouachita National Recreation Trail, which winds 224 miles through pine-hardwood forest from **Talimena State Park** in Oklahoma to **Pinnacle Mountain State Park** near Little Rock, Arkansas. (The easternmost 32 miles lie outside the national forest.) But the trail crosses roads and highways all along the way, making day hikes and weekend overnight camping trips easy, and letting visitors experience segments of this regionally celebrated route.

The trail also connects with several notable areas in the national forest. Eleven miles east of the Arkansas state line, the trail crosses US 270 near Eagleton, where you'll find a parking lot and a trailhead marking the start of the 6-mile Black Fork Mountain Trail. The trail heads northeast for a mile to a spur trail running west to the **Black Fork Mountain Wilderness,** one of the six official wilderness areas in the national forest. This 13,139-acre tract centers on **Black Fork Mountain.** To reach the 2,403-foot summit, you'll need to climb 3 quite strenuous miles from the trail junction. On the top you'll find dwarf forests of mature white oaks less than 20 feet tall, stunted by a combination of poor soil, dry conditions, and exposure to winter weather. On the Oklahoma side, Black Fork's steep slopes are marked by rock glaciers, expanses of jumbled boulders created by erosion.

Another 36 miles east, the trail reaches the **Big Brushy Recreation Area,** off Ark. 270 about 14 miles west of Mount Ida. From the campground and picnic area you can follow loop trails (in part utilizing the Ouachita Trail) for hikes of 3 to 12 miles. Here, as throughout the region, the forest is a mixture of oaks, hickories, red maple, dogwood, and shortleaf pine. One trail follows **Brushy Creek,** a typically pretty mountain stream with a few nice cascades.

The trails here are open to mountain biking except for the **Brushy Mountain Trail,** which climbs to its eponymous summit with fine views along the way.

Arkansas's most famous mountain-bike route heads south from the Ouachita Trail just west of Ark. 27, near the town of Story. The **Womble Trail** winds through hills for 37 miles to North Fork Lake, 10 miles west of Mount Ida. Its challenging climbs and descents and rewarding scenery attract riders from around the country. This is a point-to-point ride, not a loop, but canoe outfitters on the Ouachita River can arrange a shuttle for a small fee.

At the eastern edge of the national forest, the Ouachita trail passes through the 9,507-acre **Flatside Wilderness,** the closest wilderness to Little Rock. The parking area on FR 94 on the east side provides good access into Flatside. Just uphill to the east rises 1,550-foot **Flatside Pinnacle,** which you can reach by a short but steep spur off the trail. You'll find a terrific view from this rocky outcrop, with the ridges of the Ouachita Mountains stretching off to the west for 50 miles or more like rolling green waves.

Little Missouri Falls Area

The **Little Missouri River** begins in a valley south of the Missouri Mountains about 15 miles southeast of Mena, Arkansas. One of the most beautiful streams in the Ouachita National Forest, it cascades over falls large and small as it makes its rocky way southeast toward its confluence with the Ouachita River. It's also the site of two of the forest's most popular recreation areas; if you visit here on a summer weekend, your pleasures will definitely not include the joy of solitude. Try to visit in the off-season or on a weekday.

A hiking trail more or less parallels the river for 15 miles (one way; no loop trip on this route), but access points make possible hikes that are as short as 4 miles (with a shuttle). Of course, you can walk any distance you want, even just a few hundred yards, along the Little Missouri and backtrack to your car. You're not likely to be bored by the views in either direction.

From Langley, Ark. 369 leads north to the **Albert Pike Recreation Area,** a popular camping spot and one access point for the trail. Continue northwest on FR 73, FR 43, and FR 25 about 7 more miles to reach Little Missouri Falls picnic area, another trailhead. You'll quickly see why people flock to the superb swimming holes around this waterfall; if you walk upstream or downstream you'll find others just as nice and more private.

Lined by old-growth shortleaf pines and spreading beeches, the Little Missouri earns its designation as an official National Wild and Scenic River. Its relatively pristine surroundings and pure water make it home to some of the Ouachitas' distinctive species such as the Caddo madtom, the Ouachita darter, and five types of crayfish.

Talimena Scenic Byway

The 54-mile ridge-running stretch of highway called Talimena unquestionably offers magnificent views, offbeat local history, and some lessons in geology and botany. Between Mena, Arkansas, and Talihina, Oklahoma, the road climbs **Rich Mountain** at 2,681 feet, the highest peak in Ouachita.

Leaving Mena on Ark. 88, you'll soon reach the eastern visitor information station, open from spring through fall. (There's another station at the western end of the drive.) Here you can pick up maps and other material, and access the 2.7-mile loop **Earthquake Ridge Trail,** popular with hikers and mountain bikers.

Two miles into the drive is **Blue Haze Vista,** the first of more than 20 overlook points along the way. From all of them the parallel east-west ridges of the Ouachita Mountains lie beneath you.

You'll reach the state line 17 miles west of Mena, where the highway becomes Okla. 1. At Milepost 30, the **Robert S. Kerr Memorial Arboretum, Nature Center, and Botanical Area** is a very worthwhile stop. Exhibits and three short trails interpret the Ouachita Mountains environment, and the adjacent 8,026-acre natural area has examples of locally distinctive plant communities, from shortleaf pine forest to seeps surrounded by wildflowers.

■ **1.8 million acres** ■ **West-central Arkansas and eastern Oklahoma** ■ **Best seasons summer and fall** ■ **Camping, hiking, canoeing, mountain biking** ■ **Contact the national forest, P.O. Box 1270, Hot Springs, AR 71902; 501-321-5202. www.fs.fed.us/oonf/ouachita.htm**

Holla Bend National Wildlife Refuge

Holla Bend National Wildlife Refuge

60 miles north of Hot Springs

One of Arkansas's best wildlife-watching sites, Holla Bend National Wildlife Refuge is an excellent birding spot year-round. Fall brings great flocks of waterfowl and a variety of raptors, and the warmer months offer the chance to see an array of species of mammals and nesting birds.

The **Arkansas River** once made an extensive southward loop as it passed through this central Arkansas valley. In 1954 the U.S. Army Corps of Engineers straightened the river by cutting through the top of the bend; the area within the old channel was dedicated as a refuge in 1957.

Today Holla Bend comprises good bottomland hardwood forest, small lakes, scrub, and grassy areas. As is the case at many national wildlife refuges, part of the property is used to grow such crops as wheat, milo, and soybeans; some of that is left in the fields to feed the wildlife.

As many as 20,000 Canada and snow geese may winter on the refuge; smaller numbers of greater white-fronted and Ross's often stay here too. They're all joined by thousands of ducks: Mallard, American wigeon, northern pintail, green-winged teal, and gadwalls.

Other creatures you might see in Holla Bend are white-tailed deer, coyotes, raccoons, armadillos, striped skunks, and bobcats. You might see a river otter along the bank of a lake, or at dawn or dusk glimpse a beaver swimming across the water.

At the southeast part of the refuge, scan the tall trees along the water for bald eagles, which winter here in good numbers to feed on sick waterfowl.

Wildlife watching doesn't end when the waterfowl and eagles head north in spring. Holla Bend's list of nesting birds includes such notable species as wild turkey, greater roadrunner, Kentucky warbler, and painted bunting. From late March into the spring, white-tailed does give birth to fawns. Sliders, red-eared turtles, and their kin congregate on logs in warm weather.

You can see a lot from **refuge roads,** but you'll enjoy a visit more if you walk some of the **trails.** One follows a levee near the Arkansas River, passing through thick stands of eastern red cedar providing good winter shelter for birds. Another loops through lush forests in the southwest portion. Watch for fox squirrels in the trees here, and listen for the boisterous song of a Carolina wren. No matter when you explore Holla Bend, you'll find something to make the trip worthwhile.

■ **7,057 acres** ■ **West-central Arkansas, 8 miles southeast of Russellville**
■ **Best seasons year round** ■ **Fishing, bird-watching, wildlife viewing**
■ **Contact the refuge, 10448 Holla Bend Rd., Dardanelle, AR 72834; 479-229-4300. http://southeast.fws.gov/HollaBend/**

Armadillos

The nine-banded armadillo once was rare in Arkansas. It began creeping eastward from the arid Southwest in the latter decades of the 20th century. It is now a regular resident of Holla Bend National Wildlife Refuge.

The "little armored one" has very poor eyesight and can often be observed at close range if you approach quietly from downwind.

Armadillos' long claws make them excellent diggers, and spots where they have torn into the soil to search for beetles and other food are abundant in woods and fields. The bony plates that cover their bodies make them look reptilian, but armadillos are mammals that give birth in spring, almost always to four genetically identical quadruplets.

The species has been used in medical research because it's the only animal in addition to man that can contract Hansen's disease, or leprosy.

Mount Magazine State Park

75 miles northwest of Hot Springs

Although 2,753-foot-high **Mount Magazine** is the highest point in Arkansas, don't expect long-distance vistas. Dense forest dominated by oaks, hickories, and shortleaf pine surrounds you all along the gentle grade, making this more of a nature walk than a mountaineering trek.

This flat-topped highland occupies an exceptional place in regional natural history. Scientists are studying several rare or unusual plants and animals found here, such as the tiny invertebrates that live in mountaintop springs and the inconspicuous small-headed pipewort plant that's only a few inches tall.

Once you've driven the winding highway to the mountaintop, you can follow a 2.5-mile **loop drive** to several lookout points, including the site of an old lodge on the south side and a line of tall sandstone bluffs on the north near Cameron Bluff Campground. From either of these spots, the **Signal Hill Trail** winds less than a half mile to Magazine's summit.

In spring and summer, listen for the raspy songs of male scarlet tanagers, gorgeous in deep red and black, and the *teacher-teacher* of

Ozark Wildflowers

For pure showiness, the best wildflower displays always are found on prairies and other open areas, where blooming plants enjoy abundant sunlight and have little competition from trees and shrubs. But an early-spring hike in the Ozark Mountains, when the mornings are still chilly and new leaves have barely begun to appear, can lead to some of the region's most striking wildflowers, unfolding their petals on rocky slopes and in the rich soil near streams. In contrast to the flamboyant display of many prairie plants, forest flowers tend to be smaller and more subdued, but in no way less beautiful.

In February and early March, look for white and yellow trout lilies, bloodroot, toothwort, and the aptly named harbinger of spring. Soon, these species are joined by rue anemone, Dutchman's breeches, bluebells, jack-in-the-pulpit, coral root orchid, and the delicate round-lobed hepatica. By April, trilliums, crested iris, wild ginger, columbine, golden seal, and shooting star make an Ozarks woodland hike a truly colorful experience.

ovenbirds, ground-nesting warblers. Wild hyacinth, crested iris, trilliums, violets, cardinal flower, blue phlox, purple coneflower, coreopsis, black-eyed Susan, and tall ironweed are just a few of the wildflowers that blossom from spring into fall, augmented early in the year by blooming trees such as redbud, serviceberry, dogwood, and wild plum.

Flowers, along with patchwork habitats of woodland, glades, old fields, and roadsides, make Mount Magazine a magnet for butterflies. More than 90 species have been observed here, ranging from common kinds such as pipevine swallowtail, orange sulphur, pearl crescent, and red-spotted purple to uncommon finds such as southern dogface, banded hairstreak, and mottled duskywing. Magazine's most famous winged inhabitant is the spectacular Diana fritillary.

You can see butterflies anywhere in the park, from deep woods to fields, but you'll observe them most easily on sunny days at patches of wildflowers where they pause in their near-constant flight to feed.

At the **Brown Springs picnic area** on the north side of the mountain, look for the maple-leaved oak, a tree found nowhere else in the world; the leaves resemble those of maples more than oaks. On the slopes below grow two notable ferns. Hay-scented fern, a common species of the Northeast, is very rare this far south, and mountain woodsia, which is not found anywhere else between the Appalachians and the Rockies.

Several of the park's loop trails run from the Benefield picnic area, just north of the southern park entrance. More adventurous hikers, especially those who can arrange a vehicle shuttle, may want to walk the 9.3 miles from Cameron Bluff down to the Ozark National Forest's **Cove Lake recreation area,** where there's camping, picnicking, and swimming.

Rock climbing and rappelling are popular sports on Magazine bluffs, but participants must check at the park visitor center; some areas are closed to protect rare species.

■ **2,200 acres** ■ **West-central Arkansas, 17 miles south of Paris on Ark. 309** ■ **Best seasons spring and fall** ■ **Camping, hiking, rock-climbing, bird-watching, wildlife viewing** ■ **Contact the park, 16878 Hwy. 309 South, Paris, AR 72855; 479-963-8502. www.arkansasstateparks.com**

Ozark National Forest

80 miles north of Hot Springs

You'll find some of the remotest and most rugged country in America's midsection within the Ozark National Forest, which encompasses more than a million acres of densely wooded terrain in northwestern Arkansas. The forest takes its name from the Ozark Plateau, an uplifted ancient sea bed deeply eroded over millions of years by the relentless action of rain and rivers. Tall limestone and sandstone bluffs line its narrow valleys, and countless mountain streams splash down rocky ravines to form perfect swimming holes.

Hikers, mountain bikers, and horseback riders can explore a total of more than 300 miles of trails on the forest (though some reserved for foot travel only). Included in that figure are the 185 miles of the Ozark Highlands Trail, one of the country's finest long-distance trails.

When the late-winter rains begin, canoeists and kayakers pack up and head for Ozark float streams such as the Mulberry River and Big Piney Creek. In the autumn, woods dominated by oaks, hickories, and maples blaze into endless swaths of red, orange, and yellow.

Considering the range of possible adventures, the sheer acreage in which to experience them, and the relative ease of access, few places in the south-central states have as much to offer as Ozark National Forest.

Scores of developed camping and picnic sites are scattered throughout the forest, which comprises several sections from the Oklahoma state line east to the White River near Mountain View and south to Mount Magazine *(see pp. 216–17).*

For any kind of exploration off the beaten path, you'll need to get a map at the forest's headquarters in Russellville, or in any of the ranger district offices. With it you can find designated recreation areas, as well as enjoy one of the national forest's less structured pleasures: simply driving its gravel or dirt back roads and discovering your own scenic spots. Miles of these routes cover the forest, but it's easy to get confused by their turns and intersections without the detailed map.

If you're visiting any time from fall through spring, ask about current hunting seasons. You may want to avoid hiking away from developed areas during the fall deer season and the spring turkey season.

White Rock Mountain & Vicinity

The **Ozark Highlands Trail** traverses the national forest for 185 miles, from Dockery's Gap in the west, past the **Buffalo National River** (*see pp. 220–23*), to Matney Knob in the east. Along with the **Ouachita National Recreation Trail** (*see pp. 211–12*), Ozark Highlands is one of the state's major long-distance hiking trails. Highlands is accessible from recreation areas and forest roads for out-and-back day hikes or, with a shuttle, backpacking trips of days or weeks.

One access point on the trail also happens to be the most famous panoramic viewpoint in the Ozarks. Thousands of "sunset in the Ozarks" photos have been snapped from White Rock, depicting forests ridges one after the other all the way to the horizon.

To get there from I-40 at Mulberry, take Ark. 215 north 14 miles to **Shores Lake Recreation Area** (a pretty mountain lake with a campground and swimming area). Continue north on FR 1505 and FR 1003 for 7 miles uphill to the **White Rock Mountain Recreation Area,** a wonderful destination for a picnic or camping trip. Civilian Conservation Corps-era cabins and a lodge are available for rent here *(479-369-4128)* adjacent to the national forest campground.

Whether you're here for an afternoon or a weekend, take time to walk the 2-mile **loop trail** that circles the bluffs atop this 2,260-foot peak. (Be careful near the very steep drops along the way.) The rock shelters beside the path offer spots to rest and enjoy the views, which can stretch 40 miles or more in all directions.

White Rock got its name from the lichens that encrust its sandstone bluffs, giving the mountain a pale appearance from a distance. For a closer look at the bluffs, and at the pine-oak-hickory forest that surrounds the mountain, you can hike either of two trails that follow creeks downhill to Shores Lake, or

Hiking in Ozark National Forest

combine them for a loop hike of 13 miles. But before you try this as a day hike, bear in mind that the route loses and gains 1,700 feet in elevation.

Rugged sections of the highlands trail are easy to find: Just locate a trailhead on the forest map and head out in any direction.

For a short hike, drive to Cass on Ark. 23, also called the **Pig Trail Scenic Byway,** and turn west on FR 1520. In 1.2 miles, the highlands trail crosses the road. Hike west from here and cross Fane Creek, which may require some wading. Vernal witch hazel grows along the pretty stream, blooming as early as February, and white trout lilies grow on the nearby hillside.

The trail heads uphill, steeply at times, almost 2 miles before it reaches an abandoned railroad bed. This narrow-gauge line was used for logging from 1915 to 1926, and the old right-of-way—now being reclaimed by the forest—provides flat walking for the next 2 miles or so. Tall white, northern red, and black oaks form a canopy over the path, lined in many places with picturesque sandstone ledges. Cucumber magnolias grow beside the trail in spots, and wild turkeys and pileated woodpeckers are common. You may see the remains of rail equipment, relics of a time when virgin timber still stood in these wild highlands.

■ **1.2 million acres** ■ **Northwestern Arkansas, south of Harrison** ■ **Best seasons fall and summer (use caution during fall and spring hunting seasons** ■ **Camping, hiking, canoeing, fishing, mountain biking, horseback riding** ■ **Contact the national forest, 605 W. Main, Russellville, AR 72801; 479-968-2354. www.fs.fed.us/oonf/ozark/index.html**

Buffalo National River

120 miles north of Hot Springs

In the rugged hollows of the Boston Mountains, spring rains feed tiny rivulets that bounce over rocks and ledges on their meandering paths downstream. Near the communities of Fallsville and Red Star, several of these intermittent creeks join and join again to become a substantial stream, rushing along under a dense canopy of oaks and hickories. This young brook flows for a few miles through an Ozark National Forest wilderness area, but soon passes into the administration of the National Park Service and takes on a new status as the Buffalo National River: one of the wildest, most beautiful, and most rewarding natural areas you can explore in mid-America.

If the dams proposed for the Buffalo in the 1940s and 1950s had been built, those little streams would have flowed into a deep, sprawling, relatively sterile reservoir, just like the ones that have drowned so many other Arkansas rivers. Only years of unrelenting struggle by regional conservationists, involving hostile confrontations and seemingly endless legal battles, saved the Buffalo as a free-flowing stream. In March 1972, the Buffalo was officially designated as America's first national river, protected for 135 miles to its confluence with the White River.

Even a brief encounter with the Buffalo is enough to show why so many people dedicated themselves to preserving its wildness. Smallmouth and Ozark bass, bluegills, sunfish, and a notable array of other species flit through the clear water. Countless spots along the river make perfect summer swimming holes. Limestone and sandstone bluffs rise more than 400 feet straight from the river. Black bears, minks, bobcats, and beavers live in the countryside, along with over 200 species of birds and more than 1,500 species of plants. Small tributaries and creeks run peacefully through hollows seldom traveled and seemingly unchanged for centuries.

These attributes were among those that led to a congressional report calling the river "worthy of national recognition" during the debate over its protection. Today's visitors, probably unaware of how close America came to losing the Buffalo, are happy to call it their own Ozarks playground, whether they've come to paddle, swim, fish, hike, or simply to find a rock and sit down to admire the views.

The main visitor center for Buffalo National River is located at Tyler Bend, off US 65 about 11 miles north of Marshall. Ranger stations are located at Pruitt, on Ark. 7, 13 miles south of Harrison, and Buffalo Point, off Ark. 14, 17 miles south of Yellville. Check in at one of these offices and speak to a ranger about current conditions, especially if you're planning to canoe or go for a lengthy hike. Unlike most national parks, the Buffalo National River allows hunting, so at certain times of the year hikers need to use caution.

A free visitor's guide offers useful information about park facilities and safety; you can also pick up maps and trail guides.

Ghost Town

The discovery of zinc in the Buffalo River country set off a mining boom in the late 19th century and created a new town called, appropriately enough, Rush. The community may have had a population of 2,000 at its peak during World War I, but it slowly declined and faded away completely by the 1960s.

Located off Ark. 14 a few miles north of Buffalo Point, Rush is now an important historic site, where a short interpretive trail passes several abandoned buildings and the remains of an ore processing site, including an 1886 smelter. It's important to obey trail signs here: Old mine shafts and decaying buildings can be dangerous.

Thirteen campgrounds are spaced along almost the entire length of the river, and at Buffalo Point you can stay in historic cabins the Civilian Conservation Corps built in the 1930s.

The national river encompasses three official wilderness areas: the **Upper Buffalo** above Boxley Valley; the **Ponca,** on the river's most popular canoeing segment; and the **Lower Buffalo,** a remote area located where the Buffalo flows into the White River.

Canoeing

For many people, "floating the Buffalo" is the most exciting and satisfying experience in the Ozarks. While the white water isn't daunting to experts—the top rapids are usually only Class II—superb scenery and wilderness qualities make the Buffalo a memorable destination. There's something here for all abilities, too: thrilling rapids on the famed **Ponca-to-Pruitt** stretch of the upper river for the serious adventure-seeker, and gentle ripples between quiet pools on the lower river, perfect for beginners. Rangers or canoe concessionaires *(see a list of approved rental companies in the free visitor's guide, available at the campgrounds)* can point you to an appropriate stretch of river—be honest with them about your canoeing experience; this is one area where you literally don't want to get in over your head. The upper Buffalo's rapids can be managed by skilled floaters, but there are plenty of opportunities for beginners to find trouble at spots such as the Wrecking Rock, below Ponca, and Gray Rock, just above Kyles Landing.

The Upper Buffalo is usually floatable only from winter (when canoeists must take serious precautions against hypothermia) through spring. In April and May, the Ponca-to-Pruitt section can get crowded; try to visit on a weekday. As summer arrives, rains slacken, and floaters then find adequate flows only on the middle and lower sections.

Outfitters provide canoes, life jackets, and paddles, and can arrange shuttles between all river access points. For overnight trips, camping on a gravel bar is a traditional part of the Buffalo River experience. Be aware, though, that a nighttime rain can cause the river to rise quickly. Choose a high spot and be aware of the water levels.

Hiking

The National Park Service maintains more than 100 miles of trails that range from short day hikes to long, strenuous routes. The only marked and maintained trails in the three wilderness areas are those leading to **Hemmed-In Hollow** in the Ponca Wilderness Area. Experienced hikers with topographical maps can find their own routes using abandoned roads and old logging trails.

For an exemplary Buffalo River experience, hike part of the 37-mile **Buffalo River Trail** that follows the river from **Boxley Valley,** an immensely picturesque area of family farms and pastures, all the way to the Pruitt recreation area on Ark. 7. The trail gets challenging between Ponca and the Erbie Campground, often climbing bluffs where the reward is great views of the river. Multiple trailheads make short hikes possible.

All hikes in the Buffalo River forest pass through beautiful woodland dominated by oaks, hickories, and maples, with sweetgums, beeches, dogwoods, shortleaf pines, and many other trees interspersed; sycamores, willows, and river birches line the river itself. In spring and summer watch for an array of wildflowers, from violets to sunflowers.

■ 94,294 acres, including 135 river miles ■ North-central Arkansas, between Ponca and the White River ■ Canoeing is best from March to July, and hiking is best from fall through spring ■ Hunting is allowed in many areas; check with rangers for safety precautions ■ Camping, hiking, canoeing, fishing ■ Contact the national river, 402 N. Walnut St., Suite 136, Harrison, AR 72601; 870-741-5443. www.nps.gov/buff

Blanchard Springs Caverns

125 miles northeast of Hot Springs

Ancient oceans laid down the sediments that became the Ozark Mountains more than 300 million years ago. Over the past few million years, since the mountains took on their present configuration, water flowing through subterranean cracks in the limestone has created long passages through the rock. Underground rivers still fill some of these hollows, but at Blanchard Springs Caverns, the water level has dropped over time, leaving a series of rooms accessible to visitors.

The stream that carved the caverns continues to flow, pouring from a hillside near the entrance to join with North Sylamore Creek a short distance away. Visitors ride an elevator 216 feet down, using an artificial entrance that doesn't interfere with air flow through the cave's natural openings; they then pass through an air lock that maintains high humidity that is so vital to cave creatures and the continuing growth of the formations.

Most first-time visitors take the half-mile **Dripstone Trail,** open year-round. Fairly easy and accessible to those in wheelchairs with a strong assistant, this tour passes through the higher, older part of the cave, where stalactites, stalagmites, columns, "draperies," and other formations have had more time to grow. These speleothems (the geologic term for all cave formations) develop as slightly acidic water trickles down through overlying limestone, dissolving the calcium carbonate, or calcite, that is its major component. When water reaches the cave, it leaves a fine deposit of minerals that, over thousands of years, produces the shapes that decorate cave ceilings, floors, and walls.

Consider the slow rate at which speleothems are formed, and then imagine the creation of the 65-foot-high **Giant Column** that you pass on the Dripstone Trail. While this massive formation is among the cave's most impressive, many smaller features are equally enthralling. Tiny "soda straws" (young stalactites) and delicate rimstone terraces (formed in quiet pools of water) highlight the Dripstone tour, as does the "cave popcorn" along walls.

From Memorial Day to Labor Day, guides lead tours along the caverns' **Discovery Trail,** a 1.2-mile path that is significantly more strenuous than Dripstone. Descending deeper into a "younger" part of the cave, the Discovery route in part follows the underground stream that shaped Blanchard Springs Caverns. Though you'll see fewer formations here, other features make this trail a fascinating alternative. Visitors pass a campsite early cave explorers used and see the natural opening through which they entered, using ropes and harnesses. Near the tour's end, the **Giant Flowstone** rates with the most wondrous of the cave's formations, a smoothly rounded mini-cliff in shades of white and brown.

Chances are higher along the Discovery Trail of spotting some of the animals that live in the cave, such as bats, crickets, salamanders, crayfish, spiders, and beetles. If you miss them, check out the **"Life in the Dark"** exhibit hall near the visitor center, where you'll learn how these creatures have adapted to their surroundings.

■ **1.9 miles of trails** ■ **North-central Arkansas, 11 miles north of Mountain View off Ark. 14** ■ **Year-round. Discovery Trail open Memorial Day to Labor Day. Cave temperature remains a constant 58°F; a sweater or light jacket is recommended** ■ **Caves viewing, nearby camping, hiking, swimming** ■ **Contact for caverns, Ozark-St. Francis National Forests, 650 W. Main, Russellville, AR 72560; 479-968-2354. www.fs.fed.us/oonf/ozark/recreation/caverns.html**

Blanchard Springs Caverns

Crater of Diamonds State Park

50 miles southwest of Hot Springs

It can be said with absolute finality that there's no place in the world like this small park in Arkansas's Gulf coastal plain. That's not because diamonds are found here; these precious bits of compressed carbon are mined at many sites around the globe. Rather, it's because at this spot, anybody who pays a small admission fee can sit in the middle of a diamond-bearing volcanic field, search for gems, and keep any found.

Perhaps 100 million years ago, an eruption brought ash and magma from deep within the Earth to the surface here, covering an area of about 80 acres with volcanic breccia and tuff (compacted ash and other volcanic fragments). Carried with this material came diamonds, scattered randomly throughout the vast amount of uplifted rock. After the first few were discovered in 1906, several commercial operations tried and failed to turn a profit from the deposit. In 1972, the state of Arkansas bought the site and created a park.

Mining for diamonds

More than 24,000 diamonds have been found at the park since it was established. Although most are small gems whose principal value is as souvenirs of a visit, many searchers dream of finding another like the "Uncle Sam," unearthed in 1924. At 40.23 carats, it remains the largest diamond ever found in North America.

All sorts of people grub around in the park's main 37-acre field. In 1998, a woman looking over the surface on her first day in the park found a 7.28-carat diamond. In 2000, a 5.57-carat stone was found by a local man who scoured the field six days a week. Diggers also have found jasper, agate, quartz, and amethyst.

■ 911 acres ■ Southwestern Arkansas, 2 miles southeast of Murfreesboro on Ark. 301 ■ Year-round ■ Adm. fee ■ Camping, hiking, gem-hunting ■ Contact the park, 209 State Park Rd., Murfreesboro, AR 71958; 870-285-3113. www.craterofdiamondsstatepark.com

Beavers Bend State Park

100 miles southwest of Hot Springs

Tucked into the southeast corner of Oklahoma, Beavers Bend State Park's beautiful setting on a clear, rocky stream in the rugged Ouachita Mountains would be enough to make it one of the state's most popular getaway spots. Add several miles of fine hiking trails and some of the region's best trout fishing and you have an excellent year-round destination.

Lots of visitors head for the **Mountain Fork River** to swim or canoe on mostly flat water; concessionaires rent canoes and other watercraft. Anglers travel long distances to fish for stocked rainbow and brown trout, which can grow to extraordinary size. Trout are released in the stream year-round; check with the park office for limits and regulations.

Near the river, the park's **nature center** is home to a variety of live animals, including snakes and injured birds of prey that are either being rehabilitated or are too hurt to be released. The hawks and owls are fed at designated times, and visitors can take advantage of photo opportunities with the birds, as well. In winter, park staffers lead special field trips to see the bald eagles that winter along the Mountain Fork.

More than 12 miles of hiking trails wind through the park, varying in difficulty from fairly easy to quite challenging. The nature of the terrain means that there's very little truly flat land. The 1-mile **Dogwood Nature Trail** has no steep climbs, and for part of its loop stays near the river. The **Pine Ridge Nature Trail** is also is easy. **Cedar Bluff Nature Trail** includes a few climbs. Some of the other routes, including the **Deer Crossing Trail,** offer a more strenuous challenge.

Pines dominate many of the Ouachita Mountain slopes, with varied oaks, hickories, and other hardwoods intermingled. The **Forest Heritage Trail,** a 1.1-mile loop, identifies many of the trees you'll find throughout the park. It begins at the park's **Forest Heritage Center,** where exhibits interpret the human relationship with woodlands from the perspective of the timber industry.

■ **3,482 acres** ■ **Southeastern Oklahoma, 7 miles north of Broken Bow on US 259A** ■ **Year-round** ■ **Camping, hiking, boating, fishing; golfing** ■ **Contact the park, P.O. Box 10, Broken Bow, OK 74728; 580-494-6300 or 800-435-5514. http://touroklahoma.com/pages/resort1.html**

Isle Royale

O ut of the vastness of Lake Superior rises an island known more for its immigrant wolves and moose than for its splendors as a park. But the people who discover Isle Royale treat this isolated realm like no other park: visitors typically stay here three days, while the average visit to a national park is about 4 hours.

Most people get to the 45-mile-long island aboard a commercial or National Park Service boat. As soon as they touch land in this wilderness park, they are on their own. They must pack what they need and carry out their refuse.

This is rough, untamed country. Waterways may be fogbound and trails muddy. Blackflies and mosquitoes may descend upon hikers in swarms. And, because campsites cannot be reserved, a backpacker is never certain where the day's trek may end. Fewer people visit Isle Royale in a year than Yellowstone sees in a day.

Everyone who lands on Isle Royale—even day-trippers—must stop near dockside to hear a ranger talk about low-impact hiking and camping. Such information is good for campers as well as for the park. For example, water must be boiled for 2 minutes or filtered, because chemical purifiers will not wipe out tapeworm cysts.

Humans share trails with wolves and moose, the island's most famous inhabitants. They are descendants of moose from the mainland that presumably swam to Isle Royale in the early 1900s and wolves that walked across the frozen lake between 1945 and 1950. Scientists have been studying the interplay of predator and prey since 1958 *(see sidebar p. 233)*.

On the trails, all you can expect to see are the animals' tracks and droppings, although quietly grazing moose do surprise hikers, particularly in swamps or dense forest. On beaver ponds you may spot ripples on the surface, made by the ponds' creators. At

- Northern Michigan
- 571,790 acres
- Established 1940
- Best seasons mid-April–October; transportation services available mid-June–Labor Day
- Hiking, wildlife viewing, lake cruises, camping, kayaking, swimming, stargazing
- Information: 906-482-0984 www.nps.gov/isro

Shoreline, Isle Royale National Park

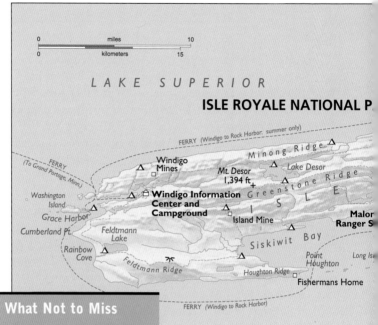

LAKE SUPERIOR

ISLE ROYALE NATIONAL P

FERRY (Windigo to Rock Harbor, summer only)

Minong Ridge

FERRY (To Grand Portage, Minn.)

Windigo Mines

Mt. Desor 1,394 ft.

Lake Desor

Greenstone Ridge

Washington Island

Windigo Information Center and Campground

I S L E

Grace Harbor

Island Mine

Malor Ranger S

Cumberland Pt.

Feldtmann Lake

Siskiwit Bay

Rainbow Cove

Feldtmann Ridge

Houghton Ridge

Point Houghton

Long Isl

Fishermans Home

FERRY (Windigo to Rock Harbor)

What Not to Miss

- Taking a scuba diving trip to the wreck sites around the island

- Staying overnight in the Rock Harbor Lodge, the only non-camping accommodation

- Boarding the shuttle boat to Raspberry Island for good picnic spots

- Hiking the Windingo Nature Trail to learn about the island's geology

- Renting a canoe or kayak to explore the shoreline

campsites watch for fox looking for a handout. Remember that feeding the animals is illegal. It is not healthy for them and increases the likelihood that they will scavenge for people's food and equipment.

How to Get There

Make reservations well in advance for passenger boats from Houghton or Copper Harbor, Mich., or Grand Portage, Minn. The port you pick determines the length of your visit.

The National Park Service's *Ranger III* offers interpretive programs during the 6-hour trip between Houghton and Isle Royale; the 165-foot-long boat is the largest piece of moving equipment the park service operates and owns.

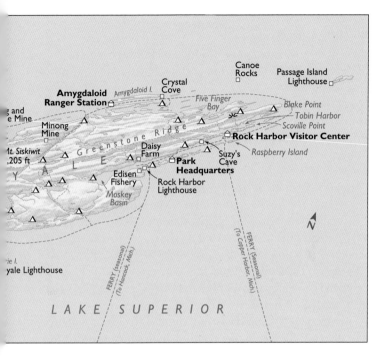

For information about boats and charter seaplane service, see **Information & Activities,** pp. 238–39.

Isle Royale is located 56 miles from Michigan's Upper Peninsula, 18 miles from Minnesota's shore, and 22 miles from Grand Portage, Minn. Airports: Houghton, Mich., and Duluth, Minn.

When to Go
Late June to September; the park closes from November to mid-April. Mosquitoes, black-flies, and gnats are most pesky in June and July. Summer can be cool (40°F at night). Blue-berries and thimbleberries ripen in late July and August.

How to Visit
Although day visits are feasible, you need a longer stay to appreciate Isle Royale. A day visitor must sandwich a couple of hours of sightseeing between boat arrival and departure. Trips take 3 to 6 hours, depending on the starting point. The best way to see the park is to backpack to campsites strung along the park's 165 miles of trails. Non-campers can reserve lodgings at Rock Harbor and explore on tour boats and on foot.

EXPLORING THE PARK

Windigo: **A full day**

Take the *Wenonah,* a passenger boat that makes the trip from Grand Portage, Minnesota, in 3 hours, the shortest from any port serving Isle Royale.

On the way into fjord-like **Washington Harbor,** watch for the buoy marking the resting place of the *America,* a 183-foot lake steamer that went down June 7, 1928, after hitting a shoal. All the passengers and crew survived. Now, the wreck rests at a sharp angle, its ghostly bow about 2 feet below the surface.

The *America* is one of ten shipwrecks that rest in the chilly waters around Isle Royale National Park. The remains of the steel-hull passenger ship became a favorite spot for divers. However, the constant diving began taking its toll on the fragile wreck late in the last century. This prompted the Great Lakes Shipwreck Preservation Society to tackle the unusual task of saving a boat that was underwater. The unique project began in 1996, and members continue to work on it today.

As soon as you land on the island, check at the ranger station for the the next **Windigo Nature Walk,** a 1-hour ramble around this western entrance to the park that explores many of the area's natural and cultural resources.

If you miss the ranger-guided walk, try the **Windigo Nature Trail,** a 1.25-mile loop that shows the power that Lake Superior exerts on an island molded by fire and ice.

As glacial ice retreated some 10,000 years ago, Isle Royale rose above what would become Lake Superior. Gouges in the barren rocks became lakes. Early migrants—lichens, mosses, birdborne seeds—drifted into cracks and crannies, beginning the long work of building soil. Animals also found their way onto Isle Royale, and an ecosystem emerged.

It continues to evolves, with some animals appearing, such as the wolves and moose, and some animals disappearing, as did caribou and coyotes. Be sure to take the short side trip to the fenced-in **Moose Exclosure,** which shows how differently a forest grows when moose don't munch on it.

Your stay—about 2.5 hours—will depend on your boat's schedule. So you may have time to stroll westward a while along the **Feldtmann Lake Trail.** This shoreline stretch gives you a view of **Beaver Island** and the harbor's forested northern shore.

Superior Symbiosis

Insulated from civilization's effects, Isle Royale serves as an ideal living laboratory of how plants and animals interrelate in nature's cycles. The United Nations designated Isle Royale an International Biosphere Reserve in 1980.

Cow moose and calf

The world's longest running wildlife research project involves Isle Royale's moose and wolf populations. Since 1958, biologists have been monitoring their numbers, tracking them by plane during the winter months when they are easier to see. Many of the wolves have been fitted with radio collars.

When moose first swam to the island in the early 1900s, they found an ample food supply in the vegetation and no natural predators. By the 1920s, there were between 1,000 and 3,000 on Royale.

But the moose ravaged their food source, and their numbers dropped. A fire in the 1930s spurred a lush growth of vegetation, which in turn boosted the moose population again.

This cycle might have continued in perpetuity had it not been for the arrival of the eastern timber wolf. During the frigid winter of 1948–49, an ice bridge formed on Lake Superior between Ontario and Isle Royale, allowing a small pack of wolves to cross to the island. The terrain suited them, as did the bountiful food source: moose. In response, the wolf population began burgeoning.

Thus began an age-old interdependent cycle. With a large moose herd, wolves prevent overpopulation by culling the sick, the old, and the young.

A smaller, stronger herd, by contrast, means difficult hunting for the wolves, curtailing their breeding rate. The wolf population peaked at about 50 animals in 1970, but the number had dropped to 14 by 1998.

Meanwhile the moose herd has grown to about 900 from 850 animals; in a dance as old as time, the wolf numbers may follow suit.

Tobin Harbor, Isle Royale National Park

Rock Harbor: **1 or more days**

A 1-day visit to Rock Harbor, the park's eastern gateway, can be tight. The voyage aboard *Isle Royale Queen III* from Copper Harbor, Mich., takes about 4.5 hours, leaving you with about 2.5 hours to explore the Rock Harbor area.

If you can stay longer and aren't a backpacker, Rock Harbor offers many relatively easy sojourns. Make reservations at the Rock Harbor Lodge, with views of the lake and the only restaurant on the island. (The lodge also offers guided fishing and

sightseeing tours, as well as boat rentals.)

Begin with a walk along **Stoll Trail,** a 4-mile loop that starts at the lodge and winds through forest and plank-pathed bog. After about half a mile, you'll come to an area where Native Americans once chipped away, stone on stone, at shallow mining pits to extract outcrops of copper. Unmarked, these pits are hard to detect.

Mining here began around 2500 BC and continued for at least 1,500 years. The copper, traded along the upper Mississippi River Valley, was formed into fishhooks, knives, and awls. More than a thousand mining pits have been found on Isle Royale.

Rock Harbor Trail, Isle Royale National Park

Continue another 1.5 miles, mostly along a rocky shore, to craggy **Scoville Point,** a fine spot for viewing some of the 200 rocky islets that form the Isle Royale archipelago. On the way back you can switch to a branch trail that clings to the forested shore of **Tobin Harbor.** As the trail nears the lodge, you can see traces of **Smithwick Mine,** one of many relics of 19th-century mining ventures.

For a small fee, you can take a shuttle boat from Rock Harbor across half a mile of usually calm water to **Raspberry Island,** where a mile-long trail introduces you to a boreal forest of white spruce, balsam fir, paper birch, and aspen, as well as a bog. You'll also see a pit would-be miners dug in a vain search for copper. This provides a nice backdrop for a picnic.

Also for a fee, you can take another boat on a half-day, guided tour around the island. The first stop is **Edisen Fishery** that belonged to the late Pete Edisen, one of the last commercial fishermen on Isle Royale. The Park Service has restored his jumble of moss-chinked log cabins and shacks made of odds and ends. Here park employees demonstrate mid-20th-century fishing techniques for visitors; whatever gets caught winds up on the tables at Rock Harbor Lodge.

A short trail leads to the **Rock Harbor Lighthouse,** which contains a maritime exhibit. Erected in 1855 to guide ore ships, the lighthouse closed in 1859 when the mines shut down and re-opened between 1874 and 1879 during a second mining venture.

Into the Backcountry: 3 to 5 days

To savor Isle Royale's isolated grandeur, you must venture into the backwoods. Plan your stay around the boat schedules.

A sample 5-day itinerary starts at Rock Harbor on Monday aboard the *Isle Royale Queen III* and a hike southwest along the **Rock Harbor Trail** through forest, bog, and slanted rocks and roots. After almost 2 miles, look for a sign to **Suzy's Cave,** about 80 yards up a side trail. The cave is an unusual, water-carved arch.

At 3 miles, you reach Three Mile Campground. Stay here and head out next morning on the 4.5-mile shore trail to **Daisy Farm;** in this spot daisies have flourished where vegetables never could survive. You can camp here for 3 days and start back early Friday to meet the returning *Queen.* Or you can split the hike into 2 days by spending Thursday night back at Three Mile.

While you're at Daisy Farm, climb **Mount Ojibway Trail;** it is a moderate 1.75-mile ascent up the 1,136-foot mountain that has a lookout tower on the summit. Visitors can climb as far as the cabin, which houses a solar-powered, air-monitoring station. The Park Service runs a network of these stations to check on air quality in 65 national park areas.

From the tower, take the **Greenstone Ridge Trail** that runs about 40 miles along the backbone of the island. About 1.5 miles west of the tower, look for the wooden post marking the **Daisy Farm Trail,** which leads you back to the campground.

Royale Gems

Scour Isle Royale's beaches and you may discover the greenstone, a lustrous pebble about as big as a pea with a distinctive segmented turtle-shell pattern. More properly called chlorastrolite, it was formed in the gas cavities of lava flows.

Not to be confused with the greenish rock found on Greenstone Ridge and elsewhere on the island, chlorastrolite has been found on certain islands in the South Pacific also. In 1972, the governor of Michigan made the semiprecious stone the official state gem.

INFORMATION & ACTIVITIES

Headquarters
800 E. Lakeshore Dr.
Houghton, MI 49931
906-482-0984
www.nps.gov/isro

Visitor & Information Centers
Windigo Visitor Center at west end of island, **Rock Harbor Visitor Center** at east end. Both open daily all season. Phone park headquarters for information.

Seasons & Accessibility
Park open mid-April through October; it can be reached by boat or seaplane only. Full services available mid-June through August. Weather and rough waters may delay departures; allow extra time. Mainland headquarters open year-round.

Boat & Seaplane Information
Reservations required (one to two months in advance suggested). Write or call headquarters for boat schedule from Houghton to Rock Harbor. (The park service's boat, *Ranger III,* will transport boats less than 20 feet long between those points.) For boats from Copper Harbor to Rock Harbor, write to the Isle Royale Line, Box 24, Copper Harbor, MI 49918, call 906-289-4437, or visit www.isleroyale.com. For boats from Grand Portage, Minn., to Windigo and Rock Harbor, write to GPIR Transport Lines, 1507 N. First St., Superior, WI 54880, call 715-392-2100, or visit www.grand-isle-royale.com

Entrance fees
Fee is $4 per day.

Pets
Not allowed on boats or within park boundaries, which extend 4.5 miles into Lake Superior.

Facilities for Disabled
Park headquarters at Houghton, Rock Harbor Lodge, both visitor centers, and a campsite at Daisy Farm are wheelchair accessible. Boats to island require assistance.

Things to Do
Free naturalist-led nature walks and evening programs. Canoe tour; lighthouse, copper mine, and Edisen Fishery tours; and films. Also, boating *(motorized crafts permitted on Lake Superior only),* canoeing *(rentals at Windigo and Rock Harbor; permit required),* hiking, scuba diving, fishing *(license required for Lake Superior only),* boat cruises to the outer islands.

Special Advisories

Expect sudden squalls and rough waters on Lake Superior. Do not attempt to take boats less than 20 feet long across it. Have the park service transport small boats; see above. No public phone service in the park.

Camping

Thirty-six backcountry camping areas; 1-day to 5-day limit. Camping allowed from mid-April through October. First come, first served. No fees. Permit required; available at ranger stations. Seventeen of the areas permit group camping; contact park headquarters for information.

Hotels, Motels, & Inns

(Unless otherwise noted, rates for two people in a double room, high season.)

INSIDE THE PARK:
■ **Rock Harbor Lodge**
P.O. Box 605, Houghton, MI 49931. 906-337-4993. From October to April write c/o Mammoth Cave, KY 42259. 270-773-2191. 60 lodge rooms $203 with meals; 20 cabins with kitchenettes $130. Restaurant. Open mid-June to mid-September.

OUTSIDE THE PARK
In Copper Harbor, MI 49918:
■ **Bella Vista Motel**
P.O. Box 26. 906-289-4213. 22 units, 8 cabins. $42-$60. Open May through October.
■ **Keweenaw Mountain Lodge**
US 41. 906-289-4403. 42 units $85; Cottages $105. Restaurant. Open May to mid-October.
■ **Lake Fanny Hooe Resort & Campground** (off US 41) 505 Second St. 800-426-4451. 17 units $69-$89; 64 campsites $22-$32. Open mid-May to mid-October.

In Grand Portage, MN 55605:
■ **Grand Portage Lodge & Casino**
70 Casino Dr. 218-475-2401 or 800-543-1384. 85 units. $66.50-$76.50. Pool, restaurant.

In Houghton, MI 49931:
■ **Best Western-Franklin Square Inn** 820 Shelden Ave. 906-487-1700 or 888-487-1700. 103 units. $89-$189. AC, pool, restaurant.

Excursions from Isle Royale

Keweenaw Peninsula

60 miles south of Isle Royale

Rising off the back of Michigan's Upper Peninsula like a dorsal fin, the Keweenaw (pronounced KEY-wha-naw) Peninsula was the epicenter of the nation's copper mining industry in the mid-1800s. Today the Keweenaw's wealth is measured not in metals but in its mother lode of natural beauty.

One of the highest points of the uplifted Superior Basin, the Keweenaw contains the classic complement of Upper Peninsula landscapes: Birch, aspen, and pockets of sugar maple clinging to corrugated ridgelines, white pine forests stretching 80 feet or more to the sky, and clear rivers coursing toward Lake Superior. Miles of deserted beaches—some sand, some rocky cliff-tops—rim the peninsula.

Those interested primarily in relaxation on their visit to the peninsula will find it. Some pretty little tourist towns invite exploration, and nearly every paved road could be labeled a scenic drive. Even a casual walk or brief lakeside picnic lunch will leave you with fond memories of the area's beauty.

Many of the Keweenaw's loveliest spots, however, are hidden from view. The forests are filled with miles of trails that loop through groves of old-growth pines, passing unmarked waterfalls

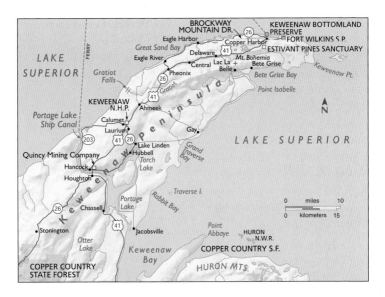

and fantastic stretches of otherwise inaccessible Lake Superior beaches. Few of the trails are marked, much less maintained, and some simply peter out in the middle of nowhere.

To get a true taste of this remote area, you need a sense of adventure and a good map, for you are entering territory almost as pristine as it was for the early copper miners. Today it remains a remarkable land of discovery.

Though the Keweenaw Peninsula actually begins 25 miles or so to the south, the twin towns of Houghton and Hancock represent the psychological gateway. They are located on the **Portage Lake Ship Canal,** which severs the peninsula from the mainland. This 21-mile canal largely follows an old Indian paddle-and-portage route that spared travelers a time-consuming 100-mile trip around the peninsula.

Just north of the twin towns on US 41, the skeleton of the Quincy Mine shaft house lurches skyward, dwarfing even the super-steep bluffs of Hancock. This ranked as one of the world's richest copper mines in the late 1800s, producing more than half a million tons of copper. The **Quincy Mining Company** *(201 Royce Rd., Hancock, MI. 906-482-3101. Adm. fee)* is a key site in **Keweenaw National Historical Park** *(see sidebar, p. 242)*. An excellent tour takes you through the world's largest steam hoist (used for hauling out miners and their equipment), down a steep bluff in a glass-enclosed tram, and then thousands of feet into the mine. Here you'll get a sense of what it was like to work in the damp, dark environment with only hand tools and candles.

Copper isn't the only notable mineral veining the Keweenaw. Its spine of Precambrian rock is one of the most geologically rich and fascinating regions in the world. The **A. E. Seaman Mineral Museum** *(5th Floor, Electrical Energy Resources Center, 1400 Towson Dr., Houghton. 906-487-2572. www.museum.mtu.edu),* on the campus of Michigan Technological University holds the premier collection of area minerals, including crystallized copper, silver, datolites, and agates.

Heading up the peninsula on US 41, you'll pass through **Calumet,** once the heart of Keweenaw copper mining. Much of the area, including the mine's industrial core and its once glamorous downtown, now belongs to the historical park. The sturdy buildings have held up well; many of them were made from red sandstone quarried in nearby Jacobsville.

Continuing up the road, turn northwest at the town of Ahmeek, cross the Gratiot River, and head for Superior's shore. Well-hidden hiking and mountain biking trails run along the river to beautiful **Upper** and **Lower Gratiot Falls.**

The road traces a sandy stretch of shoreline to the town of **Eagle River.** Along with **Eagle Harbor,** 7 miles up the road, it served as an important mining port. The towns' names reflect the area's healthy population of bald eagles, often seen riding lakeshore updrafts.

From Eagle River, continue along the lake on **Sand Dunes Drive** (Mich. 26), which ascends through a dune landscape above Great Sand Bay. Beach peas, sand cherries, and wild roses cling to windswept mounds of sand. Like beach grasses, the plants' spreading root systems help trap sand, stabilizing and enlarging the dunes.

The Keweenaw's fault line tilts precipitously in this part of the peninsula. To the south rises the exposed basalt face of the Cliff Range, while to the north the fault line drops away so quickly that Great Sand Bay reaches depths of more than 1,000 feet.

North of Eagle Harbor, the road forks into two distinctly different drives. Mich. 26 continues to parallel the shoreline, now rocky with bony fingers of reddish volcanic rock reaching into the lake.

Keweenaw National Historical Park

Not so much a place on a map as a place in time, Keweenaw National Historical Park was established in 1992 "to commemorate the heritage of copper mining on the Keweenaw Peninsula—its mines, its machinery and its people."

Rather than a park with simply defined boundaries, Keweenaw National Historical Park consists of cultural attractions throughout the peninsula. Two units anchor the park: the **Quincy Unit** at the Quincy Mine in Hancock, and the **Calumet Unit** in historic downtown Calumet.

Much of the park's 1,700 acres remain in private hands. The park has also designated "cooperating sites" throughout the peninsula, including various mine tours and museums with artifacts from the mining rush that began in the 1840s.

For information, contact the Keweenaw Tourism Council, 56638 Calumet Ave., Calumet, MI 49913; 800-338-7982. www.nps.gov/kewe

Eagle Harbor Light Station, Keweenaw Peninsula

Balsams grow gnarled and stunted like bonsai trees in this exposed and windswept environment. The coves here are littered with agates, banded rocks that formed as different minerals seeped into gas bubbles in cooling lava.

The other fork turns briefly inland, then up the steep backbone of Brockway Mountain. The 10-mile **Brockway Mountain Drive** rises 726 feet above Lake Superior, making it the highest paved road between the Rocky and Allegheny Mountains. A wide variety of plants thrive here, including Indian pipe and several kinds of orchid.

From **Brockway Mountain Lookout,** you'll get an outstanding view of Superior's rocky shoreline, the town of Copper Harbor, a handful of inland lakes, and the Keweenaw interior as it narrows to a point. Watch for hawks and other raptors soaring below you. The area is a spring migration route for red-tailed and sharp-shinned hawks, which effortlessly ride the thermals around the mountain before striking out across Lake Superior for points north.

One of Michigan's most appealing towns, **Copper Harbor** wedges between its namesake harbor and an inland lake named Fanny Hooe. When copper prospectors poured into the region in the mid-1800s, the federal government, fearing fights between the miners

The Lake Effect

The Great Lakes are big insulators. Slow to warm up and slow to cool down, they create a noticeable difference in the temperatures from the lakeshore and the interior. Five miles inland during warm weather, you may be perfectly comfortable in shorts and a T-shirt, but go to the beach, and you'd be shivering in a sweatshirt and pants. The reverse holds true in the winter, when the lakes moderate cold air.

These massive bodies of water also have a dramatic effect on snowfall. Traveling on prevailing western winds, dry winter air moves over the lakes, soaking up moisture. When it hits land, the air dumps its load of precipitation as snow. Surprisingly localized, these snowfalls often target a narrow band along a lake's leeward shore. Meteorologists refer to this phenomenon as "lake-effect snow." Jutting far out into Lake Superior, Keweenaw Peninsula often gets slammed by lake-effect snow. Whereas Detroit averages less than 40 inches of snow a year, the Upper Peninsula gets 160 inches. A giant snow gauge on US 41 near the town of Phoenix marks the area's record snowfall of 390.5 inches in the winter of 1977-78.

In the shade of pine forests, patches of snow may last beyond Memorial Day.

and local tribes, ordered the construction of a fort. Fortunately, it was never needed. Today the whitewashed structure is the highlight of **Fort Wilkins State Park** (906-289-4215; mid-May–mid-Oct.), which also includes pleasant walking trails and campgrounds along **Lake Fanny Hooe.**

The road may end at Copper Harbor, but the Keweenaw Peninsula continues another 10 miles or so. Here a 60-square-mile tract is veined with miles of trails that range from old logging and mining roads to single-track paths and deer trails. Mountain bikes and hiking boots offer the best means for exploring this area, owned by a paper company and open to the public.

■ 80-mile long peninsula ■ Northwest Upper Peninsula of Michigan
■ Excellent colors in fall ■ Hiking, camping, backpacking, skiing, wildlife viewing ■ Contact Keweenaw Peninsula Chamber of Commerce, 326 Shelden Ave. Houghton, MI 49931; 866-304-5722. www.keweenaw.org

Huron Mountains

100 miles southeast of Isle Royale Created by volcanoes and scoured by glaciers, the vast humpback of the Huron Mountains rears up from the north shore of Michigan's Upper Peninsula, covered with washboard peaks and valleys, virgin white pine forests, hundreds of lakes, dazzling waterfalls, and the headwaters of half a dozen rivers. Virtually devoid of roads, much less towns, the Huron Mountains instead harbor wildness: Wolves, moose, loons, and many other animals seek the solitude of these remote mountains.

Preservation did not occur by happenstance. Beginning around 1880, the Huron Mountains became the wilderness retreat of choice for several wealthy industrialists. While some such as Cyrus McCormick, head of the farm implement company that would become International Harvester, amassed their own wilderness holdings, dozens of others owned camps at the exclusive Huron Mountain Club. The powerful club members easily stopped construction of a road that was to link Marquette with L'Anse to the west: Co. Rd. 550 ends abruptly just west of Big Bay at a security gate.

Craig Lake State Park

For more than a century, the club has kept away miners, loggers, and developers. As a result, this 25,000-acre enclave boasts blue-ribbon trout streams, 80-foot white pines, carpets of orchids, miles of untouched Lake Superior beach, and waterfalls that appear on no map. Today, descendants of the original families still protect and preserve this spectacular land as a private club.

But not to worry; the Huron Mountains and plenty of other

near-pristine wilderness extend far beyond the club's boundaries. Though every local has an opinion about where the Huron Mountains begin and end, it's safe to say they fall within the fuzzy boundaries of Lake Superior to the north and US 41 to the south and west. That's a chunk of land roughly 30 miles wide by 25 miles long, with plenty of protected terrain.

County Road 550 links Marquette with the tiny town of Big Bay. This 30-mile paved route offers plenty of good jumping-off points into the Huron Mountains. Dozens of old logging roads and single-track trails spin off Co. Rd. 550 to the west; you'll find them perfect for mountain biking and visiting the falls of the **Little Garlic River,** halfway between Marquette and Big Bay.

From Big Bay, your best bets for venturing into the backcountry are Co. Rd. 510, which branches off Co. Rd. 550 southeast of town, and the Triple A Road, off Co. Rd. 510. Both are well maintained (but slow-going) dirt roads. Co. Rd. 510 leads to Yellow Dog River, a trout stream that splashes and tumbles over cliffs and through canyons from Yellow Dog Plains to Lake Independence.

On the south side of the mountains, **Craig Lake State Park** *(906-339-4461)* encompasses half a dozen gorgeous lakes. **Craig Lake** is the largest, a 374-acre lake studded with rocky islands and hemmed in by towering granite bluffs, thin ribbons of sand beach, and a wooded shoreline of aspen, hemlock, and pine.

Getting to the park involves a slow, bumpy trip down a 7-mile dirt road. The route tends to be confusing, so pick up a map at nearby **Van Riper State Park** before setting out.

Use a canoe or kayak here. After exploring Craig Lake and its islands, try the short, hilly portage at the north end of the lake to reach **Clair Lake,** or at the east side to reach **Crooked Lake.** Other good paddling lakes, **Teddy** and **Keewaydin,** have separate boat launches off the main road.

Craig Lake Trail is a well-marked, 7-mile path that crosses the Peshekee River, dips into ferny ravines, and offers lots of lake views through the pines.

■ **700 square miles** ■ **Michigan's Upper Peninsula, northwest of Marquette via Co. Rd. 550** ■ **Best seasons summer and fall** ■ **Camping, hiking, kayaking, canoeing, fishing, mountain biking, cross-country skiing, snowshoeing, wildlife viewing** ■ **Contact Marquette Country Visitors Bureau, 2552 US 41, Marquette, MI 49855; 800-544-4321. www.marquettecountry.org**

Sturgeon River Gorge Wilderness Area

100 miles
south of
Isle Royale

A web of free-flowing rivers stitches across the Upper Peninsula of Michigan, each with its own inviting picnic rock or casting spot, each a bit lovelier than the last. If you explore only one, make it the **Sturgeon River.**

This lovely body of water travels a circuitous route through one of three wilderness areas in **Ottawa National Forest,** cutting and tumbling through a 300-foot-high basalt gorge. From the eastern lip of the gorge, you get an eagle's-eye view of the river's frothing rapids and its dark, curlicue path squiggling off through the forest. **Sturgeon Falls Trail** leads half a mile or so from the gorge down to the river's edge, where it pours over a series of small cascades, then plummets over 22-foot-high **Sturgeon Falls.**

The gorge's isolation adds to its appeal. From Mich. 28 near Sidnaw, follow FR 2200 north to FR 2270. This wanders along the eastern boundary of the 14,000-acre wilderness that encompasses the Sturgeon and its tributaries. Several unmarked footpaths on the left side of the road eventually bring you to the river. (If you're not in the mood for that challenge, you can drive until you reach a small marked parking area.)

To experience the river as it manifests a completely different character, follow US 41 north to the **Sturgeon River Sloughs Wildlife Area** outside the national forest near Chassell, where the river bleeds through lowlands before emptying into Portage Lake. The 1.5-mile **De Vriendt Nature Trail** follows dikes and boardwalks back into the slough.

■ **14,159 acres** ■ **Michigan's Upper Peninsula, north of Mich. 28** ■ **Best seasons spring, summer, and fall** ■ **Camping, hiking, bird-watching** ■ **Contact Kenton District, Ottawa National Forest, Kenton, MI 49967; 906-852-3500. www.fs.fed.us/r9/ottawa/**

Sturgeon River Gorge

Porcupine Mountains Wilderness State Park

55 miles southwest of Isle Royale

The largest property in Michigan's excellent state park system is Porcupine Mountains Wilderness State Park. It preserves wild rivers, 23 miles of undeveloped Lake Superior shoreline, secluded lakes, and the largest tract of virgin timber between the Rocky Mountains and the Adirondacks.

The Ojibwa named the range, deciding this rumpled landscape of low mountains and tall pines had the silhouette of a porcupine.

Two roads lead to the park's east and west ends; both deposit you near the shores of Lake Superior. South Boundary Road connects these roads (as you might expect) along the park's southern edge. And that's about it; to see the rest of the park, you'll need hiking boots (with one exception).

Begin your visit at the east end at the visitor center. From here, a mile-long interpretive **nature trail** introduces you to the plants and animals commonly found in the park, looping through a mixed forest of hemlock, spruce, black ash, paper birch, white cedar, and sugar maple. The park's abundant wildlife includes bears, deer, coyotes, ruffed grouse, and bald eagles.

Near the visitor center, mile-long **Union Mine Trail** provides interpretive signs that chronicle the activities of the copper mining that was done here in the 1840s. You can still see shafts and other diggings along this delightful trail as it loops through the **Little Union Gorge,** where the Union River flows clear and cold

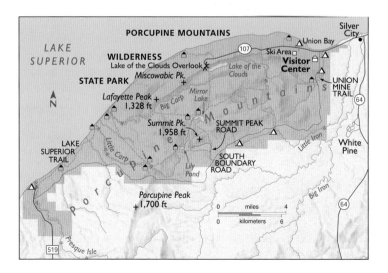

Copper Fever

When many Americans were hearing the siren call of mineral wealth from the western wilderness, copper miners were making their way to the Porkies. All they ever found were some low-grade flecks in the basalt. But they dug ten mines in search of something better, inspired by the story of a huge copper mass sitting along the Ontonagon River just east of the mountains. The 3,708-pound boulder was discovered by Alexander Henry in the 18th century and then rolled to the river mouth by entrepreneur Julius Eldred.

It was removed in 1843 and eventually ended up at the Smithsonian Institution in Washington, D.C. Luckily for the wilderness, another was never found.

from a spring two miles upstream.

The park's only interior road goes 7 miles west from the visitor center to the Porkies' marquee view, the **Lake of the Clouds Overlook.** Hundreds of feet below this 1,400-foot-high escarpment, the lake divides a thick patch of jade forest that extends for miles in three directions.

Some of the park's most rugged trails begin at the overlook. **Big Carp River Trail** climbs and dips for 9 miles over volcanic rock, lined with the wild roses and berries that manage to survive in the thin soil and parched southern exposure. The 4-mile **Escarpment Trail** skims several peaks as it follows the north shoreline of the lake from high above.

More than 25 miles of hiking trails at the east end of the park are groomed for cross-country skiers. Some lead to Lake Superior, where waves create dramatic ice sculptures along the shore. Rarely freezing over, Superior shines a deep cobalt blue beyond the shoreline ice pack. Downhill skiers may be surprised to find a state-run ski hill within the park, with trails spanning a north-facing flank. Sweeping views of Lake Superior rimmed by white shore and dark forest make a winter foray here well worth the cost of a lift ticket.

■ **63,000 acres** ■ **Michigan's Upper Peninsula, 25 miles west of Ontonagon via Mich. 64 and Mich. 107** ■ **Best seasons winter and summer** ■ **Camping, hiking, backpacking, skiing, snowshoeing** ■ **Contact park, 412 S Boundary Road, Ontonagon, MI 49953; 906-885-5275. www.porcupinemountains.com**

Black River Waterfalls

70 miles southwest of Isle Royale

The handsome Black River ends its run with a flourish, tumbling and crashing over seven falls in 6 miles before bursting into Lake Superior.

Five of the seven falls lie north of US 2 and the town of Bessemer, accessible from the **Black River Road National Scenic Byway** (Co. Rd. 513) that parallels the river on its west side. The maples that line the road and extend into the forest seem to glow electric crimson and yellow in autumn. The waterfalls, too, are brilliantly backdropped in fall, but they're at their most spectacular in spring, when snowmelt turns them into raging torrents.

The first, Chippewa Falls, is on private land and inaccessible. **Algonquin** is next. Lying off the **North Country National Scenic Trail** at the north end of Copper Peak Road, it can be difficult to find. The next five falls are more accessible, thanks to well-marked hiking trails, a few staircases, and observation decks.

Great Conglomerate Falls is named for the pebbly rock fragments found here that are cemented together by finer sand and other material, called conglomerate or "pudding stone." In a wild, noisy show, water roars over this textured rock and squeezes into a gorge. Half a mile downstream lies lovely **Potawatomi Falls,** its delicate fretwork of foam cascading over remnants of an ancient lava flow. Continue downstream for 200 yards from Potawatomi to **Gorge Falls,** where the river narrows to 29 feet from 130 feet, churning the water into a torrent as it charges through the gorge.

The geology changes at **Sandstone Falls,** where the powerful erosive forces of the Black River are slowly sculpting the softer rock of the river bed. Here sparkling water spills through bowls and potholes, while white pines lean out over the golden sandstone banks.

The final and largest cataract in the group is **Rainbow Falls.** This cascade plummets 40 feet, its rebounding spray sometimes revealing its luminous namesake rainbow. You can get the best view from the east bank of the river. To reach it, cross the suspended footbridge near the mouth, but pause long enough to enjoy the sight of Lake Superior from this unique mid-river vantage point.

■ **6-mile stretch of Black River** ■ **Michigan's Upper Peninsula, from Bessemer north on Co. Rd. 513** ■ **Best seasons spring and fall** ■ **Hiking, wildlife viewing** ■ **Contact Ottawa National Forest, E6248 US 2, Ironwood, MI 49938; 906-932-1330. www.fs.fed.us/r9/ottawa/**

Apostle Islands National Lakeshore

100 miles southwest of Isle Royale

Wisconsin has a small corner of Lake Superior's vast shoreline, yet what it lacks in quantity it makes up for in quality. Like emeralds in a sapphire sea, 22 forested islands lie scattered off the tip of Bayfield Peninsula. All but the largest, Madeline Island, are undeveloped and uninhabited, and feature sculpted sandstone sea caves, pristine stretches of sandy beach, and remnant old-growth hemlocks and hardwoods.

Jesuit missionaries and French fur traders named the islands after the 12 apostles of Jesus. The honor, though reverential, is not particularly appropriate: Historians believe the missionaries did indeed realize there were more than 12 islands. The national lakeshore now protects 12 miles of mainland shore and the entire archipelago, with the exception of Madeline Island that already had year-round residents when Congress created the national lakeshore in 1970. The protected islands range in size from 3-acre Gull to 10,000-acre Stockton.

The Apostles are visible remnants of the last ice age. As the glaciers advanced, they left high hills of sand and gravel, and carved a deep, broad basin; when they retreated about 10,000 years ago, melted water filled the basin, and the high spots became islands.

The relatively hard red sandstone of the Apostles became a popular building material in the late 1800s. "Brownstone" quarried from Stockton, Basswood, and Hermit Islands was used to construct many buildings throughout the East and Midwest, including those rebuilt in Chicago after the great fire of 1871. The old county courthouse in Bayfield, now the National Lakeshore Visitor Center, is made of brownstone from the Apostle Islands.

The islands became an important fur-trading post in the 1600s. The Ojibwa tribe lived on Madeline Island, and the Huron came here to trade with French-Canadian voyageurs. The fur trade lasted nearly two centuries. As it declined, commercial fishing began to develop in the 1830s. Two decades later the fishing industry was harvesting enormous stocks of whitefish, herring, and lake trout. You can visit restored fish camps at **Little Sand Bay** on the mainland and on **Manitou Island.**

All those boats on the water prompted the construction of lighthouses, and the Apostles now lay claim to one of the nation's highest concentrations of beacons. Six lighthouses—the largest collection in the National Park System—are located within the national lakeshore.

Logging followed fishing, and clear-cutting the islands was almost too easy. By the 1930s, the islands were so denuded of trees that the National Park Service resisted the idea of making them into a national park when Herbert Hoover's administration suggested it.

Today these areas are protected as the **Apostle Islands Maritime Forest State Natural Area,** and they include Devils Island, Raspberry Island, and portions of Outer and Sand Islands.

Fortunately, wilderness has slowly reclaimed the Apostles, and native species thrive once again in this transition zone between the boreal forest of fir and spruce and the northern highland forest of maple, hemlock, birch, and pine. **Devils Island** showcases bluff-top boreal forest, with balsam fir and spruce clinging to its exposed rock, while Arctic plants such as butterwort and sedges grow from raw, north-facing cliffs.

The Mainland

Head for the mainland's Little Sand Bay, 13 miles north of Bayfield, where the national lakeshore begins. Here the **National Lakeshore Visitor Center** offers a variety of fishing and shipping displays, as well as a restored fishery.

Farther west, the 13 miles of shoreline at **Mawikwe Bay** include a dramatic stretch of sandstone sea caves. Exposed to the furious weather of the open lake, the brilliant red sandstone has been shaped into gaping chasms and flying buttresses that rise as high as 65 feet. In winter, ice and snow sculptures build up along the cliff faces and ooze off the top like icing on a cake. The best view of the sea caves is from a kayak on the lake.

Visiting the Islands

Allow at least half a day to see the islands. The Apostle Islands Cruise Service *(715-779-3925)* offers 3-hour or all-day tours from mid-May through mid-October. The tours wind past lighthouses and dramatic rock formations as narrators share information on the area's history and natural resources. Through the same company, you can arrange for a shuttle to drop you at an island for a few hours or a few days, also.

Oak Island is the highest, rising nearly 500 feet above the lake surface. It was the first to emerge as lake levels fell. Remnants of different lake stages can be seen in several places on the island.

With more than 11 miles of maintained trails, it's one of the best destinations for hikers.

On **Sand** and **Raspberry Islands,** you can tour restored lighthouses and learn from naturalists about the life of a 19th-century lightkeeper. The 1881 sandstone lighthouse at the north end of Sand is one of Lake Superior's most picturesque.

With its year-round residents, resorts, restaurants, roads, and cars, **Madeline Island** seems downright urban compared with the rest of the Apostles. Still, this is a fine place to explore, especially around **Big Bay State Park.** Here, trails skirt a lagoon, pass sandstone formations and sea caves, and wind through pine forest. The eponymous bay offers more than a mile of protected sand beach along the lake's sparkling waters.

■ **69,372 acres** ■ **Northwestern Wisconsin, along tip of Bayfield Peninsula and 21 islands in Lake Superior** ■ **Best months May–Oct.** ■ **Camping, hiking, boating, diving, fishing** ■ **Contact the national lakeshore, Route 1, Box 4, Bayfield, WI 54814; 715-779-3397. www.nps.gov/apis**

Lighthouse on Raspberry Island, Apostle Islands National Lakeshore

Apostle Islands Country Drive

Begins 120 miles southwest of Isle Royale

95 miles one way; half a day Wisconsin Route 13 traces Lake Superior's southern shore, a remote North Woods landscape of windswept fishing villages and vistas of the low-lying Apostle Islands. Starting just west of Ashland—where the Soo Line Iron Ore Dock serves as a reminder of the area's mining and shipping legacy—the route follows Lake Superior's Chequamegon Bay north, its shimmering water visible through the trees.

Washburn, about 10 miles ahead, has an old bank building, courthouse, and other edifices made of brownstone originally quarried nearby and on Basswood Island. In the 19th century, Basswood stone was used in building construction all over the country.

The road moves on past farms cut out of the forest, their individualism expressed in the art painted on their barns. Where the road returns to the bay shore, you can see forested **Van Tassells Point** ahead, a great hogback hill protruding toward the lake.

The drive continues through the hilly woods, with glimpses of the water and islands, then twists and turns back down the bluff to sheltered Pikes Bay. Here, at **Bayfield State Fish Hatchery** *(715-779-4021),* you can learn how they raise fish to stock lakes.

Victorian-style inns and shops signal the approach to **Bayfield,** a fishing and tourist village with fairy-tale mansions once owned by lumber magnates. Stroll along the deep-water harbor, where the Apostle Islands appear to float offshore *(see pp. 251–53).* Most prominent are Madeline and Basswood, resembling green pancakes.

Red Cliff Indian Reservation encircles the tip of Bayfield Peninsula, north of where Wisc. 13 heads west. La Pointe Chippewa have lived here since 1854, when Chief Buffalo negotiated a treaty that gave them 14,142 acres. Beyond the town of Red Cliff, turn right on Co. Rd. K and right on Little Sand Bay Road to reach the Little Sand Bay Visitor Center *(715-779-3459).* Stroll along the sandy crescent overlooking the lake.

Back on Wisc. 13, zigzag across the peninsula, then descend to Siskiwit Bay and tiny **Cornucopia.** Here, a 19th-century fishing village has been reborn with craft shops and a café. St. Mary's Greek Orthodox Church is an odd centerpiece in this town established by Scandinavian immigrants.

Wetlands border the road west of Cornucopia, where Lost Creek No. 1, Lost Creek No. 2, and Lost Creek No. 3 wander through a wide floodplain cut by a postglacial river and now drained by a river and a creek. Down the road, tiny **Herbster** has a nice beach at the end of Lake Avenue.

West of the small fishing village of Port Wing, Wisc. 13 enters dense new-growth forest similar to what the first settlers encountered more than a century ago. The road crosses the Iron River and, soon after entering **Brule River State Forest** *(715-372-4866),* veers south. Watch for Brule River Road, which leads 4 miles to the mouth of the **Bois Brule River** at Lake Superior. Five presidents have fished in the state's premier trout stream, beginning with Ulysses S. Grant. Brook, brown, and rainbow trout migrate up the river from the lake each year, along with coho and chinook salmon.

Beyond the river, the road dips into stream-filled valleys and climbs over high glacial hills covered with trees and wildflowers. After crossing the Amnicon River, look to the left for the green-roofed **Davidson windmill,** built in 1885 by a Finnish settler who hand-carved the gears.

The last stop before Superior is **Amnicon Falls State Park** *(3 miles S on Co. Rd. U. 715-398-3000),* where the Amnicon River tumbles through a red sandstone and basaltic lava escarpment. Ancient volcanic activity and thick glaciers created this lovely landscape. Make sure you cross the 55-foot **covered bridge** over the water; the Horton or bowstring bridge was secured with hooks and clips instead of rivets and bolts. It was moved here in 1930.

About 3 miles ahead, on the world's largest freshwater lake, Superior has the world's largest grain elevators, iron ore docks, and coal-shipping terminal. You can see them from **Barkers Island** or **Connors Point.**

■ 95 miles one way; half a day ■ Spring through fall. In winter, when average temperature is 17°F, you can walk to the islands on the frozen lake. Check locally to be sure the water is thoroughly frozen before venturing across the ice.

Mammoth Cave

U nder a swath of Kentucky hills and hollows lies the world's largest known cave system. While the surface of Mammoth Cave National Park encompasses about 80 square miles, nobody knows how many lie beneath. More than 365 miles of the five-level cave system have been mapped, and new caves are continually being discovered.

Two layers of stone underlie Mammoth's hilly woodlands. A sandstone and shale cap, as thick as 50 feet in places, acts as an umbrella over limestone ridges. The umbrella leaks at places called sinkholes, from which surface water makes its way underground, eroding the limestone into a honeycomb of caverns.

Now a United Nations World Heritage site and core area of an international biosphere reserve, Mammoth Cave is as "grand, gloomy, and peculiar" as it was when Stephen Bishop, a young slave and early guide, described it. By a flickering lard-oil lamp he found and mapped some of Mammoth's passages.

Bishop died in 1857. His grave, like his life, is part of Mammoth; it lies in the Old Guide's Cemetery near the entrance.

Most visitors see the eerie beauty of the caverns on some of the 10 miles of passages that are open for tours. Rangers dispense geological lore and tell tales about real and imagined happenings 200 or 300 feet down. The tours are hikes inside the Earth; uphill stretches can be hard going for some visitors. Few seem frightened; people terrified by darkness or tight spots naturally avoid caves. Rangers say they rarely have problems guiding the 500,000 men, women, and children who venture below yearly.

Mammoth does not glamorize the underworld with garish lighting. You never forget that you are deep in the Earth. And nowhere else can you get a better lesson in the totality of darkness

- South-central Kentucky

- 52,830 acres

- Established 1941

- Best season summer when cool cave temperatures are refreshing

- Caving, camping, hiking, backpacking, boating, fishing, horseback riding, bird-watching

- Information: 270-758-2180 www.nps.gov/maca

Moonlight Dome, Mammoth Cave National Park

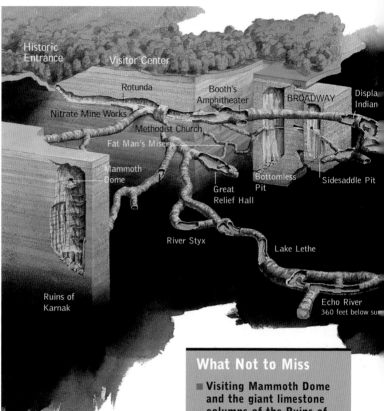

Historic Entrance
Visitor Center
Rotunda
Booth's Amphitheater
BROADWAY
Displa Indian
Nitrate Mine Works
Methodist Church
Fat Man's Misery
Mammoth Dome
Great Relief Hall
Bottomless Pit
Sidesaddle Pit
River Styx
Lake Lethe
Ruins of Karnak
Echo River
360 feet below su

What Not to Miss

- Visiting Mammoth Dome and the giant limestone columns of the Ruins of Karnak on the 2-hour Historic Tour

- Getting dirty and up-close on the Introduction to Caving and Wild Cave tours

- Taking a guided cruise along the Green River and witnessing the cave geology from the surface

- Exploring river canyons on the 4-hour, 4-mile Grand Avenue Tour

- Hiking along River Styx Spring Trail to see water spouting from the cave

and the power of light. Usually on a tour, a ranger gathers everyone and, after a warning, switches off the lights. The darkness is sudden, absolute. Then the ranger lights a match, and the tiny dot of light magically spreads, illuminating a circle of astonished faces.

How to Get There

Mammoth Cave is 9 miles northwest of I-65. It is nearly

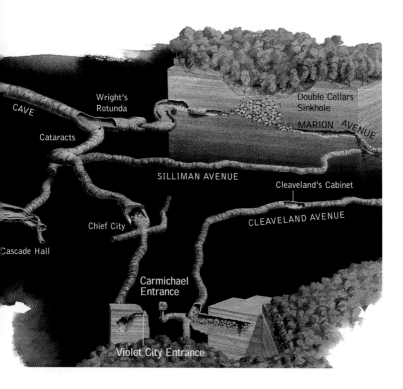

CAVE

Wright's
Rotunda

Double Cellars
Sinkhole

MARION AVENUE

Cataracts

SILLIMAN AVENUE

Cleaveland's Cabinet

Chief City

CLEAVELAND AVENUE

Cascade Hall

Carmichael
Entrance

Violet City Entrance

equidistant (about 85 miles) between Louisville, Ky., and Nashville, Tenn. From the south, take the exit at Park City and head northwest on Ky. 255 to the park; from the north, take the exit at Cave City and head northwest on Ky. 70 to the park. Don't be misled by signs proclaiming commercial "mammoth" caves. Airports: Nashville, Tenn., and Louisville, Ky.

When to Go

All-year park. Beneath the surface, the temperatures fluctuate from the mid-50s to the low 60s. Summer brings the most people, and frequent tours are offered. Though there are fewer tours the rest of the year, they are less crowded.

How to Visit

The tours vary greatly; pick ones to fit your time and

Service Elevator Entrance

Thorpe's Pit

Wild Cave Tour

BOONE AVENUE

Snowball Dining Room
267 feet below surface

KENTUCKY AVENUE

Stalactites in Mammoth Cave

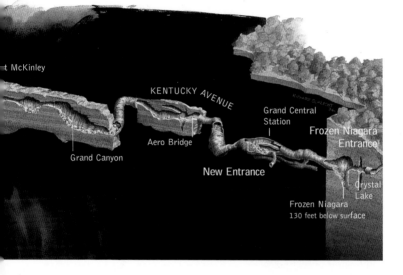

t McKinley

KENTUCKY AVENUE

Grand Central
Station

Frozen Niagara
Entrance

Aero Bridge

Grand Canyon

New Entrance

Crystal
Lake

Frozen Niagara
130 feet below surface

stamina. All require you to buy a ticket. It's best to make reservations in the summer, on holidays, and on spring and fall weekends.

For a half-day visit, you might take the **Historic Tour,** which combines geology with Mammoth's rich history, or the **Introduction to Caving Tour.** If you plan to stay longer, consider the fairly strenuous **Grand Avenue Tour;** there are three steep hills, each nearly 90 feet high.

To enjoy the caves safely and comfortably, wear shoes with nonskid soles and take a jacket. Top off your underground trips with a river trip or a walk on the **River Styx Spring Trail.**

The least arduous cave tour (a quarter mile, 75 minutes) is the **Travertine Tour.** A modified version of the **Frozen Niagara Tour,** it has only 18 steps each way (plus an optional 49) and is designed for visitors who want a short and easy trip. The toughest challenge is the 5-mile, 6-hour, belly-crawling **Wild Cave Tour,** offered daily in summer and weekends year-round by reservation.

EXPLORING THE PARK

Historic Tour: **2 miles; 2 hours**

You leave daylight and walk into dimly lit gloom at the **Historic Entrance,** which Native Americans discovered thousands of years before. A few steps inside is the **Rotunda,** a room 142 feet long and nearly as wide. This was the room where 70 slaves equipped with candles or burning rags mined saltpeter to make gunpowder. They hauled in logs, built leaching vats, and filled them with cave dirt. Water, poured into the vats, trickled into a trough as brine. Two pipelines of hollowed-out logs carried water in and brine out. The residue went into the gunpowder.

The underground avenue of **Broadway** leads to a spot called **Methodist Church,** where frontier folk may have held services in the 1800s. Farther on, **Booth's Amphitheater** recalls the visit of actor Edwin Booth. Here, the brother of assassin John Wilkes Booth recited Hamlet's famous soliloquy.

Cedar Sink Trail, Mammoth Cave National Park

The next stop on the path is the **Bottomless Pit,** a 105-foot deep hole that was created by groundwater seeping downward through cracks and sinks in the sandstone capping the cave system. From here, look up into its dome 38 feet above the surface. (In cave lingo, a bottom of the shaft is called the pit and the top, the dome.)

On your way back toward the entrance you pass through **Fat Man's Misery,** a passage polished smooth by generations of squirming spelunkers. You emerge into **Great Relief Hall,** a large chamber where you are able to stand upright. Then back on the trail for the final spectacles: **Mammoth Dome**—192 feet from floor to ceiling—carved by water dripping through a sinkhole, and the **Ruins of Karnak,** a cluster of gleaming limestone pillars that looks like an Egyptian temple.

Introduction to Caving Tour: **1 mile; about 3 hours**

Cave exploring or spelunking can be fun and challenging. The

Introduction to Caving Tour gives visitors ages 10 and above some first-hand experience in underground exploration. Offered daily in summer and on weekends in spring and fall, this trip involves hand-and-knees crawling, climbing, stooping, and even canyon-walking, with feet on different ledges and nothing but air in between. Straying from traditional walking paths, you visit the twisting, convoluted canyons and crawls of **Fox Avenue,** emerging at **Frozen Niagara.** Along the way rangers explain the geologic processes that result in the varied subterranean spaces. You also learn the basic rules of safe caving, including what to do if you get lost.

Helmets and lights are provided. Participants should bring knee pads (the kind used with in-line skates or hard plastic knee pads are not allowed). You'll need long pants and boots; it's wise to bring gloves, too. There are no rest rooms, and children between the ages of 10 and 15 must be accompanied by an adult.

Grand Avenue Tour: 4 miles; 4.5 hours

This tour is likely to be very crowded in the summer. It begins with a 5- to 10-minute bus ride from the visitor center to the **Carmichael Entrance,** a concrete bunker and stairway. The path then leads down to **Cleaveland Avenue,** a long, tubular chamber tunneled out by a river. Its walls sparkle with flowery patches of gypsum; the white mineral crystallizes below the surface of the limestone from seeping moisture, then gradually forms one cubic inch per thousand years.

About a mile beyond is the **Snowball Room,** where the tour stops for lunch. Food service here is limited to sandwiches, candy, and drinks. The growths on the roof that look like snowballs used to be a dull gray, the residue of phosphates found in the lint from visitors' clothing. The growths have since been cleaned; in hopes of preventing another massive cleaning or worse yet, damage to the growths, environmentalists continue to lobbying for the restaurant's removal.

Another river canyon, Boone Avenue, takes you 300 feet into the Earth along a passage so narrow you can touch both walls. The tour ends at **Frozen Niagara,** a 75-foot tall and 50-foot wide cascade of orange-white flowstone formed by the mineral-laden waters that seeped here, vanished, and left behind the shimmering stalactites

Trapped

Many Americans did not know about Mammoth Cave until January 1925 when William Floyd Collins became trapped in Sand Cave on what is now the southeast edge of the park. Stuck in a narrow tunnel, his legs pinned by a big rock, the caver waited while rescuers tried to save him. For 17 days, people around the country followed the Collins saga in the newspapers and on the radio.

Unfortunately the rescuers were unable to free Collins, and he died. But the media blitz shone a spotlight on the Mammoth area, and the following year legislation was under way to create a new national park.

and stalagmites. Such formations build up at the rate of about a cubic inch every 200 years.

Boat Trip & Hikes

South of the visitor center, you can take a 1-hour cruise aboard the *Miss Green River II* along that slow-moving body of water that flows 24 miles through the park past cliffs and valleys. Tickets are sold in the center.

Most of the park's 70 miles of trails are in the backcountry across the river. Since there are no bridges over the river in the park, you can drive onto the Green River Ferry at a crossing southwest of the visitor center or go to Houchins Ferry at the western edge of the park. The boats are the most recent incarnations of those that have carried people across since the 1800s.

While at the Green River Ferry landing, try the short **Echo River Spring Trail** that leads past a series of pools formed when the underground river emerges from the caves.

After you've crossed on the Green River Ferry, drive a few miles southwest to **Cedar Sinkhole Road** and take the 0.8-mile **Cedar Sink Trail;** it's one way. Then take the 1-mile long **Turnhole Bend loop** just north on a kink in the river. The water from the sink travels through unseen passages below and surfaces here.

If you want to explore more from here, go to the section of park that's north of the river. This hilly, wooded countryside is laced with pretty trails and threaded by the **Nolin River** and other tributaries of the Green.

Should you not want to cross the river, pick up the **Mammoth Sink Trail** near the visitor center. This trail goes down into an open forest of oaks, hickories, and tulip poplars. In about half a mile, you'll descend into a bowl-shaped pit filled with trees and plants.

To see the interplay between surface features and the underworld, pick up the **River Styx Spring Trail** near the Historic Entrance. At the **River Styx Spring,** you'll see water emerging from the cave and flowing into the Green River. Farther along is **Cave Island,** formed of waterborne logs, silt, and other materials.

Before leaving the park, go to **Sloan's Crossing Pond,** at the junction of West and South Entrance Roads. The depression in the sandstone has collected enough water to create a tiny ecosystem; frogs hide in the cattails that hem the edges, and red-winged blackbirds scout for mayflies.

INFORMATION & ACTIVITIES

Headquarters
1 Mammoth Cave Parkway
Mammoth Cave, KY 42259
270-758-2180
www.nps.gov/maca

Visitor & Information Centers
Visitor center open daily. If space is available, you can buy tickets there on the day for all tours except Wild Cave, which requires advance reservations. Tours sell out quickly, especially in summer, on holidays, and on spring and fall weekends. So, if at all possible, buy tickets in advance through the National Parks Reservation Service (see p. 13) or online at www.nps.gov/maca.

For more information on ranger-led activities, call 270-758-2328.

Seasons & Accessibility
Park open year-round. Visitors must join a tour to view the caves; tours offered daily.

Entrance Fees
None. Fees required for tours, $4-$22 for adults and youths; children under 6 free. Higher fees for special tours; Wild Cave Tour is $45 per person.

Pets
Permitted on leashes except in caves and visitor center. Kennel facilities through the Mammoth Cave Hotel (see opposite).

Facilities for Disabled
Visitor center, some sites at Headquarters Campground, and rest rooms are accessible. The half-mile Pond Walk, quarter-mile Heritage Trail, and 0.1-mile Sand Cave Trail are fully accessible.

Things to Do
Naturalist-led activities: cave tours, (12 daily in summer, 5 the rest of the year), children's exploration program, nature walks, evening programs. Nature trails, fishing, horseback riding, Green River boat trip, bicycling, occasional special events.

Special Advisory
■ Cave tours are strenuous; talk with a ranger before selecting one if you have difficulty walking or trouble with your heart or lungs. Wear sturdy shoes and bring a jacket.

Overnight Backpacking
Permits required. They are free and available at the visitor center.

Campgrounds
Three campgrounds, all with a 14-day limit. Fees $11-$25 per night. Tent and RV sites at headquarters. No hookups;

showers nearby for a fee; open March through November.

Tents only at Maple Spring Group Campgrounds, open March through November; and at Houchins Ferry, open all year, first come, first served. Use the National Parks Reservation Service *(see p. 13)* to reserve at headquarters and Maple Spring. Food services in park.

Hotels, Motels, & Inns
(Unless otherwise noted, rates for two people in a double room, high season.)

INSIDE THE PARK:
■ Mammoth Cave Hotel
Mammoth Cave, KY 42259. 270-758-2225. 112 units. Hotel $68; motor lodge $75; cottages $59. AC, restaurant.

OUTSIDE THE PARK
In Cave City, KY 42127:
■ Best Western Kentucky Inn
1009 Doyle Ave. 270-773-3161 or 800-528-1234. 51 units. $75-$80. AC, pool.
■ Days Inn Cave City
822 Mammoth Cave St. 270-773-2151 or 800-329-7466. 110 units. $35-$69. AC, pool.
■ Knight's Inn
1006A Doyle Rd. 270-773-2181 or 800-321-4245. 100 units. $80. AC, pool, restaurant, playground.

■ Quality Inn
102 Gardner Ln. 270-773-3101 or 800-228-5151. 105 units. $59. AC, pool.

In Park City, KY 42160:
■ Park Mammoth Resort
I-65 and US 31W, P.O. Box 307. 270-749-4101. 92 units. $68. AC, pool, restaurant, 2 golf courses.

In Bowling Green, KY 42104:
■ Bowling Green Bed & Breakfast
3313 Savannah Dr. 270-781-3861. 3 rooms. $60, includes breakfast. AC.
■ New's Inn
3160 Scottsville Rd. 270-781-3460. 49 units. $42-$69. AC, pool.

For additional accommodations, call the Chambers of Commerce of Cave City at 270-773-5159 and Bowling Green at 270-781-3200.

Excursions from Mammoth Cave

Dale Hollow Lake State Resort

60 miles southeast of Mammoth

An out-of-the-way gem of a park, Dale Hollow features a turquoise lake rimmed by wooded peninsulas and steep rocky bluffs.

Before World War II, there was no lake here in the Cumberland foothills, just a couple of small rivers and their tributaries twisting their way west to the Cumberland River nearby. Then, in 1943, the U.S. Army Corps of Engineers built a reservoir on the Obey River for flood control and hydroelectric power. The result is this lovely 28,000-acre lake and its 620 miles of undeveloped shoreline.

Most of the lake is in Tennessee, and the park is in Kentucky with its largest peninsula jutting down across the state line. Some of the trails actually cross into Tennessee. When the area was flooded for the reservoir, the high and dry parts were narrow ridges. The 15-mile **trail system** follows old logging roads over these ridges. In between are steep hollows that are difficult to walk and that erode easily with wear and tear.

Stop in the lodge for information, then head over to the campground. From here, the 1.8-mile **Eagle Point Trail** goes to a rock shelter, or overhang, poised above the lake. This bluff affords an excellent view of the island-dotted lake and the low hills of Tennessee disappearing in the distance. In winter you may see some of the bald eagles that set up temporary residence here. Back in the woods lives a vibrant population of white-tailed deer, grouse, quail, and wild turkey.

Since the park's trails tend to lead out to overlooks on peninsulas, you'll need to backtrack to your starting point. From Eagle Point, this means another 1.8 miles back to the campground. You're welcome to cheat a bit by parking off the road, thereby cutting the hike to only 0.8 mile each way.

At the marina, you can rent a pontoon boat and try your luck with the lake's whopping smallmouth bass, crappie, catfish, trout, walleye, and muskellunge. The water's extreme clarity makes for good scuba diving and snorkeling.

■ **3,398 acres** ■ **South-central Kentucky, 14 miles southeast of Burkesville** ■ **Best seasons summer and fall** ■ **Camping, hiking, boating, swimming, scuba diving, fishing** ■ **Contact the resort, 6371 State Park Rd., Burkesville, KY 42717; 270-433-7431. http://parks.ky.gov/dalehol.htm**

Bald Eagles

One of the country's most extraordinary birds, the bald eagle lives only in North America.

The eagle isn't actually bald; the moniker comes from the way the white feathered head looks. As with many other birds of prey, females are larger than males; in flight, the females wings can span 8 feet, and the males, 6.5 feet. The two sexes look alike.

Bald eagles are primarily fishing birds, hooking their catch in their sharp talons. They use sticks to build huge platform nests in trees, returning year after year to the same site. The largest known nest measured ten feet wide and 20 feet high.

Both parents help build the nest and incubate the eggs.

For a while, the outlook for bald eagles was pretty bleak. They were illegally hunted, their habitats were diminished, and, perhaps worst of all, their eggs were fatally weakened by the pesticide DDT. By the early 1960s, there were about 450 breeding pairs left in the 48 contiguous states.

After DDT was banned and the federal government put the birds on the endangered species list, their numbers began to grow. In 2000, there were more than 6,500 pairs in the contiguous United States. By this time, the birds had been upgraded to threatened rather than endangered.

Dale Hollow Lake and other waterways in central and western Kentucky and Tennessee are good places to spot an eagle, especially in the winter.

Bald eagles

Bernheim Arboretum and Research Forest

50 miles northeast of Mammoth

Although it's hard to improve on nature's handiwork, a little extra attention here and there can yield breathtaking results. Bernheim achieves that deeply satisfying mix of wildness and horticulture. From scenic high spots, you can behold long rolling sweeps of green punctuated by flowering trees and mirror-smooth lakes. The woodlands all around buffer the vast cultivated areas, framing a landscape that seems almost too perfect to be real.

But this is one picture that you can step—and drive—into. Among the arboretum's 2,000 labeled varieties of trees, shrubs, and other plants are collections of crab apples, maples, dogwoods, and dwarf conifers, as well as the most extensive collection of hollies (250) in North America. Scientists here work on a number of projects including the search for a blight-resistant American chestnut hybrid, and maintaining wild turkeys for restocking in other parts of the state.

All this incredible beauty was created from the sale of I. W. Harper bourbon, the popular brand distilled by Isaac Wolfe Bernheim. The German immigrant arrived in New York in 1867, an 18-year-old with four dollars to his name. After several years peddling in the east, he came to Kentucky and learned to distill whiskey. By 1928, he was a successful 80-year-old businessman. He then bought a huge tract of land and set up a foundation to turn the acreage into a place that would restore the connections between people and nature. Much of the land had been heavily logged, mined, and farmed; the soil was thin, hillsides eroded.

Though Bernheim would not live to see his vision completed, slowly but surely the land was renewed. In 1950 Bernheim Forest opened to the public.

What to see and do

Pick up trail maps and auto tour brochures at the **visitor center,** which also houses some interesting displays. The **auto tour** circulates around the big meadow and varies with the season. In spring you'll see snowy banks of white fringe tree and dogwood, both native to the state, as well as pink and red crab apples, and the small aptly-named Carolina silverbell tree. The shrubby white serviceberry sends a sweet scent over the meadow, while high up, the tulip poplar—one of the tallest hardwoods in the country—displays its wide orange-and-green flowers. In fall, the maples, oaks, sourwoods, and Kentucky coffee trees paint the landscape with strokes of orange, gold, and crimson. From the **Big Meadow Overlook** you have a delicious view of the color quilt all around, tinged with such autumn wildflowers as goldenrod, aster, and ironweed.

The sculpture here and in other places around the arboretum enhances the connection between art and nature. For more work on your identification skills, stop by the gardens of the **Arboretum Center,** which feature a number of wildflowers and grasses.

Some 35 miles of trails loop around Bernheim's wooded knobs and hollows. Several interpretive trails near the visitor center make for easy, informative strolls through both open and woodsy terrain. They vary in length from the half-mile **Bent Twig Trail** just behind the visitor center to the 1.5 mile **Cull Hollow Trail** off the right side of Tower Hill Road. Continue up this road and park at the end to take a 1-mile loop to the 1929 **fire tower.** You can climb the tower on weekends with a guide.

■ **14,000 acres** ■ **North-central Kentucky, on Ky. 245, 1 mile east of I-65**
■ **Best seasons spring and winter** ■ **Hiking, scenic drive, museum, bird-watching** ■ **Contact arboretum and research forest, Clermont, KY 40110; 502-955-8512. www.bernheim.org/**

Big Bone Lick State Park

 125 miles northeast of Mammoth

The Pleistocene was a great time for mammals in North America. All manner of creatures thundered, ambled, and trod across the land from two million years ago up through the Ice Age.

When the glaciers started pushing south about 20,000 years ago, the animals scooted out of the way. The ice made it to just north of the Ohio Valley. In the lee of a sharp northern bend in the Ohio, there was a swampy area with mineral springs that looked and tasted awfully good to the animals. Wooly mammoths, mastodons, ground sloths, bison, giant stag moose, and primitive horses were among the visitors to these salt- and mineral-rich springs.

Mastodons and mammoths (differing from mastodons mainly in their molars), nearly as big as elephants, were especially vulnerable in this soupy ground. Many of them got stuck and died. But their bones, covered in the morass, were preserved for thousands of years.

Big Bone Lick was a gathering place for hordes of these big mammals for about 8,000 years. This left plenty of time for lots of bones to accumulate. Explorers began discovering the fossilized bones as far back as 1739; especially noteworthy were the long curving tusks of the mastodon.

Some bones collected in the 1760s were sent to Benjamin Franklin, who was so confused by their elephantine nature that he imagined the Earth had been "in another position and the climates differently placed."

Thomas Jefferson became so excited by the bones that he charged Meriweather Lewis and William Clark to find out if any prehistoric "monsters" were still living in the West. Like many other

Wildflowers, Big Bone Lick State Park

intellects of the day, Jefferson had a hard time accepting extinction; "Such is the economy of nature," he wrote, "that no instance can be produced of her having permitted any one race of her animals to become extinct."

He later sent Clark back to Bone Lick on likely the first organized paleontological expedition in the country. The team gathered more than 300 bones and established Big Bone Lick as the birthplace of the study of American vertebrate paleontology.

Scientists and paleontologists still puzzle over what happened to the mastodon and mammoth. One of the most tantalizing theories came from a question Jefferson asked a delegation of Lenape Indians: "Do you know, or have you heard, of the Mammoth, the creature whose huge bones have been found at the Saltlicks, on the Ohio?" The chief told a story about a herd of tremendous animals destroying the bear, deer, elk, and other animals "which had been created for the use of Indians." Then the "Great Man above" slaughtered all but the big bull, who bounded over the Ohio, "and finally over the great lakes, where he is living at this day."

Begin in the **museum** *(adm. fee),* which has an introductory video and a small but interesting collection of fossilized bones. Just outside, take the paved 1-mile **Discovery Trail** to learn more about Big Bone Lick's past and present. Life-size models of mammoth, mastodon, and giant sloth give you a sense of what the scene may have looked like long ago. A shaggy-haired mammoth stands drinking in a swamp, its stout legs deep in muck. In the low light of early morning or late afternoon, you can almost believe it's real.

Elsewhere, a small herd of live (and fenced) bison lend authenticity to the Pleistocene landscape. Trees, grasses, and wildflowers have now filled in what used to be a wide swamp, and the ancient salt/sulphur spring has all but dried up.

At the other end of the park, a 2-mile trail encircles the 7.5-acre lake, where you can angle *(license required)* for largemouth bass, bluegill, and catfish.

■ **525 acres** ■ **Northern Kentucky, south of Union off Ky. 338** ■ **Best seasons spring and summer** ■ **Camping, hiking, swimming, fishing, prehistoric animal site** ■ **Contact the park, 3380 Beaver Rd., Union, KY 41091-9627; 859-384-3522. www.state.ky.us/agencies/parks/bigbone.htm**

Daniel Boone National Forest

110 miles east of Mammoth

Kentucky's only national forest runs east of the Bluegrass region in a narrow, 140-mile-long strip from the Tennessee border up nearly to the Ohio border. Within this hilly, rural countryside on the western edge of the Cumberland Plateau are towering sandstone bluffs, deep gorges, mature hardwood forests, and inviting waterfalls. More than 32 species of rare, threatened, or endangered wildlife live here, including red-cockaded woodpeckers, wintering bald eagles, and gray and Indiana bats; among the rare plants are running buffalo clover and white-haired goldenrod. Some 23 of the forest's 89 mussel species are federally endangered.

Now a healthy mix of young and old forest, the Daniel Boone was in pretty sad shape by the time it was turned over to the government in the 1930s. For decades, the old-growth woodlands had been clear-cut, the hillsides stripped for iron ore and coal. The soil on this barren, stump-filled landscape washed off, clogging streams and killing fish and other aquatic dwellers.

Timber harvesting continues on the national forest, but in a much more controlled way to allow cut sections to recover. There is still some coal mining being done within the forest's confines, though tourism is becoming more and more vital to the area's economy.

What to see and do

Private and federal lands are interspersed in the six ranger districts (including an outlying district to the east) in about a two to one ratio. This means you can travel into and out of public land on roads, trails, even lakes and rivers without being aware of it. To protect watersheds, geological features, and rare species, the forest service is slowly acquiring more land, filling in the gaps on your map. Meantime, you can help by respecting private property; stay on trails and observe posted signs.

South End

The forest around the **Big South Fork National River and Recreation Area** is laced with trails that allow you to explore a wide variety of scenery, from high narrow ridges to steep gorges and rapid-filled rivers.

The **Laurel Creek Trail** gives you a good sample of what the area

Daniel Boone, Man & Myth

Hunter, farmer, surveyor, trailblazer, town-builder, state legislator, and father of nine, Daniel Boone was America's preeminent frontiersman.

Legend, however, obscured a life of ups and downs. Few of the vast land claims Boone made worked out. Unjustly accused of treason during the Revolutionary War and robbed of $20,000 entrusted to him by investors, Boone spent most of his life in debt.

While business ventures failed, his reputation drew admirers wherever he went. He died in 1820 at 85 in Missouri, holding his daughters' hands.

has to offer, and it's easy to reach. Driving north on US 27, turn right on Co. Rd. 696 about 2 miles north of Ky. 92. After 2.2 miles, you'll reach the trailhead on the right. Cross a ridge and walk down to babbling **Laurel Creek** in the first half-mile. The trail follows the creek on a gentle downhill grade, passing good swimming holes and noteworthy rock shelters. Bright red cardinal flowers and fire-pinks dazzle the eye, the latter shaped like little stars. The white flowers of the low-growing evergreen partridgeberry give way in fall and winter to its scarlet fruit. After about 4 miles heading northwest along the creek, you reach Ky. 478 and the end of the trail.

Cumberland Falls State Resort Park

The main destination in this part of the forest is the 125-foot-wide waterfall. Water tumbles over a seven-story ledge with such sudden force that mist forms a constant shimmering cloud downstream and on the nearby trails. On clear nights during or around a full moon you can see a rare phenomenon called a moonbow, a ghostly light that arcs out from the base of the falls.

Situated on a boulder-strewn bend of the **Cumberland River,** the park is a good place to try out some Class III white water. Guided rafting trips *(fee)* are available from May to October; these are a wise choice for beginners who want a feel for the river. Experienced river runners can rent a canoe or kayak from one of the nearby outfitters. Riffles and small waves make the section above the falls a fun ride; just make sure to pull over to the right at the

Cumberland Falls

take-out point 200 yards above the falls.

Downstream lie some challenging squeezes—it's 11.6 miles to the Cumberland's confluence with the Laurel River, about 4 to 6 hours away.

For a great 3-mile walk, take the **Eagle Falls Trail** on the opposite side of the river. Along the way you'll see views of Cumberland Falls and 44-foot-high **Eagle Falls.** On the near side of the river, you can pick up the scenic **Moonbow Trail** and take it down the river as far as you like. It's actually part of the 269-mile **Sheltowee Trace** that runs the entire length of the national forest. The name comes from the Shawnee for "big turtle," an honorary name the Native Americans gave to Daniel Boone.

West of Cumberland Falls, past US 27, the Natural Arch Scenic Area has 9.5 miles of trails around one of the many impressive sandstone arches in the region. You can visit the stalwart 50-foot by 90-foot arch on the 1-mile **Natural Arch Trail;** keep your eyes peeled for wildflowers, deer, grouse, and wild turkey.

One of the forest's two designated wilderness areas, the 4,800-acre **Beaver Creek Wilderness** lies to the northeast below the Laurel River off US 27. Take FR 50 and 51 to the interpretive **Three Forks Loop Trail** (No. 512), a 2-mile jaunt along a sandstone cliff to a lofty overlook of the Beaver Creek system. Throughout the wilderness are rock shelters that Native Americans used as far back as 9,000 years. Here and there remain stone fences, road tracks, and a few other traces of the coal and logging industries.

Not far to the northeast, **Laurel River Lake** covers 5,600 acres of clear, deep water rimmed by a 192-mile shore of cliffs. Geese, ducks, and ospreys call in at the lake. Within the water dwell black crappie, bluegill, rainbow trout, muskelunge, channel catfish, large-mouth bass, and walleye.

A few miles west, the tortuous **Rockcastle River** travels south to the Cumberland. The state of Kentucky has designated this 17-mile section north of the Bee Rock Campground a Wild River. It is one of Kentucky's most exciting white-water runs. Class III and IV rapids, rocks, and dangerous hydraulics await your skilled eyes and arms. For a safer look, hike one of the trails up along **Rockcastle Narrows** north of the campground. The Rockcastle above and below this stretch is much tamer.

North End

One of the best bases for exploring the region's geological high-lights, **Natural Bridge State Resort Park** (*2.5 miles SE of Slade on Ky. 11. 606-663-2214*) has 2,100 forested acres surrounding the feature presentation.

One of the great things about this park is that, despite its popu-larity, you still have to make an effort to see its wonders. The almost 1-mile long **Original Trail,** blazed in the 1890s by the Lexing-ton & Eastern Railroad, is the quickest way, but it's an uphill climb. The wide trail ascends through a forest of yellow poplar, red maple, basswood, sugar maple, white oak, and black walnut. Pitted and fis-sured sandstone cliffs line the trail, splotched with lichens in shades of green and orange. At the top stands a massive 65-foot-high

Bat Caves

Of the 14 bat species that live in Daniel Boone National Forest, three are considered endangered: the Virginia big-eared, the gray, and the Indiana. They depend upon the area's many caves for their hibernation. Some known bat habitats are gated, while others may be posted.

Hikers who do stumble upon sleeping bats should stay away. Noise can disturb the bats; they may then use up their small sup-ply of winter energy in needless flight and die.

Romanesque arch. Walk through it and take the rock stairway through a cleft in the stone to the top of the arch. From up here, you have wonderful views of the flat-topped Cumberland Plateau north and south, gashed with its many cliffs and ridges. You can walk across the 78-foot-long bridge; it's as wide as a country road. But there are no rails, so do your viewing from the middle.

Some 150 natural arches exist within a 5-mile radius of this point. **Natural Bridge** may be up to a million years old, while others have only recently formed. They generally begin as an opening in a rock; such openings are called rock houses or shelters. If the rock house stands on an exposed ridge, wind and rain over thousands of years can eventually whittle out a deeper opening that is capped by erosion-resistant sandstone.

Formations with a small hole are termed lighthouses. As more time goes by, the lighthouse can become a true arch or bridge. Eventually the arch becomes too eroded to support the top, and it collapses.

Tobacco curing barn, Daniel Boone National Forest

For variety, take the **Balanced Rock Trail** back down. A series of stairways helps you make the steep descent. The cliff walls along here seem like works of art: fantastic flower-like whorls, wormholed boulders, and honeycombed and fluted formations sprouting up from the ground. The balanced rock resembles a behemoth mushroom.

Among the park's 17 more miles of trail, take the **Laurel Ridge Trail** to Lover's Leap for an outstanding view of the canyon formed by the Red River's middle fork. In addition to the standard forest mix, there are also some chestnuts, red oaks, white ash, cucumber tree, and yellow buckeye; rhododendron, white pine, and hemlock grow in shaded coves, while laurel, pitch pine, Virginia pine, and shortleaf pine take to the higher ridges. About half the park is a designated state nature preserve, home to the federally endangered Virginia big-eared bat and the state-endangered yellow lady's slipper.

Up near the extreme north end of the forest, the **Cave Run Lake** area has a number of worthy attractions. To get to the lake, take the 11-mile **Zilpo National Scenic Byway,** which runs east of Ky. 211 about 5 miles south of US 60. The road winds along a ridge out to a wooded peninsula jutting into the lake. After about 6 miles, pull to the right for the **Tater Knob Fire Tower.** Built in 1934, this last remaining lookout in the Daniel Boone forest is no longer used for locating fires; planes do that. But you can climb the 35-foot structure for great views of the hills all around.

Across the road, trails weave through the woods. The surrounding 7,610 acres belong to the designated **Pioneer Weapons Wildlife Management Area;** hunters who use bows and arrows or muzzle-loading firearms come here to pursue white-tailed deer, wild turkey, and other game in season.

The road ends at the **Zilpo Recreation Area,** where there are hiking trails and a sandy beach on **Cave Run Lake.** The U.S. Army Corps of Engineers completed the 8,270-acre lake primarily to control flooding in the Licking River Valley northwest.

■ **699,575 acres** ■ **Eastern Kentucky** ■ **Best seasons spring and summer** ■ **Camping, hiking, white-water canoeing and kayaking, rock climbing, hunting, wildlife viewing** ■ **Contact the national forest, 1700 Bypass Rd., Winchester, KY 40391; 859-745-3100. www.southern region.fs.fed.us/boone**

Pine Mountain State Resort Park

150 miles east of Mammoth

Situated near the southern end of Pine Mountain, Kentucky's first state park is full of geological treasures such as rock houses, tremendous boulders, and high sandstone cliffs that are within easy walking distance.

The park lies on Pine Mountain's southeastern slope, which means lots of sun but not much soil. Pines proliferate on the high dry ridges, as do low-growing red azaleas and mountain laurels. There are several ravines and recesses carved out by streams, where hemlocks predominate, towering over thickets of rhododendron. In between the exposed ridges and the sheltered ravines you can find a typical upland mix of oaks, hickories, beeches, and large tulip trees. Under these grow such springtime stars as dogwood, serviceberry, and the white-flowering sourwood, which makes a delicious honey. Red maples contribute to the color scheme in fall.

More than any other geological feature, Pine Mountain defines the southeast corner of Kentucky. It stretches 120 miles, southwest to northeast, varying in elevation from 2,000 to 3,270 feet. The mountain is actually the leading edge of a 12-mile-thick sheet or wedge of earth that was uplifted and tilted more than 300 million years ago.

Pick up maps and information at the lodge and poke your head in the small, old-fashioned **nature center** to see exhibits on local woods, mushrooms, lichens, and birds of prey. Just outside, notice the tremendous fossilized tree trunk, a 300-million-year-old lycopod. Kentucky's coal owes its existence to an ancient forest of such trees, compacted over the eons into rich seams of black carbon.

The park has 13 short trails, varying in length from a half to 1.75 miles. One of the nicest, the 0.75 **Hemlock Garden Trail,** starts just behind the lodge. The trail loops through a hemlock-shaded ravine, crosses little footbridges, and passes trickling streams. To appreciate this walk, you need to go slowly. There are no grand vistas, just exquisite little moments. Water glides over a mossy rockslide, while a thrush sings somewhere down the slope. At **Inspiration Point,** moss covers a boulder like bright green velvet; up at the head of the ravine you can just make out a sandstone wall hiding in the trees.

Farther along the trail, house-sized boulders, some turned upon their roofs, have their own gardens growing on top. Some of the

Winter on Pine Mountain, Cumberland Mountains

boulders are pitted with fist-size erosion holes that make nice recesses for snails and insects. A stone stairway squeezes up a dark crevice between two giant boulders. Here and there are patches of rhododendron, as well as thick carpets of partridgeberry, an ever-green ground cover that flowers into little white trumpets in late spring. The nearby **Fern Garden Trail,** also a hemlock-filled ravine, is a prime habitat for cinnamon and royal ferns.

About half the trail system is on the east side of the park, a 4-mile drive from the lodge. Here you'll find the most dramatic views. The half-mile **Chained Rock Trail** goes out to a series of massive rocks that billow like a cloud up to a cliff. You can scramble up the tilted rock face for fine views of Pineville and US 25E, part of the old **Wilderness Road** that was the main overland avenue to the west in the late 1700s. On clear days you can see Cumberland Mountain to the south. The huge chain was stretched across the rock in 1933, reputedly to protect Pineville from a rock fall. On the way back, look for such wildflowers as pink lady's slipper, jack-in-the-pulpit, and large-flowered trillium.

■ 1,519 acres ■ Southeast Kentucky, 1 mile south of Pineville via US 25E ■ Best seasons spring–fall ■ Camping, hiking, swimming ■ Contact the park, 1050 State Park Rd., Pineville, KY 40977; 606-337-3066. www.state .ky.us/agencies/parks/pinemtn2.htm

Shenandoah

S kyline Drive, the 105-mile-long spine of Shenandoah National Park, is a park itself. But many of the drivers on the road are passing the real Shenandoah. To see that, it's necessary to get out of the car and hike along some of the nearly 500 miles of trails that roll out from either side of Skyline, then twist through the Blue Ridge Mountains.

The long, narrow park flows outward, upward, and downward from the highway that divides it. The drive follows ridge trails that Native Americans and early settlers from Europe once used. To the east lies the Piedmont and the coastal plain. Beyond the mountains' western flanks rolls the lazy, pretty Shenandoah River, for which the park was named; the Native American word means "daughter of the stars."

To create the park, Virginia state officials acquired 1,088 privately owned tracts and donated the land to the nation. Never before had a large, populated expanse of private land been converted into a national park. And never before had planners made a park out of land so heavily used by people.

In the decade before the park opened, some 465 families moved or were moved from their cabins and resettled outside the proposed park boundaries. A few mountaineers, though, lived out their lives in the park and were buried in the secluded graveyards of Shenandoah's vanished settlements.

Much of Shenandoah consisted of farmland and second- or third-growth forests logged since the early 1700s. Today the marks of lumbering, grazing, and farming have mostly disappeared, as forests have slowly come back.

Spring arrives first in the park valleys and then moves upward. Walking up a valley trail, a visitor can follow spring's path and see, in a single day, a variety of flowers that bloom elsewhere over a span of weeks.

■ Western Virginia

■ 199,038 acres

■ Established 1935

■ Best seasons early spring and fall. Wildflowers peak in April and May

■ Hiking, backpacking, climbing, fishing, horseback riding, bird-watching, scenic drives

■ Information: 540-999-3500 www.nps.gov/shen

Page Valley, Shenandoah National Park

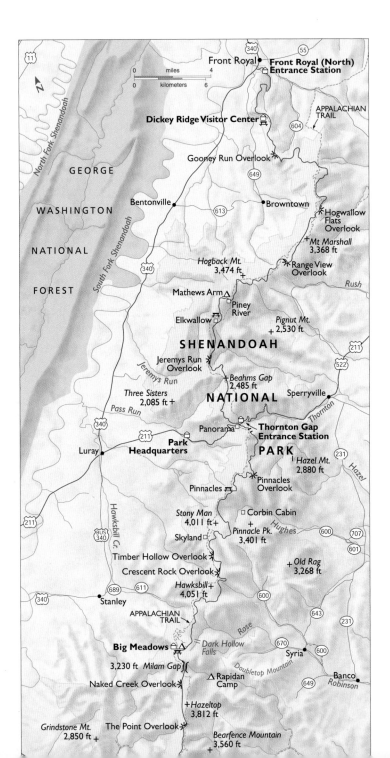

Front Royal

**Front Royal (North)
Entrance Station**

APPALACHIAN
TRAIL

Dickey Ridge Visitor Center

Gooney Run Overlook

GEORGE

Bentonville

Browntown

WASHINGTON

Hogwallow
Flats
Overlook

NATIONAL

Mt Marshall
3,368 ft

Hogback Mt.
3,474 ft

Range View
Overlook

FOREST

Rush

Mathews Arm

Piney
River

Elkwallow

Pignut Mt.
2,530 ft

SHENANDOAH

Jeremys Run
Overlook

Beahms Gap
2,485 ft

Three Sisters
2,085 ft

NATIONAL

Sperryville

Pass Run

Thornton

Panorama

**Thornton Gap
Entrance Station**

**Park
Headquarters**

PARK

Luray

Hazel Mt.
2,880 ft

Hazel

Pinnacles

Pinnacles
Overlook

Stony Man
4,011 ft

Corbin Cabin

Hughes

Pinnacle Pk.
3,401 ft

Skyland

Timber Hollow Overlook

Old Rag
3,268 ft

Crescent Rock Overlook

Hawksbill
4,051 ft

Stanley

APPALACHIAN
TRAIL

Rose

Big Meadows

Dark Hollow
Falls

Syria

3,230 ft Milam Gap

Rapidan
Camp

Doubletop Mountain

Banco

Naked Creek Overlook

Robinson

Hazeltop
3,812 ft

Grindstone Mt.
2,850 ft   The Point Overlook

Bearfence Mountain
3,560 ft

North Fork Shenandoah

South Fork Shenandoah

Jeremys Run

Hawksbill Cr.

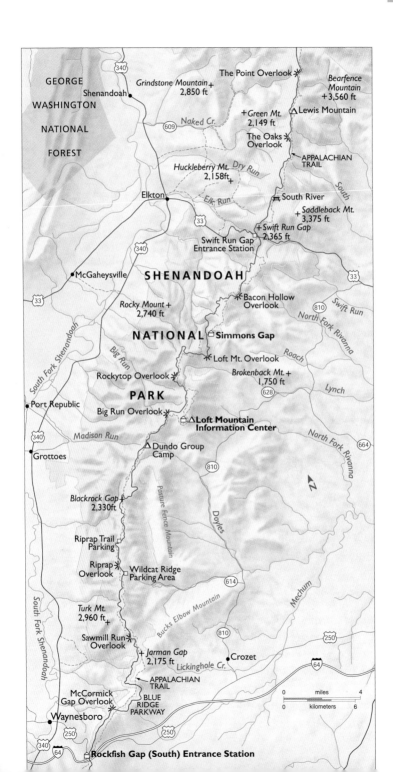

How to Get There

From Washington, D.C. (about 70 miles away), take I-66 west to US 340, then head south to the park's Front Royal (North) Entrance. From Charlottesville, take I-64 to the Rockfish Gap (South) Entrance. From the west, take US 211 through Luray to the Thornton Gap (Middle) Entrance or head east on US 33 to the Swift Run Gap Entrance. Airports: Dulles near Washington, D.C., and Charlottesville, Va.

When to Go

Of the nearly two million people who visit the park each year, 400,000 go in October to see the foliage. To avoid fall traffic jams, arrive early (preferably on a weekday), park at an overlook, and walk a trail.

Snowstorms sometimes close Skyline Drive, the park's north-south highway. Facilities close in winter.

Campgrounds fill on summer weekends, but day-trippers still have plenty of park. Wildflowers bloom from early spring to late fall.

How to Visit

On a day's drive-in visit, whatever entrance you use, get out and walk a trail. Even if you venture only a few hundred feet from an overlook, you will

What Not to Miss

- Driving the length of Skyline Drive and stopping at some of the fine overlooks, such as Range View, Hogback, and Big Run

- Hiking the 1.5-mile Stony Man Nature Trail to the summit of Stony Man

- Having a picnic at the Pinnacles

- Visiting waterfalls such as the 70-foot-high cascade on the Dark Hollow Falls Trail

- Reveling in the expansive views to the north, east, and west of the park at Big Meadows

- Taking the Corbin Cabin Cutoff Trail to see one of the few log cabins in the park

see a different Shenandoah beyond the scenic drive.

For a longer stay, make a base at one place, such as **Big Meadows** or **Skyland,** and explore from there. And be sure to reach Big Meadows about halfway through the park; the views north east and west from this large tract of land cannot be beat, especially at sunset.

EXPLORING THE PARK

Skyline Drive from Front Royal to Big Meadows:
51 miles; a full day

Not quite 5 miles south of the **Front Royal Entrance Station** is the **Dickey Ridge Visitor Center,** where exhibits introduce you to the park and its facilities along Skyline Drive. To walk a path of mountain life, cross the drive at the visitor center and start the self-guided, 1.3-mile **Fox Hollow Trail,** named for the family that first settled this hollow in 1837. Their houses have disappeared, but you can see relics of their toil: large, well-stacked piles of rock cleared from farmland. Other stones—rough and dimly lettered— jut from the family graveyard.

Along the drive, stop at overlooks for views of the **Shenandoah Valley** and the peaks looming above it. The views are magnificent (except when pollution levels or fog mar visibility). At many overlooks there are signposts for well-marked trails. Daubs of paint on trees identify the trails: white, the **Appalachian Trail;** blue, a park hiking trail; yellow, a horse trail *(hiking also allowed).*

At Mathews Arm Campground, 22 miles from Front Royal, the easily accessible 1.75-mile **Traces Trail** takes you through an oak forest back to the time of the earliest white settlers. The traces are faint: an old road and some tumbling stone walls.

For a more rugged hike into the past, stop at the parking area past Milepost 37 and take the **Corbin Cabin Cutoff Trail** into Nicholson Hollow. The steep trip *(1.5 miles each way)* ends at **Corbin Cabin,** a typical mountain residence built of chestnut logs.

This isolated hollow once held more than 20 homesteads. When the Park Service took over, it razed many of the existing cabins and let all but a few deteriorate. In the 1950s, the agency gave the Potomac Appalachian Trail Club, a volunteer organization, permission to renovate one of the remaining cabins in Nicholson Hollow for hikers to use.

Inside, a portrait of the cabin's builder, George T. Corbin, hangs over the mantel. He was the grandson of Aaron Nicholson, the ruling patriarch of this backwoods community that some called Free State Hollow because it was too wild for even the local sheriff.

Corbin married three times. His second wife died in childbirth during a snow storm. After burying her nearby, Corbin hurried down the hollow through snow drifts up to his waist to find milk for the newborn child.

Deer, Shenandoah National Park

The Corbin family, like many others in the region, lived on what they grew or made, including brandy from peaches and apples. They also brewed corn whiskey and chose not to pay taxes on it. What they didn't drink, they packed on mules and carried across the mountains for resale.

Bring your own aperitif and hunker down for a night or two in Corbin's cabin. The trail club rents it, as well as five others scattered through the park *(703-242-0693. www.patc.net)*.

For less rustic accommodations, visit **Skyland** *(near Mile 42),* which dates from the 1890s. The resort has guest rooms, cabins, and a dining room; it is open from April through November. The 1.5-mile **Stony Man Nature Trail** begins near the parking area and, climbing about 340 feet, reaches the cliffs of **Stony Man's** 4,011-foot summit, the second highest point in the park. From an outcrop on the cliffs, you get a sweeping view. The trail loops back around to the start.

The **Limberlost Trail** *(near Mile 43),* a gently winding walkway of crushed green stone, passes through old-growth hemlocks before crossing Whiteoak Canyon Run on a wooden bridge. The 1.3-mile trail is wheelchair accessible with numerous benches located at intervals for hikers to rest and contemplate their surroundings.

Stop at **Crescent Rock Overlook** *(near Mile 44)* for a look at 4,051-foot-high **Hawksbill Mountain,** the park's highest point. Then, 6 miles farther, stop at the parking area for the **Dark Hollow Falls Trail,** a 1.5-mile round-trip to the falls. Thomas Jefferson once stood below this 70-foot cascade, admiring its beauty. The trail is the shortest route to any falls in the park. It takes you past clusters of ferns, mosses, and liverworts. Split-log benches offer a rest en route.

Big Meadows *(Mile 51)* has trails, a campground, lodge, facilities for visitors, and the **Byrd Visitor Center,** where changing exhibits tell the stories of the park. Blueberries and strawberries grow up here, and deer often graze on the edge of the meadow.

The defoliated trees you see here and elsewhere in the park attest to the presence of a natural phenomenon: the gypsy moth. However, unlike the chestnut tree blight early in the 20th century *(see sidebar p. 188)*, the destructive gypsy moths will not wipe out an entire species of trees. Healthy ones should renew the forest in future decades.

You can end your day at Big Meadows with a wildflower walk through the gently undulating meadowlands that give the area its name. On the way, you may startle a deer or even a black bear.

Rapidan Camp to Rockfish Gap: 54 miles; a full day

Park at the west side of Skyline Drive at **Milam Gap** *(Mile 52.8)*. Cross the drive to a trail marker to begin the 4-mile round-trip to Rapidan Camp (formerly Camp Hoover). You walk a short distance on the Appalachian Trail, then turn left onto the **Mill Prong Trail.** This passes through a wooded tract, descends to a small waterfall, crosses three streams, and meets a road. Turn right and continue toward the cabins of **Rapidan Camp,** a national historic landmark.

The camp satisfied President Herbert Hoover's three require-ments for a hideaway: It had to be within 100 miles of Washington, have a trout stream, and be high enough to discourage mosquitoes. The president and his wife, Lou, used the camp as a summer White House in 1931. You can walk around and look at the outside of the three remaining cabins, now restored to the way they looked in 1931. Two are open to the public for ranger-led tours. Check on times for these at the Byrd Visitor Center.

A wonderful view of the Blue Ridge's classic smoky peaks appears at **Hazeltop Ridge Overlook** *(Mile 54.4)*. And as you con-tinue along the top of the ridge, look for **Bearfence Mountain.** An 0.8-mile, 90-minute hike to Bearfence starts at Mile 56.4 before the Lewis Mountain Campground. It demands some scrambling over rocks but finally rewards climbers with a spectacular 360-degree view.

A bit farther along, at Milepost 59, the easy 2-mile round-trip to the **Pocosin Mission** takes you to the ruins of a missionary church and graveyard.

The **Swift Run Gap Entrance** *(near Mile 65)* is an old Blue Ridge crossing now paved by US 33. In May, wildflower seekers climb the nearby **Hightop Summit Trail** (3 miles round-trip) to see the blooms.

Loft Mountain *(near Mile 79),* with a campground and information center, is a southern base for exploring the park. Near a service complex along Skyline Drive, look for the trailhead to the **Frazier Discovery Trail,** a 1.5 mile loop that demonstrates how pasture lands are turning back into woods. After the demise of the chestnut trees, other trees and shrubs began repopulating the land. You can see it happening here, and from a rocky vantage point on the trail; you can also see it happening on a grand scale throughout the park. Two summit viewpoints offer views to the west, over the Shenandoah Valley to undulating peaks beyond.

At **Rockfish Gap,** near the **Rockfish Entrance Station,** a bison path evolved into a colonial road, and later a modern highway. Here, at the park's southern end, begins the **Blue Ridge Parkway,** a National Park Service highway that connects Shenandoah to Great Smoky Mountains National Park *(see pp. 162–173)* to the south in Tennessee and North Carolina.

Lichen-covered boles, Shenandoah National Park

INFORMATION & ACTIVITIES

Headquarters
3655 US 211E
Luray, VA 22835
540-999-3500
www.nps.gov/shen

Visitor & Information Centers
Dickey Ridge Visitor Center, near North Entrance *(Mile 4.6)*, open daily late March through November. Byrd Visitor Center at Big Meadows, near center of park *(Mile 51)*, open daily late March through November. Loft Mountain Information Center *(Mile 79.5)*. Opening and closing dates vary each year.

Seasons & Accessibility
Park open year-round. For recorded information call 540-999-3500. Skyline Drive may close temporarily during heavy snow or hazardous ice conditions. For weather and road information, call 540-999-3500.

Entrance Fee
$10 per car allows 7-day access.

Pets
Must be kept on leash; not allowed on posted trails or in park buildings.

Facilities for Disabled
Visitor centers, amphitheaters, picnic areas, and campgrounds are accessible to wheelchairs. Rest rooms, lodges, and restaurants are also accessible. The Limberlost Trail is accessible.

Things to Do
Free ranger-led activities: interpretive walks, talks, evening programs *(summer–fall only)*. Also available, fishing, horseback riding, hiking on some 500 miles of trails.

Special Advisories
■ Rocks around waterfalls are very slippery and dangerous.
■ Pull off the road completely when stopping for a view.
■ Do not feed or chase wildlife.

Overnight Backpacking
Permits are required and available free of charge from headquarters, visitor centers, and entrance stations.

Campgrounds
Five campgrounds, all with 14-day limit. **Mathews Arm, Lewis Mountain,** and **Loft Mountain** open mid-May through October, first-come, first-served. **Big Meadows** open late March through November. Reservations recommended from Memorial Day weekend through October, available through the National Parks Reservation Service *(see p. 13)*; other times, first come, first

served. Fees $14-$17 per night. Tent and RV sites; no hookups. Camp stores and restaurants near the campground. **Dundo Group Campground,** open April through November. $30 a night, reservations required. Call the National Parks Reservation Service *(see p. 13),* or write Shenandoah National Park, Swift Run Entrance Station, Virginia Route 3, Box 311, Elkton, VA 22827. Showers and laundry facilities (except at Mathews Arm and Dundo).

Hotels, Motels, & Inns
(Unless otherwise noted, rates are for two person in a double room, high season.)

INSIDE THE PARK:
■ P.O. Box 727, Luray, VA 22835. 540-743-5108 or 800-999-4714.
■ **Big Meadows Lodge**
(Mile 51.3) 97 units. Lodge rooms $67-$125; cabins $75-$87; suites $105-$142. Restaurant. Late April through October.
■ **Lewis Mountain Cabin**
(Mile 57.6) 10 cabins with outdoor grills. $61-$94. Mid-May through October.
■ **Skyland Lodge**
(Miles 41.7 and 42.5) 175 units. Lodge units $79-$122; suites $116-$170; cabins $53-$103. Restaurant. Early April through November.

OUTSIDE THE PARK
In Front Royal, VA 22630:
■ **Quality Inn**
10 Commerce Ave. 540-635-3161 or 800-821-4488. 108 units. $65-$85. AC, pool, restaurant.
■ **Woodward House on Manor Grade** 413 S. Royal Ave. 540-635-7010 or 800-635-7011. 8 units. $95-$175, includes breakfast. AC.

In Sperryville, VA 22740:
■ **Conyers House Inn and Stable LLC** 3131 Slate Mills Rd. 540-987-8025. 7 units. $150-$300, includes breakfast. AC, restaurant.

In Stanley, VA 22851:
■ **Jordan Hollow Farm Inn**
326 Hawksbill Park Rd. 540-778-2285 or 888-418-7000. 15 rooms. $133-$190, includes breakfast. AC, restaurant.

In Waynesboro, VA 22980:
■ **The Inn at Afton**
I-64 at US 250. 540-942-5201 or 800-860-8559. 118 units. $83-$91. AC, pool, restaurant.

Excursions from Shenandoah

George Washington & Jefferson National Forests

West and southwest of Shenandoah

One of the largest holdings of public land in the east, the combined George Washington and Jefferson National Forests sprawl throughout the mountains of Virginia, spilling across the state borders into West Virginia and Kentucky.

In the north, George Washington National Forest covers large portions of the Allegheny, Shenandoah, Massanutten, and Blue Ridge ranges; to the south, Jefferson includes the state's highest peak of Mount Rogers (5,729 feet). Within these vast acreages are more than 40 tree species—about 80 percent of them hardwoods—and some 2,000 species of shrubs and herbaceous plants. About 200 species of birds make homes here, including many neotropical migrants. The 55 mammal species range from black bear and white-tailed deer to rock voles and water shrews.

Scots-Irish and German settlers began pouring into the Shenandoah Valley in the early 18th century, clearing its forests for farms and pushing up into the hills. In the next century, more and more forestland gave way to timber companies and iron furnaces. Slopes started to erode, and silt clogged the streams. With the forest went wildlife; elk, deer, and wild turkeys were practically eradicated from the area.

Lands in northern Virginia were among the first purchased as part of a federal forest reserve system; in 1917 three units were collectively called the Shenandoah National Forest, which was later renamed the George Washington National Forest.

In southwestern Virginia, much the same thing was going on. The federal government bought land for a national forest. But it was being cut for timber as quickly as it was being bought. From the early 1900s to the mid-1930s, more than 63 percent of the current Jefferson National Forest lands were cleared. Then, shortly after the land was established as a national forest in 1936, the chestnut blight obliterated the region's dominant tree, thus destroying huge tracts of the remaining forest *(see sidebar, p. 188.)*

With more careful stewardship, the forests and the creatures that call the lands home are returning. Timber production is still a big part of the multiple-use policy; almost 40 percent of

George Washington and Jefferson is managed for logging. Some 5 percent, or about 140 square miles, is completely protected as wilderness.

In terms of recreation, the possibilities are nearly endless. More than 2,000 miles of hiking trails wind through the highland forests and meadows, including 330 miles of the famous **Appalachian Trail.** There are also 1,000 miles of trout streams, dozens of picnic areas and campgrounds, and numerous lakes for swimming and fishing.

What to see and do

You can pick up maps and information at the 11 ranger district offices spread throughout the forest, or at the visitor centers in New Market, Warm Springs, Buena Vista, or Wytheville.

Birding is the highlight at some 17 areas within the forest; contact one of the offices or visitor centers to find out which area is nearest. Many of these areas have interpretive nature trails, boardwalks, and viewing platforms for spying on waterfowl, migratory songbirds, and such year-round residents as turkeys, pileated woodpeckers, eastern bluebirds, and Carolina chickadees. To see hundreds of migrating hawks, go up on just about any high peak in mid-September.

In the **Lee District,** the closest to Washington, D.C., the land is surprisingly uncrowded. On the west side of the district, you can

Otter Lake, off the Blue Ridge Parkway

Frost-bitten fern

find some superlative outdoor adventures. From the **Wolf Gap Recreation Area** *(8 miles W of Columbia Furnace on Va. 675)* take the **Big Schloss Trail** as it makes a steep ascent up along the border of Virginia and West Virginia. It's about 6 miles to the top of **Big Schloss** (German for "castle"), a huge rock outcrop that affords stupendous panoramas of the wooded mountains dropping off on both sides of a thin ridge. A wooden footbridge takes you from one outcrop to another. You can make a 12-mile loop for a long, satisfying day hike, or an easy overnight.

About 217 miles of the **Blue Ridge Parkway** runs through Virginia on its way to North Carolina, passing through some of the state's most brilliant scenery. The forest flanks the parkway from about Waynesboro to Roanoke, offering motorists a chance to do more than stretch their legs at an overlook. If you stop at Milepost 6, *(starting from parkway's N end at I-64),* the 2-mile round-trip to **Humpback Rocks** is a quick, if somewhat steep, way to sample the ageless beauty of the Blue Ridge. The trail climbs from 2,360 to 3,210 feet to cliffs that provide grandstand views of the Shenandoah Valley and the distant Allegheny Mountains. Keep a close eye on children on these steep, well-worn cliffs.

Though the views are the most dramatic at Humpback, you can continue on another mile to the top of the mountain and make a loop back to the car. Great in any season, the hike up is especially pleasant in spring when thousands of rhododendrons and azaleas cheer up the understory.

There are no views from Mount Rogers' forested peak. However, if you like superlatives and want to climb the tallest mountain in Virginia, some of the trails leading to the summit have gorgeous scenery. The **Mount Rogers National Recreation Trail** makes a 6.7-mile ascent from Grindstone Campground 6 miles east of Troutdale on Va. 603. **Wilburn Ridge Trail** is very scenic and also perhaps the best way up. It begins in **Grayson Highlands State Park** *(276-579-7092. www.dcr.state.va.us/parks/graysonh.htm)* and makes its way to the top in 4.2 miles.

Crabtree Falls Trail

For a change from the long views atop the Blue Ridge, try the equally spectacular scenery of **Crabtree Falls** (*6.6 miles E of the parkway or 9.5 miles W of Massies Mill on Va. 56*). The series of five exuberant cascades rank as one of Virginia's highest falls. From the parking lot, it's an easy stroll to the first waterfall, but as you peer 1,500 feet up the narrow ravine, you can't help wanting to climb higher. The trail follows Crabtree Creek, pausing at four overlooks. Avoid the temptation to go off the trail and scramble around the rocks; many people have fallen to their deaths from the slick ledges.

Between falls, the creek provides loquacious commentary, its mist watering thick carpets of moss and little gardens of Christmas and polypody ferns, trout lilies, and rattlesnake plantains. In the fall, look for the stringy yellow flowers of witch hazel and bright red partridgeberries. The smaller but similarly red winterberry is a shrub; crush one of the berries for a refreshing smell reminiscent of lip balm. You may also find a few fallen clusters of muscadine grapes that have escaped the attention of birds and other creatures. They make a delicious snack.

Sweet birches grow near the creek; look for elliptical, saw-toothed leaves. Crack open a twig and enjoy the odor of wintergreen as you walk. Taller yellow birches push to the canopy, as do tulip poplars, oaks, and hemlocks. At the top overlook, there is a fine view of the upper falls and the folded hills that define the Tye River Valley. Slashing up one slope is a brigade of dead hemlocks, destroyed by the balsam woolly adelgid (*see sidebar p. 299*). From this vantage you have a vivid picture of the damage an introduced pest can inflict.

From the parking lot to the final overlook is 1.5 miles. The waterfalls distract you from the uphill effort, and the return trip is downhill. From the top waterfall, you have the option of continuing another 1.5 miles to **Crabtree Meadows.** The meadows are accessible by car, 3.8 miles west of the lower parking lot, then south on Va. 826 for 4 miles. On busy summer and fall weekends if the lower parking lot is full, you can start the hike from the meadows; the return is uphill.

At Milepost 86 of the Blue Ridge Parkway, park at the camp store opposite the Peaks of Otter Visitor Center and embark on the 1.6-mile (one way) **Sharp Top Trail.** This popular trail is one of the region's greatest. In the warm season, you can hop a shuttle bus *(fare)* to the top and still get some exercise by walking down. In winter, you may have the whole trail to yourself, with snow squeaking underfoot and boulders rimed with glossy carapaces of ice. The partly paved trail zigzags steeply to a series of steps. At the top, a pulpit of stone offers an uplifting 360-degree scan of the Piedmont, Blue Ridge, and Alleghenies across the valley. Huge lichened boulders adorn the bald peak.

Spotlighting some of the finest mountain terrain of southwestern Virginia, the **Big Walker Mountain Scenic Byway** makes a 16-mile loop in the forest just north of Wytheville. Take Va. 717 west from I-77 (exit 47), then north on US 52 to Big Walker's 3,405-foot peak. The 100-foot **observation tower** here provides sensational views of mountains pitching and rolling off into several states. The route continues down the north side of the mountain and turns east on Rte. 42.

■ 1,770,673 acres ■ Western Virginia ■ Best seasons spring and fall
■ Hiking, camping, bird-watching, fishing, swimming, boating, mountain biking, cross-country skiing, horseback riding ■ Contact the national forests supervisor, 5162 Valleypointe Parkway, Roanoke, VA 24019; 888-265-0019. www.southernregion.fs.fed.us/gwj/

Ramsey's Draft Wilderness Area

35 miles west of Shenandoah

A local take on the word "creek," the draft that runs through the middle of this wooded wilderness freshens the air and keeps hikers company as it washes over smooth stones and big rock slabs. Set within the **George Washington National Forest,** the Ramsey's Draft area embraces one of the state's largest tracts of virgin forest; some huge trees are more than 300 years old. Large hardwoods such as tulip poplar, red oak, and basswood mix with hemlocks that tower over lush ferns and mosses.

Elevations in the wilderness vary from 2,200 feet to 4,282 feet at the top of **Hardscrabble Knob,** a hard 7-mile walk up the draft. In keeping with a designated wilderness, trails are minimally maintained and signs are few. A major flood in 1985 washed out portions of an old road that had made hiking up the draft relatively easy. Forest managers have left debris from various storms, providing more challenge to a trail that already required several fords. The resulting area is a wilder wilderness, one in which many hikers

Attack of the Woolly Adelgids

Why are so many hemlocks dying? Look closely at a healthy branch and you may see the reason. Attached to the base of the leaves, like so many pieces of speckled lint, are the tiny killers: balsam woolly adelgids.

These aphid-like insects were introduced from Asia in the 1920s and have begun taking a serious toll on southern Appalachian forests. The pests suck sap from young twigs, primarily in spring; the weakened trees often live only a few years.

While oaks can be sprayed for gypsy moths, there is no known effective chemical control for adelgids. Researchers are testing adelgid-eating beetles that may help check the blight.

Faced with the seemingly unstoppable blight, many scientists try to take the long view. The eastern forest has always changed and continues to do so. The chestnut blight of the early 20th century destroyed chestnuts, but promoted the rise of hickories and other species. There is always an opportunist ready to fill a new niche.

choose to skip the trails and find their way through thick woods to high meadows and open views.

From the Mountain House picnic area (off US 250), the **Ramsey's Draft Trail** starts off as a wide, easy walk on the left side of the stream. In fall, the woods flame with orange and yellow foliage against a sharp blue sky, while asters and goldenrod add color to the forest floor. Spring brings out a panoply of wildflowers as well as a host of warblers and other migrating songbirds. Rock overhangs make reflections in the limpid water. As you cross, look for trout and crayfish.

The draft is wide enough for some open views of ridges even within the first mile. After 1.5 miles, the trail crosses the creek again and continues up, following the right prong of the stream. Or you go left on **Jerry's Run Trail** instead; this follows a tributary west to a junction with the **Shenandoah Mountain Trail.** Continuing left will bring you to the **Road Hollow Trail,** then back around to the parking lot for a total outing of about 8 miles.

In all, there are more than 21 miles of trails within the wilderness. Beech, birch, maple, and even a few spruce are some of the

Wonderful Beeches

One of the region's handsomest shade trees, the American beech *(Fagus grandifolia)* makes an aesthetically pleasing sight whether on a city sidewalk or quiet mountain slope. The smooth light gray trunk, often the target of initial carvers, rises to a soaring domed crown of leafy branches. The serrated, pointy leaves are light green underneath and measure about 2 to 6 inches. In fall look for them to turn a uniform brilliant yellow. They brown in winter, often hanging on well into spring.

The American beech grows up to 80 feet in height, about average for the beech family that includes oaks, chestnuts, and chinkapins.

Animals appreciate the fall crop of beechnuts, little triangular nuts that grow in pairs in prickly burs or husks. Every few years, a tree produces a bumper crop, dropping plenty of food for squirrels, chipmunks, bears, birds, and people.

Choose nuts that have grown enough to split their brown casings. Peel away the casing with your thumb, and then enjoy the nut's sweet taste.

American beeches, Shenandoah National Park

more northerly tree species you encounter in the higher elevations. The farther up you go, the more solitary your wilderness experience will be.

■ **6,519 acres** ■ **West-central Virginia, 15 miles west of Churchville** ■ **Best seasons spring and fall** ■ **Camping, hiking** ■ **Contact George Washington National Forest, Deerfield Ranger District, Va. 6, Box 419, Staunton, VA 24401; 540-885-8028. www.southernregion.fs.fed.us/gwj/ forest/recreation/wilderness/ramseys_draft.shtml**

Douthat State Park

60 miles southwest of Shenandoah

Snug in the heart of the Alleghenies yet easily accessible from I-64, Douthat State Park offers a nice package of day hikes and lake activities in a particularly scenic section of the mountains. One of Virginia's original half dozen state parks, Douthat was the work of the Civilian Conservation Corps (CCC) in the 1930s and early '40s. The detailed craftsmanship of the CCC men, such as the hand-carved doors and hinges, is still evident in the rustic lodge, restaurant, cabins, and trails, all of which helped the park achieve National Historic Landmark status in 1986.

Douthat's 24 trails explore some 40 miles of woods, passing by cascading waterfalls and climbing to open ridges more than 3,000 feet high. In spring the park comes to vibrant life as its dogwoods, rhododendrons, and laurels slip on lovely costumes of pink and white. Wildflowers break out along trailsides from spring to autumn. In fall, the hardwoods cover themselves in the colors of the sunset; every tree from oaks and tulip poplars to dogwoods, birches, sassafras, and maples gets into the act. In winter, the tall hemlocks and white pines keep their greenery, while their neighbors go bare and the forest takes on a breathtaking silence. If you stand a while and listen carefully, you can hear birds hunting for seeds and perhaps a deer out foraging along the stone cold ground. Other animals that inhabit the park include grouse, turkeys, bobcats, bears, and foxes.

To bone up on the area's tree species, take the short **Buck Lick Interpretive Trail** across the road from Douthat Lake View Restaurant. The nearby 0.8-mile (one way) **Heron Run Trail** traipses through hemlocks and maples along the edge of the 50-acre lake.

(The lake itself has a fine sand beach and is good for a swim later.)
A dam at one end of the lake makes it impossible for you to do
a loop, so you'll need to backtrack; but this offers a different
perspective on the woods and lake and surrounding mountains.
Look carefully for signs of beaver activity. Fisherman can work the
lake, or cast for trout over on **Wilson Creek.**

For something a bit more adventurous, take the **Blue Suck Falls
Trail** about 1.5 miles through thick woods up to a lovely cascade
plunging from a rhododendron-lined ravine over a series of stone
slabs. The falls originate from one of the area's many small sulfur-
rich springs known as "suck licks," where animals often come to
drink. About a half mile beyond the falls you can stand atop
Lookout Rock for fine views of the mountains all around. Try to
time your visit here at sunset when the sun casts a brilliant gold
sheen on the landscape to the east.

A manageable loop hike can be made by combining the **Guest
Lodge, Mountain Top,** and **Mountain Side Trails** for about a 4.5-mile
outing and some excellent views in the northeast part of the park.
Or, instead of starting from the lodge, you can begin with the **Buck
Hollow Trail,** just off the Buck Lick Interpretive Trail.

■ **4,493 acres** ■ **West-central Virginia, 7 miles north of Clifton Forge**
■ **Best seasons spring and summer** ■ **Camping, hiking, boating,
swimming, fishing** ■ **Contact the park, Route 1, Box 212, Millboro, VA
24460; 540-862-8100. www.dcr.state.va.us/parks/douthat.htm**

Mountain Lake Wilderness

110 miles
southwest of
Shenandoah

This remote highland plateau is the largest wilderness area in the **Jefferson National Forest** (see pp.
294–98). A primitive, roadless area, it features a
mountain bog and virgin stands of towering hemlocks, spruce,
and fir set amid a gorgeous oak-hickory forest floored with
azalea, mountain laurel, and blueberries.

The wilderness actually lies to the northeast of **Mountain Lake,**
the site of the resort that was used in the movie *Dirty Dancing.* The
wilderness begins a mile or so beyond the lake and runs for about
8 miles across a plateau, dropping sharply to the east in drainages
for Johns Creek. The tract straddles the Eastern Continental Divide
and the Virginia-West Virginia border.

Mountain Lake Birds

A Mountain Lake area bird count on a recent day in June tallied about 70 species and 1,400 individuals. The 12 observers turned up species varying from yellow-billed cuckoo and eastern bluebird to American goldfinch and indigo bunting. They also spotted a number of hawks, woodpeckers, and warblers.

Of the common grackle and European starling, species common in urban areas, the observers sighted only one each; yet there were 125 red-eyed vireos, a record for the mountain. A tireless minstrel, this woodland bird is recognized by its black-outlined white eyebrows, dark olive back, and white underparts.

The observers also saw good representation by American robins, blue jays, woodpeckers, and black-capped chickadees, hardy species that stay active in the mountains throughout the year, even in the coldest days of winter. During a snowfall, the tiny chickadee ruffles out its feathers to keep warm, then darts bravely from shrub to shrub in search of things to eat.

Five miles of the **Appalachian Trail** run through Mountain Lake Wilderness. From the second parking lot *(5 miles N of Mountain Lake)* you can get on the trail. In about half a mile, you ascend an outcrop called **Wind Rock** that affords a fabulous view of Stony Creek Valley below Potts Mountain.

From the first parking lot *(3 miles N of Mountain Lake)*, the **War Spur Trail** takes you up to another magnificent view from the cliffs. Make a 2.5-mile loop by connecting with the **Chestnut Trail,** a delightful outing that takes you through groves of ancient conifers. Or you can take the **Appalachian Trail Connector** north to the trail, then follow the road back for about a 7-mile circuit. Elevations in the wilderness vary from 4,100 feet (at Wind Rock) to 2,200 feet on the east side. Animals that live here include black bear, deer, fox, bobcat, wild turkey, ruffed grouse, and woodcock.

■ 11,035 acres ■ Southwestern Virginia, east of Pearisburg ■ Best seasons spring and summer ■ Camping, hiking ■ Contact Blacksburg Ranger District, Jefferson National Forest, 110 Southpark Dr., Blacksburg, VA 24060; 703-552-4641. www.southernregion.fs.fed.us/gwj/forest/recreation/wilderness/mountain_lakes.html

Blackwater Falls State Park

80 miles
northwest of
Shenandoah

One of the most dramatic gorges east of the Mississippi slices through the Potomac Highlands in this park. Half a mile wide and 8 miles long, the canyon was cut by the Blackwater River, with an equally dramatic five-story-high waterfall. Hugging the rims of the canyon, the park provides endless views of the gorge, and trails lead you close enough to the falls to let you feel their cool, misty breath on your face.

The "black" or distinctive reddish brown river water is stained by leaching from upcountry hemlocks and spruce. Rhododendron also frill the canyon edges, buffeting them in greenery year-round. In winter, mist from the falls veils the surrounding greenery in a lace of ice.

One of West Virginia's signature "resort parks," Blackwater boasts a beautifully situated stone-and-wood lodge overlooking the canyon and an active Nordic center, with 20 miles of cross-country skiing trails.

What to See and Do

Obviously, **Blackwater Falls** are the park's major attraction, and maps available in the lodge information center list a number of relatively short trails weaving down into the gorge. The most accessible and therefore the most popular is the paved quarter-mile **Gentle Trail,** which begins on Blackwater Falls Road before reaching the lodge and leads to an observation platform above the falls. Or, if stairs don't bother you, you can follow the more than 200 steps from the Trading Post parking lot to the roaring water. A final platform at the base of the falls offers a good sense of their power and beauty.

Two other trails worth following lie just west of the lodge on Blackwater Falls Road. The mile-long **Balanced Rock Trail** leads to a large sandstone boulder that seems to perch precariously on a smaller rock. As you leave the rock, you can take the trail spur to your left and make a quick loop around the **Rhododendron Trail,** especially appealing in spring. The nearby **Elakala Trail** takes you down to a footbridge across the **Upper Elakala Falls.** From here, you weave back through a garden of huge boulders and equally impressive hemlocks. For hikers looking for something a little more challenging, pick up the 8-mile (one way) **Blackwater/Canaan Trail** at the horse stables and follow it south through mountain

Blackwater Falls, Blackwater Falls State Park

scenery and into the wide-open Canaan Valley Resort State Park.

In the park's northwest corner, **Pendleton Lake** offers a cooling alternative to hiking, and keeps swimmers and boaters occupied all through the summer. In winter, cross-country skiers flock to the park to take advantage of trails covered with evergreen boughs and the area's abundant snowfall. A toboggan run and rope tow *(fee)* provide more winter sport.

There are 65 tent and RV sites with shower facilities that are open from May to October, with shower facilities. Blackwater Lodge offers 54 rooms and 26 cabins.

■ **1,688 acres** ■ **North-central West Virginia near the Maryland border** ■ **Best seasons spring and winter** ■ **Camping, hiking, swimming, fishing, mountain biking, horseback riding, cross-country skiing, sledding** ■ **Contact the park, P. O. Drawer 490, Davis, WV 26260; 304-259-5216 or 800-225-5982. www.blackwaterfalls.com**

Virgin Islands

igh green hills that drop down to enchanting turquoise bays. White powdery beaches. Coral reefs. These all are part of the tropical beauty that is St. John, one of about a hundred specks of land known as the Virgin Islands.

Despite its small size—19 square miles—St. John's wide range of rainfall and exposure gives it surprising variety. More than 800 subtropical plant species grow in areas from moist, high-elevation forests to arid terrain to mangrove swamps. On that list of species, you'll find mangoes, soursops, turpentine trees, wild tamarind, century plants, and sea grapes. Around the island live the fringing coral reefs—beautiful, complex, and exceedingly fragile communities of plants and animals, which St. John's famous beaches depend upon.

In 1493, Christopher Columbus saw the large cluster of islands and cays and named it after St. Ursula and the 11,000 virgins who were martyred with her, according to legend. Since then, Spain, France, Holland, England, Denmark, and the United States have controlled various islands at different times. The Danes began colonization in the 17th century; in 1717 planters arrived on St. John. By the middle of the century, 88 plantations had been established there. Slaves stripped the steep hillsides of virgin growth and cultivated the cane.

By the time the Danes abolished slavery in 1848, the sugar industry was doomed. Afterward, the island went into a century-long period known as the "subsistence era."

During World War I, the United States bought St. John, St. Croix, St. Thomas, and about 50 smaller islands from Denmark for $25 million; the government did this because the leaders were concerned that Germans might capture the islands and be a bit too close to home.

- Caribbean Sea
- 14,689 acres
- Established 1956
- Best seasons spring and winter. Hurricane season typically runs June–Nov.
- Camping, hiking, boating, scuba diving, snorkeling, fishing, bird-watching
- Information: 340-776-6201 www.nps.gov/viis

Near Caneel Bay, Virgin Islands National Park

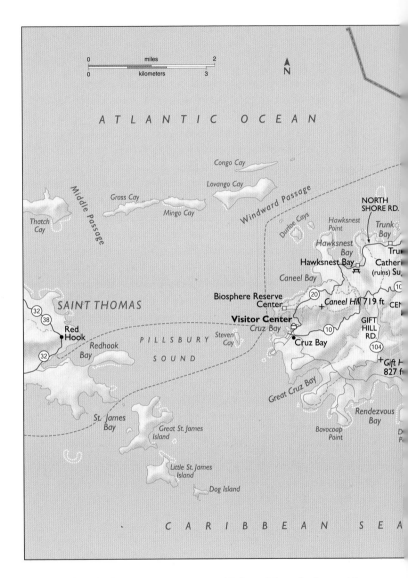

Four decades later, conservationist Laurance S. Rockefeller donated more than 5,000 acres for a national park on St. John; in 1962 the park acquired 5,650 undersea acres off the north and south coasts.

Today, although the park's boundary includes three-quarters of St. John, the federal government owns only slightly more than half the island. Officials and conservationists both worry about the escalating pace

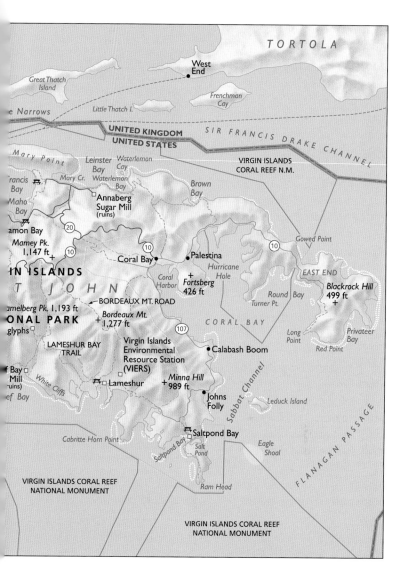

of development on private holdings within the park. They also are concerned about the pressure from the many cruise ships that disgorge large numbers of visitors at once, badly straining the park's resources.

When to Go
All-year park. High season is mid-December to mid-April.

How to Get There
By plane to Charlotte Amalie, St. Thomas, then taxi or bus to

Red Hook, then ferry across Pillsbury Sound to Cruz Bay, a 20-minute ride. Or, try to catch one of the less frequently scheduled ferries from Charlotte Amalie; the boat takes 45 minutes, but the dock is much nearer the airport.

How to Visit

If you have only 1 day, drive the **North Shore Road** as far as the **Annaberg Sugar Mill Ruins.** Be sure to take time to stretch your legs on some of the trails along the Caribbean and perhaps do a little snorkeling. Return via **Centerline Road** and stop at the ruins of **Catherineberg Sugar Mill.**

Should you have a second day to spend in the park, consider hiking the **Reef Bay Trail** and exploring the island's East End. Visit **Saltpond Bay** and walk to **Ram Head.**

If you have more time, sign up for some of the excellent tours and activities that park rangers conduct.

When you're driving around the island yourself, be prepared; the roads are steep and riddled with potholes. Stay on the left. There are several blind curves to watch for, as well. Because you never know when some livestock or a wild donkey may be around the next bend, it's important to stick to the 20

What Not to Miss
▪ **Driving the North Shore and Centerline Road Circuit for great overlooks and views of the island and surrounding Caribbean**
▪ **Hiking at sunset up Caneel Hill for views of Caneel Bay**
▪ **Snorkeling at Francis Bay in the early morning or late afternoon to see green turtles**
▪ **Scuba diving and visiting Whistling Cay and Waterlemon Bay**
▪ **Walking the Reef Bay Trail to see petroglyphs made by the Arawak**
▪ **Cruising at sunset on Cinnamon Bay from Cruz or Coral Bay**
▪ **Taking an interpretive walk around the partially restored ruins of Annaberg Sugar Mill**

miles per hour speed limit. If you should encounter a donkey, give it its due: While they may look approachable and tame, wild donkeys are more than capable of ruining your day with a swift kick or a hard bite.

A more restful alternative may well be to hire a taxi and a guide.

EXPLORING THE PARK

North Shore Road-Centerline Road Loop:
15 miles; 3 hours to a full day

Begin your visit with a stop at the park visitor center in Cruz Bay to pick up a map, trail brochure, and find out what activities are scheduled for the day.

Head north out of town along the **North Shore Road**. This road is in good condition, but it is very steep in places. Near the top of the hill, pull off at the overlook for a bird's-eye view of the picturesque town and harbor, the many small adjacent islands, and the big island of **St. Thomas** across the sound. For an even better view of **St. John's West End,** climb **Caneel Hill;** the 0.8-mile, moderately strenuous trail begins a short distance ahead on the right, across the road from the Park Service sign. (Or save this hike for sunset, when it's cooler and the view from the top of the hill is spectacular.)

Stop at the next overlook a half mile farther along the road for a view of **Caneel Bay** and, to the northeast, the big island of **Jost van Dyke,** one of the British Virgins. Caneel has been the site of a famous resort since the 1930s. Before, it was a sugar plantation for most of the 18th and 19th centuries. The name is both Dutch and Danish for "cinnamon," and comes from the cinnamony leaves of the bay tree, a member of the myrtle family. From the 1860s to the 1930s, oil from the leaves was used to make the famous St. John Bay Rum cologne.

The entrance to the resort is down the hill on the left, past Milepost 1.5. The land belongs to the park but is leased to the resort, owned until recently by the Rockefellers. To get a look at its lovely beaches, bays, and palm-studded grounds flowered with bougainvillea and pink oleander, walk the mostly level **Turtle Point Trail** around **Hawksnest Point.** This takes about an hour. The resort management asks only that you register as a day guest at the front desk; ask the staff there for directions to the trailhead.

From Caneel Bay, the road climbs steeply and descends to **Hawksnest Beach,** where you can swim, snorkel, and picnic. Visitors tend to bypass this beach, but locals flock here on weekends. Exhibits describe the damage that's being done to the island's fragile reefs by pollutants, swimmers, snorkelers, and the anchors of careless boaters—and strongly urge visitors not to touch, stand, or sit on the coral.

One of the Caribbean's premier vistas unfolds a mile farther up the road. From the overlook, **Trunk Bay** with its lush palm-fringed crescent beach and dozens of bobbing sailboats lies before you. Off in the distance is **Whistling Cay,** where in the 19th century a customs shed stopped boats plying the passage between the Danish and British Virgins.

The bay's beauty draws many visitors, especially on days when cruise ships are in. The park has set up an underwater nature trail for snorkelers here; some 16 plaques identify the reef's plants and animals. If you're a serious snorkeler, however, you might want to skip this reef for a less traveled one farther along.

Beyond Trunk Bay's entrance be prepared for the road to get very steep. Near the top of the hill is the multimillion-dollar development at **Peter Bay,** a private holding that has been a model for preventing the sediment runoff that other developments have allowed. Park officials and environmentalists say that runoff damages the reefs and sea-grass beds.

At **Cinnamon Bay** (Mile 4.5), there is a campground and, across the road, the ruins of the Danish Cinnamon Bay sugar factory, one of the oldest on the island. Plaques along the 1-mile trail tell you its history and point out native trees such as bay, lime, teyer palm, and calabash, which produces a fruit that's shaped like a gourd and can be carved into bowls. If you're lucky enough to be there for a tour led by one of the Virgin Islanders on the park staff, you'll learn some colorful local lore, too.

Continue down the road a half mile to yet another stunning, sweeping view of **Maho Bay, Francis Bay** (where sea turtles come to feed), and **Mary Point.** You'll see diving pelicans and frigatebirds that, to avoid weighing down their own enormous wings, harass other seabirds for food. The red roofs visible through the trees belong to a house built in 1952 by Ethel McCully, an eccentric American who swam ashore and stayed. Since no paved roads or automobiles existed on St. John then, donkeys hauled the materials from Cruz Bay—a 4-hour trip.

Down the hill, the road flattens and passes a stretch of beach on the left. Continue on for a mile to the road's end and then turn right toward **Annaberg.** On the right, you'll see a thick mangrove swamp, one of many on the island. Its large, tangled roots help protect the shoreline and provide a breeding ground for fish.

On the left, about 100 yards from the turnoff, look for the

Trunk Bay, St. John, Virgin Islands

marker identifying one of the toxic manchineel trees that are common in the Caribbean. Columbus called their green fruit "death apples." Do not stand under this tree in the rain, because runoff can raise painful blisters on your skin.

Just ahead is **Mary Creek** with a view of Mary Point. An important marine community inhabits the shallow reefs and seagrass beds of the creek, site of a weekly naturalist-led seashore walk. If you wade out, be sure to wear something on your feet. You can find brilliantly colored conchs, spiny black sea urchins, and brittle stars that regenerate their tentacles. Coral rocks host many tiny animals. Pick up and examine the rocks, but put them back as you found them.

From here, consider an easy walk along the 0.8-mile **Leinster Bay Trail,** which follows the seashore east to **Waterlemon Bay** and some of the best snorkeling in the park. You can swim and snorkel off the sandy beach at the trail's end. If you have the stamina, walk out to the point and swim across the narrow channel to snorkel around little **Waterlemon Cay.**

Back at the Leinster Bay Trailhead, park in the lot and walk up the hill to the partially restored ruins of the **Annaberg Sugar Mill.** A quarter-mile self-guided walk introduces you to the slave quarters, windmill, horse mill, oven, cistern, and factory that for much of two centuries produced raw sugar, molasses, and rum for Denmark. Native stone, ballast brick, and coral went into building the thick walls.

From the overlook you can see a number of other Virgin Islands across the narrows, including **Tortola,** largest of the British Virgins, and the dinosaur shape of Britain's **Great Thatch** on the left. In winter, humpback whales sometimes cruise by. Before leaving the overlook, treat yourself to the scent of a frangipani blossom from the nearby tree.

To return to Cruz Bay, drive the more level **Centerline Road** and watch out for blind curves. Slow speeds should pose no hardship, however. Views of the island's **East End** are truly spectacular. If you have time, look for the **Catherineberg Road** on the right after driving about 3 miles. A short way up this road are the ruins of the area's 18th-century **Catherineberg Sugar Mill.** The outer shell of the windmill has been restored, and there are 4-foot stone walls, handsome archways, a massive stone pillar, and some original beams.

East End—Coral Bay & Saltpond Bay:

26 miles round-trip; at least a half-day

Take Centerline Road out of Cruz Bay, stopping after nearly 3 miles at the Catherineberg Sugar Mill (*see above*). About a half mile farther is the **Konge Vey Overlook,** where a wayside exhibit points out Jost van Dyke, Great Thatch, and other points to the north.

The popular **Reef Bay Trail** begins after another 1.25 miles. It descends into a steep V-shaped valley through moist, subtropical

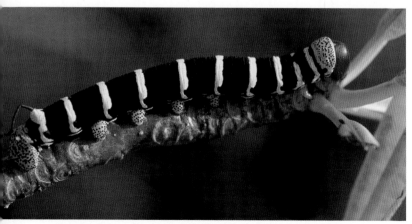

Frangipani caterpillar, Virgin Islands National Park

forest to dry forest to acacia scrub near the coast. Ruins of sugar estates can be seen along the 2.5-mile path. Nearby, there are some mysterious petroglyphs, made by the Arawak Indians centuries ago. Walk this trail at least partway to experience the lush forest, or even better, save it for a guided tour (*fee*), when a boat meets you at the coast and spares you the hike back up.

Back in your car, continue on to the overlook near **Mamey Peak** for a lovely view of Coral Bay and the island's East End. The name of the bay stems from *kraal,* the Dutch word for corral.

The Danes established their first plantations at this end of the island, among them the vast Estate Carolina, once the property of the king. They built a fort—called **Fort Frederik**—on **Fortsberg Hill** on the bay's eastern shore. In 1733, a bloody slave uprising began here, reputedly the first in the New World. It would have succeeded—1,087 of the island's 1,295 inhabitants were slaves— had the French not sailed in to quell it.

Continue on Centerline Road as it winds eastward outside the park to the village of **Coral Bay,** about 2 miles away. You might see a mongoose scuttering across the road. Introduced a century ago to kill rats, the mongoose has multiplied explosively, to the detriment of some native island fauna. At Coral Bay, stop to see the handsome pink-roofed **Emmaus Church** that Moravian missionaries built in the 1780s.

If you continued on, you'd be rewarded with magnificent views of **Hurricane Hole, Round Bay,** and the British Virgins. But for now backtrack a short distance and turn left at the intersection of Route 108. Drive 4 miles along the coast to the trailhead for **Saltpond Bay** and a wilder part of the island.

About a 0.2 mile beyond the parking area, the horseshoe bay is fringed by a wide, sandy beach. Continue around the beach and onto the rocky 0.9-mile **Ram Head Trail** that winds up a promontory and down the other side. There, a blue pebbly beach and an arid environment await you. Plants include several kinds of cactuses and the century plant, which takes 15 to 20 years to bloom and then dies.

Continue to the crest of the hill for a grand view of the Caribbean Sea. However, watch your footing on this windswept point 200 feet above the water. Here at **Ram Head** you'll be standing on rock that emerged some 108 million years ago, the oldest land on St. John.

INFORMATION & ACTIVITIES

Headquarters
1300 Cruz Bay Creek
St. John, VI 00830
340-776-6201
www.nps.gov/viis

Visitor Center
Cruz Bay Visitor Center, at west end of St. John, open daily year round. Call 340-776-6201.

Seasons & Accessibility
Park open year-round. Access by boat. Climate does not vary much during the year, though summers can be hot. Hurricane season here runs typically from June through November.

Entrance Fee
There is no entrance fee for the park. However, there is a user fee to enter both Trunk Bay and the Annaberg Sugar Mill ruins.

Pets
Not allowed on public beaches, in picnic areas, or in campgrounds. Permitted elsewhere on leashes.

Facilities for Disabled
Some ferries to St. John are accessible to wheelchairs, with assistance. The park's visitor center, several Cinnamon Bay campsites, and the rest rooms there and at Trunk Bay and Hawksnest Bay, also are wheelchair accessible.

Things to Do
Free naturalist-led activities: interpretive talks and exhibits, nature and history walks, hikes, snorkel tours, cultural demonstrations, evening programs. Also available, self-guided nature and underwater trails, swimming, snorkeling, boating, fishing, windsurfing, bird-watching, photography workshops, archaeology digs, occasional historic bus tours.

Campgrounds
One park campground, Cinnamon Bay; 14-day limit December to mid-May; other times 21-day limit. Open all year. Reservations recommended; contact Cinnamon Bay Campground, P.O. Box 720, Cruz Bay, St. John, VI 00831. 340-776-6330 or 800-539-9998. Nightly for two persons: $27 for bare sites; $80 for tents; $110-$140 for cottages. Cold showers. Food services.

For, **Maho Bay** reservations, Maho Bay Camp, 17-A E. 73rd St., New York, N.Y. 10021. 212-472-9453 or 800-392-9004. 114 equipped tent-cottages, central baths. $110 per night December through April; $75 per night May

Snorkeler in Caribbean waters

through November. Reserve early for December through May.

Hotels, Motels, & Inns

(Unless otherwise noted, rates are for two persons in a double room, high season.)

On St. John, VI 00831:

■ **Caneel Bay**
P.O. Box 720, Cruz Bay. 340-776-6111 or 800-928-8889. 166 units. $450-$1,100. Pool, 4 restaurants.

■ **Gallows Point Suite Resort**
P.O. Box 58. 340-776-6434 or 800-323-7229. 50 units, with kitchens. $365-$465. Pool, restaurant.

■ **St. John Inn**
P.O. Box 37. 340-693-8688 or 800-666-7688. 11 units, some kitchens. $140-$200.

■ **Westin Resort St. John**
P.O. Box 8310. 340-693-8000. 379 units. $260-$600. AC, pool, 4 restaurants.

■ **Coconut Coast Villas**
P.O. Box 618, Cruz Bay. 340-693-9100, 800-858-7989. 9 waterfront units, with kitchens. $139-$500. AC, pool.

■ **Estate Lindholm Bed and Breakfast**
P.O. Box 1360, Cruz Bay. 340-776-6121. 10 units, with kitchenettes. $140-$320. AC and ceiling fans. Barbecue facilities.

Voyageurs

From the air, the forest areas of Voyageurs look like green pieces of a jigsaw puzzle scattered on a huge mirror. A North Woods realm of more than 30 lakes and more than 900 islands, Voyageurs spans a watery stretch of the U.S.–Canadian border.

A third of the park's area is water, most of it in the four large lakes of Rainy, Kabetogama, Namakan, and Sand Point, linked by narrow waterways. Smaller lakes gleam in the forests of Voyageurs' terra firma, which consists of small islands, a strip of mainland shore, and the Kabetogama Peninsula.

The splendors of this 55-mile-long park can be reached primarily by water. Motorboats (*banned in adjacent Boundary Waters Canoe Area Wilderness*) churn the lakes. Canoes and kayaks glide the narrow waterways. Fishermen sit at the rails of houseboats, hoping to hook walleye, smallmouth bass, and northern pike. Nearly every lake is haunted by the cry of the loon. And you won't have a better chance to see bald eagles on the nest and on the wing or hear wolves howl at night in any other national park in the lower 48 states.

The park is named for the voyageurs, French Canadians who paddled birch-bark canoes for fur trading companies in the late 18th and early 19th centuries. The voyageurs were famous for stamina; they often paddled up to 16 hours a day. And they were also famous for their roisterous songs. Their route between Canada's northwest and Montreal is cited as part of the U.S.–Canadian border in the treaty that ended the American Revolution.

If you're in a boat in this labyrinth of waterways and islands, you can unwittingly cross that border. Be sure to take along a high-quality map that includes navigational markers to tell you where you are.

- Northern Minnesota
- 218,200 acres
- Established 1975
- Best seasons summer and winter (for winter sports)
- Camping, backpacking, boating, kayaking, swimming, snow-mobiling, cross-country skiing, snowshoeing
- Information: 218-283-9821 www.nps.gov/voya

Rainy Lake, Voyageurs National Park

ONTARIO
MINNESOTA
Bleak Bay
Rainy Lake

Boat
ramp
Tilson Bay
Boat
ramp
Dryweed Is.
RAINY LAKE
ICE ROAD
11
96
Soldier
Point
Rainy Lake
Visitor Center
K A B E T O G A M A   P E N
Saginaw
Bay
Black Bay
War Club Lake
Rapids
KOOCHICHING
Chief Wooden
Frog Islands
VOYAGEURS
Shoepack
Lake
STATE
Cutover
Island
Ellsworth
Rock Gardens
Tom Cod
Bay
FOREST
122
Kabetogama
Boat
ramp
Sugarbush
Island
Lake
Ash
Visitor C
122
Moxie
Island
Kabetogama
Ove
Kabetogama Lake
Visitor Center
Boat
ramp
123
Daley
Bay
Beaver
Ove
Irwin   Bay
53
122
Ov
217   Ray
12
ASH RIVER TRAIL
Ash
53   KABETOGA
KOOCHICHING
STATE FOR
STATE
FOREST

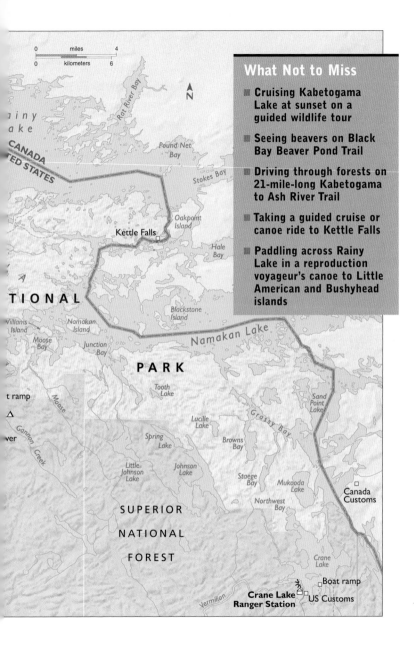

0   miles   4
0   kilometers   6

N

CANADA
UNITED STATES

Rainy Lake

Rat River Bay

Pound Net Bay

Stokes Bay

Oakpoint Island

Kettle Falls

Hale Bay

NATIONAL

Blackstone Island

Namakan Lake

Williams Island

Namakan Island

Moose Bay

Junction Bay

PARK

Tooth Lake

Sand Point Lake

t ramp

Moose

Gannon Creek

Lucille Lake

Spring Lake

Browns Bay

Grassy Bay

ver

Little Johnson Lake

Johnson Lake

Staege Bay

Mukooda Lake

Canada Customs

Northwest Bay

SUPERIOR

NATIONAL

FOREST

Crane Lake

Vermilion

Crane Lake Ranger Station

US Customs

Boat ramp

What Not to Miss

■ Cruising Kabetogama Lake at sunset on a guided wildlife tour

■ Seeing beavers on Black Bay Beaver Pond Trail

■ Driving through forests on 21-mile-long Kabetogama to Ash River Trail

■ Taking a guided cruise or canoe ride to Kettle Falls

■ Paddling across Rainy Lake in a reproduction voyageur's canoe to Little American and Bushyhead islands

How to Get There

From Duluth, drive north about 110 miles on US 53. For Crane Lake, turn east at Orr and drive 28 miles on Co. Rds. 23 and 24.

For Ash River, stay on US 53 for 25 more miles, turn right at the Ash River Trail sign, and continue for 10 miles. For Kabetogama Lake Visitor Center, stay on US 53 for 3 more miles, turn right onto Co. Rd. 122, and drive to the lakeshore.

For Rainy Lake, stay on US 53 to International Falls, then head east for 12 miles on Minn. 11 to the park's entrance road, following highway information signs; turn right to go to the visitor center. Airports: Duluth and International Falls, Minn., and Fort Frances, Ont.

When to Go

An all-year park, but most accessible from spring through the early fall. Water travel is curtailed by freeze-up in late fall and ice breakup in early spring. Winter opens the park to cross-country skiing, snowshoeing, snowmobiling, and ice fishing. And the 7-mile ice road at Rainy Lake provides a unique entry into the park: you can drive your car on the ice to places that, in other seasons, you can reach only by boat or floatplane.

How to Visit

The only way to the heart of this park is by water. **Kabetogama Lake, International Falls, Crane Lake,** and **Ash River** are resort communities that serve as entrances, even though they are not within the park's boundaries.

Begin the trip planning by choosing an entrance; each of them is widely spaced and offers a different experience. You can make motel or lodge reservations at one of the area's resorts or motels.

You can also stay in a car campground and use the resort as a base for park activities, including fishing and wildlife watching, or rent a houseboat and camp out by boat. Guides, canoes, houseboats, and motorboats are for hire. If you are sufficiently experienced, you can also tow in your own craft.

Tour boats, with park naturalists aboard, also operate out of visitor centers. Even if you have your own boat, you may want to take a commercial cruise and rely on experienced navigators; the lakes are broad with submerged rocks in shallow areas, and they're sometimes brushed by stiff winds.

EXPLORING THE PARK

Kabetogama Lake: At least a full day

At the Kabetogama Lake Visitor Center, make reservations for the Sunset Wildlife Cruise, Kettle Falls Cruise, guided canoe trip, or children's program.

If you'd rather explore the park on your own, rent one of the park's cached canoes at Locator Lake by reserving it and picking up the key at the visitor center. If you do this, you must get to the Locator Lake Trailhead on your own, with a guide, or in a rented boat. You leave the boat at the trailhead for a 2-mile hike along a spruce bog and past a beaver pond, dam, and lodge. The trail climbs to a ridge and drops to the lakeshore. There you launch your reserved cached canoe and paddle around the lake, watching for muskrat, bald eagles, loons, and blue-winged teal.

The 21-mile **Kabetogama to Ash River Trail** travels through the park and state forest lands; three trailheads, all car-accessible, offer a variety of opportunities.

Rainy Lake: At least a full day

Although this large lake is 60 miles long and 12 miles wide, you can explore it in a motorboat, houseboat, or canoe. At the Rainy Lake Visitor Center, get weather and navigation information. And be warned; northwesters can sweep down on Rainy, driving impossible waves and funneling to a climax in the Brule Narrows that lead into Saginaw Bay.

Rainy River's name derives from *koochiching*, a Cree Indian term referring to the mist rising above the falls that once roared over the Rainy River about 10 miles to the west. Early in the 20th century, a power dam buried the falls.

Paddle from the visitor center about 1.5 miles northwest to **Little American Island,** where the discovery of gold set off a short-lived gold rush in 1893. Hopefuls rushed in by dogsled, train and on foot to the island, as well as to Bushyhead nearby. The richest of seven mines yielded about $4,600 worth of gold. A short interpretive trail on the island gives a view to the past.

On **Bushyhead Island,** there's a mine shaft carved into the rock. The island got its name, according to a journal kept by one of the miners, "because it rises boldly out of the lake … and is crowned with a luxuriant growth of pine timber, giving it 'a bushy appearance, an emerald set in glass.'"

Black Bay Narrows, Voyageurs National Park

Rainy Lake's emeralds are ancient relics; 2.7 billion years ago crustal plates came together from north and south, pushing up mountains here. The granites, schists, and greenstones here lie near the southern edge of the Canadian Shield, the oldest basement rock in North America.

If you don't have your own boat, you can still explore. The park offers tour boat trips from the visitor center, as well as free trips aboard a 26-foot reproduction of a voyageur's canoe, guided trips aboard contemporary canoes, and programs for children.

Trails near Rainy Lake Visitor Center include the 2-mile Oberholtzer Trail, which travels through a variety of habitats, and the short, water-accessible Black Bay Beaver Pond Trail to an active beaver pond habitat.

Crane Lake & Ash River: **At least one or two days each**

Near the Ash River resort area is a visitor center where you can launch your boat, get information about camping, set off on hikes, and obtain charts for navigating the lakes.

For a good exploratory voyage, go to **Kettle Falls.** This waterways hub was used by Native Americans, voyageurs, loggers, fishermen, and, during Prohibition, bootleggers who were smuggling liquor from Canada.

From Crane Lake, travel north through **King Williams Narrows,** across **Sand Point Lake,** and through **Namakan Narrows,** then west across **Namakan Lake** along the U.S.–Canadian border, which veers northward here.

From Ash River, you go the length of **Sullivan Bay** to the river mouth, then weave through a string of islands into **Moose Bay.** For a scenic trip, pass through the channel on the south side of **Williams Island** (where there's a primitive campsite) into **Hoist Bay.** This body of water got its name from the amount of heavy lifting men used to do to get large logs onto trains. You can see pilings that supported a train track, which ran from the middle of the bay to a white-pine sawmill on the mainland. Then head north toward **Namakan Island,** site of other campsites, and go around the island's western side.

Both of these courses take you to the southern end of **Voyageur Narrows.** Pass through the narrows, then head east along the border through **Squirrel Narrows** to Kettle Falls. Near the dock, a dam serves a regional system regulating water flow for electric power. There's a gravel road, a portage trail, here near the dock.

Walk the road for about a quarter of a mile to a white clapboard building with a long front porch: the **Kettle Falls Hotel.** Built in 1910, the hotel welcomed many diverse guests, including lumberjacks, dam builders, fishermen, and tourists. It also took in its fair share of bootleggers, who distilled and sold liquor. Now listed on the National Register of Historic Places, the hotel is open from May to October.

Another way to reach Kettle Falls is aboard a cruise boat. Trips run several times a week from the visitor center at Kabetogama Lake. Some last only a few hours, and others go out for a day; visitors can take a picnic lunch or eat at the hotel. Reservations are strongly recommended.

There are three short trails near **Ash River Visitor Center: Voyageurs Forest, Beaver Pond,** and **Kabetogama Lake Overlook.** Each one leaves from pull-offs on the road to the visitor center. The 2-mile **Blind Ash Bay Trail,** from the visitor center to the mouth of Blind Ash Bay, wends along rock cliffs through pine forest.

Voyageurs: Canoemen of the North

Beginning in the mid-1600s—generations before Europeans would explore North America in earnest—French-Canadian *voyageurs* or travelers ventured deep into the wooded wilderness of present-day Canada. Working for fur-trading companies, the voyageurs had a straightforward, but arduous job: Transport beaver and other pelts from the far northwest to Montreal, capital of the fur trade. From there, the furs were shipped to Europe, where they were crafted into fashionable hats and other upper-crust accessories. With Europe's appetite for furs nearly insatiable, the pelts were considered "soft gold."

Paddling immense birch-bark canoes, the voyageurs followed a network of lakes, rivers, and streams that formed a nearly continuous waterway across North America. One of their most difficult overland hauls was at well-named Grand Portage on Superior's North Shore—an 8.5-mile trek that involved a 700-foot climb. Because they usually carried three loads, that walking distance was actually 42.5 miles.

There were two types of voyageurs, a distinction that evolved based on geography. The "Montreal Men" transported trade goods from the east to Grand Portage, and returned to Montreal with furs destined for Europe. They paddled special lake canoes that were 36 feet and could be propelled by as many as 14 men. The vessels were able to carry all that human weight plus up to three tons of cargo up the St. Lawrence Seaway and across Lakes Huron and Superior to Grand Portage.

At that busy post, the Montreal Men met up with a second group, the "Winterers," who transported the goods to Rainy Lake and farther west into the interior. Here the men spent the long, cold winter, trading for furs with Native Americans.

When the waters thawed in spring, the Winterers, now loaded with furs, retraced their route of the year before. They paddled 24-foot canoes—large enough to carry four to six men and nearly two tons of cargo, yet small enough to navigate narrow, rapid waters and the inevitable woodland portages. From as far north as the Great Slave Lake in what is now Canada's Northwest Territories, they journeyed along a web of rivers to immense Lake Winnipeg and Lake of the Woods, up the Rainy River, across the lakes of what is now Voyageurs National Park, through the

Hudson Bay Company voyageurs

rest, and socialize. Liquor flowed freely as Europeans and Native Americans alike shared in raucous entertainment.

The voyageurs relied heavily on the native Ojibwa and Cree (and other tribes farther west) to teach them survival skills and navigable routes. They learned to craft strong, light-weight canoes; they used birch bark for the skin, cedar roots to tie the bark together, and spruce resin to make the hull watertight.

The Native Americans, in turn, were forever changed by the trade goods brought by the voyageurs. Wool blankets and woven cloth replaced animal skins; iron traps and firearms changed age-old hunting practices; and kettles and tools modernized everyday life.

The fur trade went on for more than a century. By the 1820s, however, trapping had diminished the beaver population, and Europeans had moved on to new fashions. The Grand Portage post went out of business, and the vocation of the voyageur soon became obsolete.

Thanks to land donated by the Grand Portage band of Ojibwa, the site of the fur trading post is now a national monument (*see pp. 340–41*), with a palisade enclosing reconstructed buildings and exhibits.

maze of smaller lakes and portages in the Boundary Waters, and finally down the Pigeon River to Grand Portage.

The stamina and good cheer of the voyageurs became legendary. Singing folk songs as they paddled and sleeping in the wilderness with little more than upturned canoes for shelter, they labored from sunrise to sunset.

The July meeting, or rendezvous, in Grand Portage was the highlight of the year for the voyageurs. They camped for the better part of a month at the North West Company fur trade supply depot, taking full advantage of this rare chance to trade,

INFORMATION & ACTIVITIES

Headquarters
3131 Hwy. 53
International Falls, MN 56649
Phone 218-283-9821
www.nps.gov/voya

Visitor & Information Centers
Rainy Lake, on Minn. 11 at
northwest edge of park, open
daily; call 218-286-5258.
Kabetogama Lake, on Co. Rd.
123 at southwest edge of lake,
open daily mid-May through
September; call 218-875-2111.
Ash River, on southeast edge of
Kabetogama Lake, open mid-
May through September; call
218-374-3221.

Seasons & Accessibility
Park open year-round. Travel
within it is by boat, floatplane,
and foot in summer; snowmobile, snowshoes, cross-country
skis, and ski plane in winter.
Limited access during lake
freeze-up (*mid-Nov.–mid-Dec.*)
and breakup (*April*). In winter,
weather permitting, an ice road
on Rainy Lake connects the visitor center to Cranberry Bay,
7 miles into the park.

Entrance Fee
None.

Pets
Permitted on leashes in developed areas and at tent, houseboat, and day-use sites on
major lakes. Not allowed on
park trails, in backcountry, or
on interior lakes.

Facilities for Disabled
Kabetogama Lake, Rainy Lake,
and Ash River Visitor Centers
are wheelchair accessible, as is
the Kettle Falls Hotel, guided
boat trips, and a campsite.
Call Kabetogama Lake for
reservations.

Things to Do
Free naturalist-led activities:
nature walks, canoe trips
(*reserve at visitor centers*), children's and campfire programs,
films, exhibits, winter programs. Also, hiking, canoes and
rowboats (*boats on Interior
Lakes Program $10 a day*), boat
tours, rental boats, fishing and
ice fishing (*license required; ask
park staff for list of guides available*), swimming, waterskiing,
snowmobiling, cross-country
skiing, snowshoeing.

Special Advisory
■ Practice safe boating. Use
navigational maps. Be aware of
weather conditions. Make sure
your boat is well equipped and
not overloaded.

Camping & Houseboating

All park sites reached by water. 214 backcountry boat-in campsites, 14-day limit. Open all year, but mostly inaccessible during fall freeze-up and spring thaw; first come, first served. Free permit required for overnight stays, available at visitor centers and boat launches. No showers. Sites designated for tent camping or houseboats. Also, 2 small campgrounds. In winter, access mainly by snowmobile, cross-country skis, or snowshoes. Private campgrounds with tent and RV sites near park. Request "Camping, Houseboating, and Day-Use" brochure for planning.

Hotels, Motels, & Inns

(Unless otherwise noted, rates are for two persons in a double room, high season.)

INSIDE THE PARK:
■ **Kettle Falls Hotel**
(15 miles by water from the Ash River Trail) 10502 Gamma Rd. Ray, MN 56669. 888-534-6835. 18 units, some with kitchens, $150-$170.

OUTSIDE THE PARK
In International Falls, MN 56649:
■ **Holiday Inn**
1500 US 71. 218-283-8000 or 800-331-4443. 126 units.

Rooms start at $109. AC, pool, restaurant.
■ **Island View Lodge** (on Rainy Lake) 1817 Hwy. 11E. 218-286-3511 or 800-777-7856. 9 rooms $77-$95; 14 cabins with kitchens $120-$385. AC, restaurant.

In Kabetogama, MN 56669:
■ **Rocky Point Resort**
12953 Ness Rd. 218-875-2411. 8 cabins with kitchens, $545-$3,100 per week; 2 lodge rooms, $25 per person. Restaurant.
■ **Voyageur Park Lodge**
10436 Waltz Rd. 218-875-2131 or 800-331-5694. 10 cabins with kitchens. Summer only. $664-$1,655 per week.

For a listing of accommodations, call Kabetogama Tourism Bureau at 800-524-9085; Crane Lake Visitor and Tourism Bureau at 800-362-7405; International Falls Area Convention & Visitors Bureau at 800-325-5766; Ash River Commercial Club at 800-950-2061.

Excursions from Voyageurs

Lake of the Woods

80 miles northwest of Voyageurs With its wandering bays, leggy channels, and endless islands, it's difficult to tell if Lake of the Woods is a land punctuated with lakes, or a lake punctuated with land.

The confusion is understandable: Lake of the Woods is a giant among freshwater lakes, with 65,000 miles of shoreline, 80 miles of which stretch from its northernmost harbor in Kenora, Ontario, to its U.S. gateway in Baudette, Minnesota. In between, more than 14,000 islands—some of scoured granite, others covered in thick forest—stipple nearly 1,500 square miles of cool, clear water.

Lake of the Woods

A major waterway in the immense Rainy River system, Lake of the Woods absorbs three-quarters of the river's flow, then spills north into Lake Winnipeg and eventually into Hudson Bay. The lake is a remnant of glacial Lake Agassiz, which once covered the ancient bedrock of the Canadian Shield. Huge boulders left behind by the ice fields dot the landscape and give more evidence of the area's glacial past.

The lake's warming influence supports a jumble of species, ranging from southern hardwoods such as elm, ash, and basswood to northern spruce, balsam, and pine. Wild blueberries and raspberries are common, as is a wide variety of wildflowers.

The mix of species shows up in the park's birdlife. Most surprising are white pelicans; they have made permanent nesting sites within the islands and waterways. Only a few of the islands provide safe habitats for moose, deer, wolves, and other woodland animals.

31,900 acres ■ North of Rainy River, Ontario, near borders of Ontario, Manitoba, and Minnesota ■ Best season: summer ■ Camping, hiking, boating, swimming, fishing ■ Contact Lake of the Woods Tourism, P.O. Box 518, Baudette, MN 56623; 218-634-1174. www.lakeofthewoods.com

The Boundary Waters

60 miles southeast of Voyageurs

In paddling circles, Minnesota's **Boundary Waters Canoe Area Wilderness** (BWCAW) enjoys legendary status as one of the premier canoeing destinations on the planet. Comprising the northern tier of **Superior National Forest,** the wilderness area stretches 150 miles along the Canadian border, its one million acres a jumble of more than 1,000 lakes and 1,500 miles of interconnected water routes. Across the border, **Quetico Provincial Park** protects nearly a million acres of more pristine wetlands. Quetico and the Boundary Waters Canoe Area Wilderness together make up an area referred to as the Boundary Waters, the largest swath of wilderness east of the Rockies.

Like the Yellowstone ecosystem, BWCAW (or "beedub" as locals call it) serves merely as the centerpiece of a vast preserve. It is virtually surrounded by other protected lands: two million non-wilderness acres of Superior National Forest to the south and east, Voyageurs National Park to the west, and, of course, 1.2 million acres of Ontario's Quetico Provincial Park to the north.

For the avid canoeist, these statistics engender an almost irresistible pull: to paddle and portage your way hundreds of miles deep into the wild North Woods. Traveling the paths of the Native Americans and the French-Canadian voyageurs, you'll find that the landscape has remained essentially unchanged. The Boundary Waters is still devoid of roads, cars, and power lines and largely free of motorboats and airplanes. This primordial setting invites visitors to revel in timeless delights: wind sighing in the pines, fish

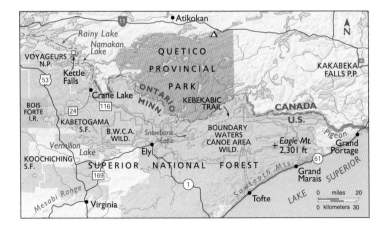

rising to feed at dusk, a moose walking through the underbrush.

Formed by ancient volcanoes and scoured by glaciers, the landscape is dominated by northern forest of spruce, pine, and birch, rock-rimmed lakes, and exposed bedrock rising up in the form of rounded knobs or shattered cliffs. Though almost all of the red and white pines that once blanketed the region were logged in the late 1800s, isolated stands of the magnificent trees still remain. In 1999, one of the most punishing windstorms in North American history (see opposite) ravaged the forest. The area is beginning to recover.

Your chances of spotting wildlife in the Boundary Waters are excellent, especially from the vantage point of a quietly floating canoe. You may see black bears browsing near the shore, beaver and muskrat gliding along the water's surface, eagles and ospreys soaring overhead, and loons, mergansers, and other birds gliding on mirror-smooth waters. In summer, almost 100 species of birds nest in the region.

Paddlers can usually count on fresh fish dinners, avoiding the blandness of freeze-dried meals. Though the fishing is best in spring and fall, catching northern pike, walleye, and smallmouth bass is generally possible all summer. But be forewarned: Mosquitoes and black flies plague the backcountry, especially in June and July. So be sure to pack plenty of repellent, and perhaps a head net.

Then again, as you rest your weary shoulders at a campsite miles from the modern world, listening to a fresh walleye sizzle in the pan over the campfire and watching the northern lights dance across the limitless sky, a few annoying insects may turn out to be a small price to pay for the sensation.

Both the BWCAW and Quetico are primarily canoeing preserves. Depending on your experience or expectations, plan a canoe trip that lasts a couple of days or several weeks. In most areas, you can map out a circular route that covers several lakes, portages, and campsites. Or paddle to a specific campsite and enjoy day trips from there, foregoing the toil of having to pack up and portage your camping gear every day.

Even if your stay is limited to one day, you can enjoy a taste of the Boundary Waters region by trying a short day paddle on one of the outermost lakes that serves as an entry point to the wilderness. These lakes don't necessarily promise the solitude you can expect from the interior, but crystal-clear waters and undeveloped shorelines make for a magical outdoor experience.

Storm of the Century

On July 4, 1999, a windstorm unlike any other blasted through the Boundary Waters. Winds reached speeds of 100 miles per hour, toppling an estimated 40 million trees and rendering 700,000 acres of forest almost unrecognizable. Within a few minutes, century-old pines were strewn across the forest floor like matchsticks.

Remarkably, although the storm occurred on a holiday weekend, no one was killed. The National Weather Service categorized the storm as a derecho, which is a a straight-line wind that can wreak far more destruction than circular or spiraling winds. It rocketed across Superior National Forest in a 40-mile-long, 10-mile-wide path from Ely, Minnesota, across the Gunflint Trail and into Ontario. The storm caused the most havoc in the Boundary Waters Canoe Area Wilderness.

Cleanup was a grueling task that entailed clearing portages and hiking paths of fallen trees. All this served as a sobering reminder of the wild inherent in wilderness.

Though renowned for its canoe routes, BWCAW contains fine hiking trails as well, from short day hikes to week-long backpacking treks. Some options are listed below under the appropriate entrance points. For maps and other suggestions, visit the Quetico office or a Forest Service office in one of the gateway towns.

Ely, Minnesota, is the self-proclaimed "canoe capital of the world" and best entryway to Boundary Waters from the southwest. Its downtown overflows with canoe concessionaires happy to help you provision your trip or orchestrate the whole adventure.

In winter, the town transforms itself into a premier dogsledding and Nordic-skiing community; polar explorers Paul Schurke and Will Steger both have businesses in town.

Ely is also home to the **International Wolf Center** (*800-359-9653*), which offers excellent exhibits, educational programs, and the chance of viewing the center's resident wolf pack. More than 400 wolves—the largest population in the lower 48 states—roam freely in the surrounding national forest.

Two of the main access roads into the region depart from Ely. The Echo Trail, or Co. Rd. 116, heads north and west toward

Voyageurs National Park. And Fernberg Road wanders east out of
Ely, leading to some of the most popular BWCAW access points,
including Fall Lake, Moose Lake, and the aptly named **Lake One.**
For an inaugural day paddle or short trip, Lake One offers a lot
of interesting inlets and islands to explore. You may see other
paddlers—likely heading for Lakes Two, Three, and points
beyond—but you'll probably have few other distractions.

The backbone of BWCAW's network is the **Kekekabic Trail**
or the Kek. The 38-mile route stretches eastward from the end of
Fernberg Trail near Snowbank Lake to the Gunflint Trail north of
Grand Marais. Built in the 1930s as an access trail for firefighters,
this rugged route ascends high hills, crosses beaver dams, and arcs
past hundreds of lakes.

Snowbank Lake Trail shares the Kekekabic's western trailhead.
The 24-mile route circles **Snowbank Lake,** climbing rocky ridges for
several fine overlooks.

Also near the west end of the Kek, you can pick up the **Old Pines
Trail,** which loops through a stand of old-growth pines to the
south, and **Disappointment Trail,** which crosses **Disappointment
Mountain** north of Kekekabic Trail. You can easily create lengthy
treks of 20 to 30 miles by combining various loop trails.

Boundary Waters marsh

From Echo Trail

Access the **Herriman Trail network,** where moderately steep loops of 3 to 14 miles follow lakeshores and the Echo River. For an all-day outing, try the rolling **Angleworm Trail,** a scenic 14-mile hike around Angleworm lake, 18 miles north of Ely.

From Tofte & Grand Marais, Minnesota

Both towns have Forest Service offices and provide access to the BWCAW from Lake Superior's North Shore.

The Sawbill Trail, or Co. Rd. 2, leads north from Tofte to well-known access points on Sawbill and Brule Lakes. Located between the two, but less trafficked than either one, **Baker Lake** (a narrow, pretty body of water easy to reach from the Sawbill Trail) is ideal for day paddles. Eight-mile-long **Brule Lake,** with its maze of bays, rocky outcrops, and islands and inlets, promises great day or overnight paddles, especially during the off-season.

Twenty miles from Grand Marais, the 7-mile out-and-back **Eagle Mountain Trail** climbs through jack pine and birch forest to the rocky knob that is Minnesota's highest point: 2,301-foot **Eagle Mountain.** From here you get a sense of the Boundary Waters' staggering scale. The seemingly endless rise and fall of forested terrain is interrupted only by dark patches of wilderness lake. On clear days Superior is visible along the southern horizon.

The **Border Route Trail** follows the U.S.–Canadian frontier for 75 miles through some of the Boundary Waters' most scenic sections, ascending high ridges that yield panoramic overlooks and passing waterfalls. The trail extends from Gunflint Trail to Pigeon River, with a half-dozen access points so you can hike a portion of the route, if the full 75 miles seems daunting.

And the **Gunflint Trail** punches north from Grand Marais to Sea Gull Lake about 75 miles away. Outfitters and lake resorts punctuate the trail. About two-thirds of the way, you cross the Laurentian Divide; waters to the north of here drain into Hudson Bay, and those south drain into the Gulf of Mexico.

■ More than 1 million acres ■ Minnesota near borders of Ontario and Manitoba, Canada ■ Best seasons: summer and fall ■ Camping, hiking, boating, swimming, fishing ■ Contact the forest, 8901 Grand Avenue Place, Duluth, MN 55808; 218-626-4300. www.superiornationalforest.org/bwca For reservations, call 877-550-6777 or visit www.bwcaw.org

Minnesota's North Shore

130 miles southeast of Voyageurs

Ah, the North Shore. To Minnesotans, the term refers to the state's precious patch of real estate along the northwest shore of Lake Superior. Though a popular vacation area peppered with resorts, cabins, and lakefront homes, this rocky coast somehow manages to remain untamed.

It's a prime example of the Canadian Shield, part of a broad band of igneous rock blanketed with boreal forest. Along the North Shore, the rock forms a high escarpment at the lake's edge, interrupted only by white-water rivers—fed by springs or snowmelt—that thrash their way toward Lake Superior.

Beginning at Lake Superior's western tip near the busy shipping port of Duluth, the North Shore extends northeastward to the Ontario border at Grand Portage. Along this 150-mile stretch lie eight of Minnesota's finest state parks, offering ample access to the big lake. Just inland, you'll see the **Superior National Forest** that spans a staggering three million acres. It climbs into the ancient Sawtooth Mountains, encompassing hundreds of glacial lakes and a wilderness that remains a stronghold of wolves, moose, deer, and other wildlife.

No wonder the North Shore ranks as such a legendary destination: Its broad appeal offers something for everyone. Sightseers, beachcombers, and hikers can remain near Minn. 61, the paved road that hugs the shoreline for almost all its length, linking state parks and charming villages. One of the nicest of these is Grand Marais, an artists colony and resort town at the base of a hill. With a picturesque natural harbor and lighthouse, fine restaurants and shops, it is a weekend destination.

Anglers, boaters, and those seeking backcountry adventure can follow the **Gunflint Trail** (FR 12) or one of the other roads that leads into the interior. Attracting distance hikers, the **Superior Hiking Trail** traces the ridgelines above Lake Superior for more than 200 miles.

Heading northeast from Duluth along Minn. 61, you'll pass several lakefront towns (notably Knife River) that serve as sportfishing hubs. Lake trout is the area's most popular native game fish. Weighing up to 20 pounds, these swift predators are the only species of trout or salmon that spawn in lakes. Lake trout reigned as Lake Superior's most valuable commercial fish from the early 1900s until the 1950s, when they were nearly wiped out by the sea lamprey, an eel-like parasite.

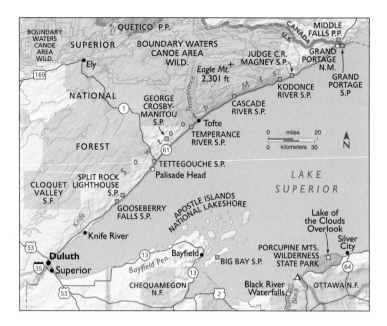

Other popular game fish—among them chinook salmon and brown, brook, and rainbow trout—were introduced to these waters for sport or to control unwanted predators. Rainbow trout have fared best, thanks to the North Shore's fine spawning streams.

Knife River is one of the few North Shore communities that still harbors a commercial fishery. Hundreds of fishermen worked along the North Shore around 1900, pulling lake trout, whitefish, and herring from the area's waters. By the mid-1900s, North Shore fishermen were netting more than five million pounds of lake herring each year. Today, only a few commercial fisheries remain.

Gooseberry Falls State Park
About 12 miles north of Two Harbors, Gooseberry Falls State Park (*218-834-3855. Adm. fee*) is known for its waterfalls. On both sides of the highway bridge, the Gooseberry River tumbles over dark lava flows, now splintered into hard-edged ledges. **Middle** and **Lower Falls,** the most impressive, lie just downstream from the bridge, where the river plunges 60 feet. Footpaths wind around the pools for several fine vantage points.

To see the most secluded cataract, follow the **Fifth Falls Trail** upstream. The 3-mile route winds up one bank and down the

Lake Superior's Tides

The Great Lakes do not experience true tides caused by the moon's gravitational pull. Still the weather on the giant bodies of water makes them rise and fall in what's called a seiche (pronounced "saysh"). A seiche occurs when wind and barometric pressure push water against the lake's shore. Behaving rather like a glass of water that's been jostled, the lake's water rebounds, sloshing back to the other side.

Seiches rarely rise and fall more than 1 foot on Lake Superior, and are usually less pronounced on the other Great Lakes. Yet to anyone who spends time along these shores, the periodic rise and fall appears to mimic a tide.

other, crossing a bridge just past the falls.

Several mountain bike trails depart from the visitor center, bound for more remote sections of the park. You'll likely spot some immense tree stumps, arboreal headstones marking the site of a large stand of old-growth white pines logged off in the 1890s. On the other side of the highway, a 1.5-mile out-and-back walk on **Gitchi Gummi Trail** (the Ojibwa name for Lake Superior) leads to a ridge-top view of the big lake. **Lower Rim Trail** (1.5 miles round-trip) follows Gooseberry River to its mouth at **Agate Beach,** where you can hunt for the lovely mineral-banded quartz stones.

Split Rock Lighthouse State Park

This nearby state park (*218-226-6377. www.dnr.state.mn.us/state_parks/split_rock_lighthouse. Adm. fee*) preserves one of the North Shore's most famous landmarks. The 1910 **Split Rock lighthouse** sits atop a dramatic bluff that rises 120 feet out of Lake Superior.

Sailors are said to have given Split Rock its name because the cliff appears split at certain angles from the water. It was first lit in 1910 after 215 men drowned during a disastrous shipping season. It warned others of the dangers along the rocky coast for 59 years until it was decommissioned. Today, visitors can go into the lighthouse from May to October.

Here, too, you can pick up a portion of the Gitchi Gummi Trail, that when complete will run the 86 miles from Two Harbors to Grand Marais. This 8.6-mile section stretches from Split Rock north to Beaver Bay.

The region's most valuable mineral is iron ore. From about 1870 to 1950, hundreds of mines across northern Minnesota's "iron ranges" produced the ore, then sent it by rail to ports on Lake Superior to be shipped to steel mills.

The steady stream of ships laden with ore led to the construction of more and more lighthouses. They were especially vital along the Lake Superior shore, where vicious storms can form quickly and the ships' highly magnetic cargoes play havoc with compass readings.

Tettegouche State Park
Just north of Silver Bay, Tettegouche's **Palisade Head** marks the highest lookout along the North Shore. Formed by ancient lava flows that reached thicknesses of more than 200 feet, Palisade Head was a well-advertised stop for motorists who cruised the scenic highway after it was completed in 1924. The sheer face now attracts accomplished rock climbers.

Cascade River State Park, North Shore

The **Baptism River** meets Lake Superior at the main entrance to Tettegouche State Park (*218-226-6365*). A small bridge here provides a good view of the river's gorge, while **Baptism High Falls Trail** leads 1.5 miles upstream to 65-foot **High Falls,** the second tallest cascade in the state. Several other trails wind farther inland through a mature forest of sugar maple, eastern white cedar, white spruce, and yellow birch to four lakes that are accessible only by foot.

At the park's east end, **Shovel Point** extends 1,000 feet into Lake

Superior. Follow the **Shovel Point Interpretive Trail** for less than a mile through three distinct ecosystems: Spruce, balsam, and other northern species grow on the cool eastern shore; a "dwarf forest" of scrub pines clings to areas of shallow soil; and little more than lichens survive on the exposed rock outcroppings. The highest point affords terrific views of Palisade Head and, on a clear day, the Apostle Islands of Wisconsin *(see pp. 251–253)* 30 miles southeast.

Temperance River State Park

Of all the North Shore rivers rushing toward Lake Superior, none is more dramatic than the **Temperance River** as it bounds through its namesake state park *(218-663-7476)*. It drops 160 feet in its last half mile, crashing through chasms and carving out potholes in the lava riverbed. **Cauldron Trail** (1.5 miles) traces the river up one bank and back down the other (keep a firm grip on children here). On the banks you will be able to spot several dry potholes, formed when the river ran higher or followed a different course.

Like many other rivers in the area, the waters of the Temperance have a reddish-brown hue. This is caused by tannin released into the water by hemlocks, cedars, tamaracks, and other trees and plants, as well as by minerals leaching from soil. Local tanneries relied on the bark of hemlocks and cedars to tan leather in the 19th century.

Grand Portage State Park

The Pigeon River forms part of the U.S.–Canadian border—and thus the end of Minnesota's North Shore. Largely undeveloped Grand Portage State Park *(218-475-2360)* was established to protect 120-foot **Pigeon Falls** (known locally as High Falls), the state's largest. Several vantage points, including one from **Middle Falls Provincial Park** in Ontario, provide views of this grand cascade.

The Pigeon River's falls and rapids required Native Americans and voyageurs to bypass this section of river as they traveled a well-established water route across North America. **Grand Portage National Monument** *(218-387-2788. Adm. fee)* commemorates the place where paddlers beached their birch-bark canoes and hauled them overland, uphill, to a navigable point more than 8 miles upstream. There are artifacts and a reconstructed stockade.

Superior National Forest & Other State Parks

Stretching along the North Shore from near Temperance River

State Park to beyond Grand Marais, and inland for some 150 miles, **Superior National Forest** is full of lakes, rivers, and bogs. In fact, almost one-sixth of the park's 3 million acres is surface water.

From the shore, four well-marked dirt roads cleave the forest: the **Sawbill, Caribou, Gunflint,** and **Arrowhead Trails.** Other roads and trails spin off these deep into the woods.

Several other state parks adorn this amazing stretch of country. **George Crosby–Manitou** *(218-226-6353)*, **Cascade River** *(218-387-3060)*, and **Judge Magney** *(218-387-3039)* State Parks each presents its own individual rustic charms. All three offer miles of backcountry hiking trails, fishing, camping, and cross-country skiing; scenic waterfalls run in both Cascade River and Judge Magney. Trekkers can keep watch for black bears, moose, wolves, and other forest wildlife.

■ **150 miles along Lake Superior** ■ **Minnesota, northwest Lake Superior, between Duluth and Grand Portage via Minn. 61** ■ **Best seasons summer and winter** ■ **Camping, hiking, boating, fishing, skiing, snowshoeing, wildlife viewing** ■ **Contact Lake Superior North Shore Association, P. O. Box 159, Duluth, MN 55801; 800-438-5884. www.LakeSuperiorDrive.com**

Split Rock Lighthouse, North Shore

Resources

USDA Forest Service Regional Offices

**Eastern Region
(Maine, Michigan, Ohio, and Wisconsin)**
626 E. Wisconsin Ave.
Milwaukee, WI 53202
414-297-3600
www.fs.fed.us/r9/

**Southern Region
(Arkansas, Florida, Kentucky, North Carolina, Oklahoma, South Carolina, Tennessee, the Virgin Islands, and Virginia)**
1720 Peachtree St.
Suite 760S
Atlanta, GA 30309
404-347-4177
www.southernregion.fs.fed.us/

Arkansas

Road Conditions
800-245-1672
www.ahtd.state.ar.us/roads.htm

Arkansas Department of Parks and Tourism
1 Capitol Mall
Little Rock, AR 72201
800-628-8725
www.arkansas.com

Arkansas Fish and Game Commission
2 Natural Resources Dr.
Little Rock, AR 72205
501-223-6300
800-364-4263
www.agfc.state.ar.us/

Division of State Parks
Arkansas Department of Parks and Tourism
1 Capitol Mall
Little Rock, AR 72201
888-287-2757
www.arkansasstateparks.com/

Ozark Highlands Trail Association
HC 33, Box 50-A
Pettigrew, AR 72752
870-861-5536
www.hikearkansas.com

Florida

Road Conditions
511 within Florida

Florida Fish and Wildlife Conservation Commission
620 S. Meridian St.
Farris Bryant Bldg.
Tallahassee, FL 32399
888-347-4356 (licensing)
850-488-3641 (info)
www.myfwc.com

Florida Trail Association
5415 SW 13th St.
Gainesville, FL 32608
877-445-3352
www.florida-trail.org

State of Florida Park System
3900 Commonwealth Blvd.
Mail Station 536
Tallahassee, FL 32399
850-245-2157
www.dep.state/fl.us/parks/

State Tourism
888-735-2872
www.flausa.com

Kentucky

Road Conditions
511 within Kentucky
Out of state: 866-737-3767
www.511.ky.gov

Kentucky Department of Fish and Wildlife
1 Game Farm Rd.
Frankfort, KY 40601
800-858-1549
www.kdfwr.state.ky.us/

Kentucky Department of Parks
Capital Plaza Tower
500 Mero St., Suite 1100
Frankfort, KY 40601
800-255-7275
www.parks.ky.gov

Kentucky Department of Tourism
Capital Plaza Tower, 22nd Floor
500 Mero St.
Frankfort, KY 40601
502-564-4930
800-225-8747
www.kytourism.com

Maine
Road Conditions
511 within Maine
Out of state: 866-282-7578
http://67.106.3.239/

Bureau of Parks and Lands
22 State House Station
Augusta, ME 04333
207-287-3821
www.state.me.us/doc/parks

Department of Inland Fisheries and Wildlife
284 State St.
41 State House Station
Augusta, ME 04333
207-287-8000
207-287-8003
www.mefishwildlife.com

Recreational Resource
www.maineoutdoors.com

Office of Tourism
59 State House Station
Augusta, ME 04333
888-624-6345
800-533-9595
www.visitmaine.com

Michigan
Road Conditions
800-381-8477
www.michigan.gov/mdot/

Department of Natural Resources—Fishing
Mason Bldg., 8th Floor,
P.O. Box 30446
Lansing MI 48909
517-373-1280
www.michigan.gov/dnr

Michigan State Parks and Trails
Department of Natural Resources—Parks and Recreation
Mason Bldg., 3rd Floor,
P.O. Box 30028
Lansing MI 48909
517-373-9900
www.michigan.gov/dnr

North Country Trail Association
229 E. Main St.
Lowell, MI 49331
866-445-3628
www.northcountrytrail.org

Travel Michigan
300 N. Washington Square
2nd Floor
Lansing, MI 48913
888-784-7328
www.travel.michigan.org

Statewide Online Campground Reservations
www.midnrreservations.com

North Carolina
Road Conditions
511 within North Carolina
www.ncsmartlink.org

Division of Parks and Recreation
512 N. Salisbury St.
Archdale Bldg.
Room 732
Raleigh, NC 27699
919-733-7275
919-733-4181
www.ils.unc.edu/parkproject/
ncparks.html

North Carolina Department of Environment and Natural Resources
1601 Mail Service Center
Raleigh, NC 27699
919-733-4984
www.enr.state.nc.us

North Carolina Travel and Tourism
301 N. Wilmington St.
Raleigh, NC 27699
800-847-4862
www.visitnc.com

North Carolina Wildlife Resources Commission
NCWRC
1707 Mail Service Station
Raleigh, NC 27699
919-662-4370 or
888-248-834
www.ncwildlife.org

North Carolina Trail Index
www.northcarolinaoutdoors.com/
pastimes/hiking/hiking.html

Ohio
Road Conditions
www.buckeyetraffic.org

Ohio Division of Travel and Tourism
P.O. Box 1001
Columbus, OH 43266
800-282-5393
www.ohiotourism.com

Ohio Division of Wildlife
2045 Morse Rd.,
Bldg. G
Columbus, OH 43229
614-265-6300
800-945-3543
www.dnr.state.oh.us/wildlife

Ohio State Parks
Department of Natural Resources
2045 Morse Rd.
Bldg. C-3
Columbus, OH 43229
614-265-6561
www.ohiostateparks.org

Guide to Ohio Trails
www.ohiodnr.com/trails

South Carolina
Road Conditions
www.dot.state.sc.us/getting
/roadcondition.html
888-977-9151

Department of Natural Resources
Hunting and Fishing Licenses
Rembert C. Dennis Bldg.
1000 Assembly St.
Columbia, SC 29201
803-734-3833
www.dnr.state.sc.us

Department of Parks, Recreation and Tourism
1205 Pendleton St.
Columbia, SC 29201
803-734-1700 or
800-872-3505
www.travelsc.com

South Carolina Forestry Commission
P. O. Box 21707
Columbia, SC 29221
803-896-8800
www.state.sc.us/forest/recreat.htm

South Carolina State Parks:
South Carolina Department of Parks,
Recreation and Tourism
1205 Pendleton St., Room 200
Columbia SC 29201
888-887-2757
www.discoversouthcarolina.com
/stateparks

South Carolina State Trails Program:
South Carolina Department of Parks,
Recreation and Tourism
1205 Pendleton St.
Columbia, SC 29201
803-734-0173
www.sctrails.net/trails/

Tennessee
Road Conditions
800-342-3258
www.tdot.state.tn.us/roadcondition
/currentmap.asp

Tennessee State Parks
401 Church St.
L & C Tower, 7th Floor
Nashville, TN 37243
888-867-2757, ext. 0
866-836-6757 (reservations)
www.state.tn.us/environment/parks

Tennessee Trails Association
P.O. Box 41446
Nashville, TN 37204
866-864-4537
www.tennesseetrails.org/

Tennessee Wildlife Resources Agency
P.O. Box 40747
Nashville, TN 37204
615-781-6500
www.state.tn.us/twra/

Virgin Islands
USVI Department of Tourism
P.O. Box 6400
St. Thomas, VI 00804
800-372-8784
www.usvitourism.vi

Virginia
Road Conditions
800-367-7623
www.virginiadot.org/comtravel
/eoc/eoc-main.asp

Department of Conservation
and Recreation
203 Governor St.
Suite 213
Richmond, VA 23219
804-786-1712
www.dcr.state.va.us/

Department of Game and
Inland Fisheries
4010 W. Broad St.,
Richmond, VA 23230
804-367-1000
www.dgif.state.va.us

Virginia State Parks
Department of Conservation
and Recreation
203 Governor St.
Suite 213
Richmond, VA 23219
800-933-7275
www.dcr.virginia.gov/parks

Virginia Tourism Corporation
901 E. Byrd St.
Richmond, VA 23219
804-786-2051
800-847-4882
www.virginia.org

List of 1,800 Places to Hike in Virginia
www.virginiatrails.org

INDEX

One of the world's largest nonprofit scientific and educational organizations, the National Geographic Society was founded in 1888 "for the increase and diffusion of geographic knowledge." Fulfilling this mission, the Society educates and inspires millions every day through its magazines, books, television programs, videos, maps and atlases, research grants, the National Geographic Bee, teacher workshops, and innovative classroom materials. The Society is supported through membership dues, charitable gifts, and income from the sale of its educational products. This support is vital to National Geographic's mission to increase global understanding and promote conservation of our planet through exploration, research, and education.

For more information, please call 800-NGS LINE (647-5463) or write to the following address:

National Geographic Society
1145 17th Street N.W.
Washington, DC 20036-4688
U.S.A.

Illustrations Credits

Front cover, Michael Melford. Back cover, Tom Jones
1 James L. Amos. 2-3 James P. Blair. 6 Layne Kennedy/CORBIS. 9 National Park Service Photo by John Brooks. 14 Michael Melford. 20-21 David Alan Harvey. 23 Raymond Gehman. 24-25, 27 Michael Melford. 29 Raymond Gehman. 32 Michael Melford. 35 David Alan Harvey. 39, 43 Michael Melford. 44 Raymond Gehman. 48 Kevin Fleming. 50-51 Ann Winterbotham. 52 National Park Service Photo by P. Bishop. 55 National Park Service Photo by Stephen Frink. 57 David Doubilet. 60 Otis Imboden. 63 Wes Skiles. 65 Nicole Duplaix/NGS Image Collection. 67 David Alan Harvey. 68, 73 Raymond Gehman. 74 Michael S. Quinton/NGS Image Collection. 77 Raymond Gehman/NGS Image Collection. 78 Raymond Gehman. 81 Donald L. Malick. 84-85, 87 Raymond Gehman. 88 Melissa Farlow/NGS Image Collection. 93, 97 Tom Jones. 102 Peter Burke. 103 (up) Jonathan K. Alderfer. 103 (ct) Diane Pierce. 103 (low) Cynthia J. House. 106 Mark R. Godfrey. 108 Emory Kristof. 112 Otis Imboden. 114-115 Matt Bradley. 117 Tom Melham. 120 Bruce Dale. 123 Raymond Gehman. 125 Paul Zahl. 126 David Alan Harvey. 128 Bates Littlehales. 129 Cynthia J. House. 130, 135 Raymond Gehman. 137 Jim Richardson. 140-141 Maltings Partnership. 142-162 (all) Raymond Gehman. 168 David Alan Harvey. 170 George F. Mobley. 171 Bruce Dale. 174-180 (all) Raymond Gehman. 184, 191 Raymond Gehman/NGS Image Collection. 194 Darlyne A. Murawski. 196 Pat O'Hara/CORBIS. 198-226 (all) Molly Roberts. 228-253 (all) Mark R. Godfrey. 256 Chip Clark. 258-261 (artwork) Richard Schlecht. 260, 262-263 Raymond Gehman. 269 N. John Schmitt. 272 Raymond Gehman. 276 Dan J. Dry. 278 Raymond Gehman. 281 Bruce Dale. 282 Vincent J. Musi. 288-300 (all) Raymond Gehman. 304 David Muench/CORBIS. 306 National Geographic Photographer Jodi Cobb. 313 Raul Touzon/NGS Image Collection. 314 Tom Melham. 317 Steven L. Raymer. 318 Layne Kennedy/CORBIS. 324 Mark R. Godfrey. 327 H.A. Ogden/National Archives of Canada. 330-341 (all) Mark R. Godfrey.

Staff Credits

National Geographic Guide to the National Parks: East and Midwest
Published by the National Geographic Society

John M. Fahey, Jr., *President and Chief Executive Officer;* Gilbert M. Grosvenor, *Chairman of the Board;* Nina D. Hoffman, *Executive Vice President, President, Books and School Publishing;* Kevin Mulroy, *Vice-President and Editor-in-Chief;* Marianne Koszorus, *Design Director;* Elizabeth L. Newhouse, *Director of Travel Publishing;* Lawrence M. Porges, *Project Director;* Robin Reid, *Editor;* Cinda Rose, *Art Director;* Carl Mehler, *Director of Maps;* Ruth Ann Thompson, *Designer;* Lise Sajewski, *Style/Copy Editor;* Matt Chwastyk, Thomas L. Gray, Joseph F. Ochlak, Nicholas P. Rosenbach, Gregory Ugiansky, Martin S. Walz, and The M Factory, *Map Research and Production;* Lewis Bassford, *Production Project Manager;* Lawrence M. Porges, *Photo Editor;* Meredith Wilcox, *Illustrations Assistant;* Dianne Hosmer, *Indexer;* Ben Archambault, Ben Bodurian, Caroline Hickey, Cindy Kittner, Barbara A. Noe, John Thompson, Mel White, Simon Williams, Jordan Zappala, *Contributors*

National Geographic guide to the national parks. East & Midwest / [prepared by the book division].
    p. cm.
  Includes index.
  ISBN 0-7922-9537-4
  1. National parks and reserves--East (U.S.)--Guidebooks. 2. National parks and reserves--Middle West--Guidebooks. 3. East (U.S.)--Guidebooks. 4. Middle West--Guidebooks. 5. United States--Guidebooks. I. Title: Guide to the national parks. East & Midwest II. National Geographic Society (U.S.) book division
  E160N243 2005
  917.404'44--dc22
                2004022726

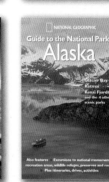

NATIONAL GEOGRAPHIC

Guides to the National Parks

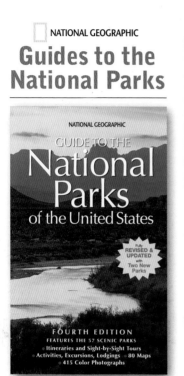

NATIONAL GEOGRAPHIC

GUIDE TO THE

National Parks

of the United States

Fully REVISED & UPDATED with Two New Parks

FOURTH EDITION
FEATURES THE 57 SCENIC PARKS
■ Itineraries and Sight-by-Sight Tours
■ Activities, Excursions, Lodgings ■ 80 Maps
■ 415 Color Photographs

- National Geographic Guide to the National Parks of the U.S. *(4th Edition)* ISBN: 0-7922-6972-1

- National Geographic Guide to the National Parks: Alaska ISBN: 0-7922-9540-4

- National Geographic Guide to the National Parks: East & Midwest ISBN: 0-7922-9537-4

- National Geographic Guide to the National Parks: Southwest ISBN: 0-7922-9539-0

- National Geographic Guide to the National Parks: West ISBN: 0-7922-9538-2

- Glacier and Waterton Lakes National Parks Road Guide ISBN: 0-7922-6637-4

- Grand Canyon National Park Road Guide ISBN: 0-7922-6642-0

- Rocky Mountain National Park Road Guide ISBN: 0-7922-6641-2

- Yellowstone and Grand Teton National Parks Road Guide ISBN: 0-7922-6639-0

- National Geographic Park Profiles: Canyon Country Parklands ISBN: 0-7922-7353-2

- National Geographic Park Profiles: Grand Canyon Country ISBN: 0-7922-7032-0

- National Geographic Park Profiles: Yellowstone Country ISBN: 0-7922-7031-2

- National Geographic Park Profiles: Yosemite ISBN: 0-7922-7030-4

- ALSO: National Geographic Guide to the State Parks of the U.S. *(2nd Edition)* ISBN: 0-7922-6628-5

AVAILABLE WHEREVER BOOKS ARE SOLD